ENGLISH ROYAL DOCUMENTS

KING JOHN—HENRY VI

1199–1461

ENGLISH ROYAL DOCUMENTS

KING JOHN–HENRY VI

1199–1461

BY

PIERRE CHAPLAIS

READER IN DIPLOMATIC IN THE UNIVERSITY OF OXFORD

OXFORD

AT THE CLARENDON PRESS

1971

Oxford University Press, Ely House, London W. 1
GLASGOW NEW YORK TORONTO MELBOURNE WELLINGTON
CAPE TOWN SALISBURY IBADAN NAIROBI DAR ES SALAAM LUSAKA ADDIS ABABA
BOMBAY CALCUTTA MADRAS KARACHI LAHORE DACCA
KUALA LUMPUR SINGAPORE HONG KONG TOKYO

PRINTED IN GREAT BRITAIN
AT THE UNIVERSITY PRESS, OXFORD
BY VIVIAN RIDLER
PRINTER TO THE UNIVERSITY

ACKNOWLEDGEMENTS

FOR permission to reproduce Plates **9***a*, **12**, **15**, **19***a*, and **25***a–c* and *e* I am indebted to the Archiviste Général du Royaume de Belgique (**12**), the Directeur Général des Archives de France (**19***a*), the Keeper of the Archives of the University of Oxford (**9***a* and **25***a–c* and *e*), and the Director of the Herzog-August-Bibliothek of Wolfenbüttel (**15**). All the other plates are reproduced by courtesy of the Keeper of the Public Records.

My search for documents suitable for reproduction in facsimile was greatly facilitated by the assistance of Dr. Patricia M. Barnes and Dr. R. F. Hunnisett, of the Public Record Office, and of Mr. D. G. Vaisey, Assistant Keeper of the Archives of the University of Oxford. To Miss D. H. Gifford and the Photographic Service of the Public Record Office I owe a special debt of gratitude for the immense pains which they have taken over the photographs of particularly difficult documents. I am also very grateful to Mr. G. D. G. Hall for lending me a copy of his Introduction to the forthcoming volume, *Early Registers of Writs*, ed. E. de Haas and G. D. G. Hall (Selden Soc., vol. 87), and for his comments on documents of a judicial nature. Mr. M. B. Parkes kindly allowed me to see before publication the whole of his book, *English Cursive Book Hands, 1250–1500* (Oxford Palaeographical Handbooks, Oxford, 1969). I am indebted to Dr. R. W. Hunt and Mr. C. H. Roberts for various suggestions which helped to make the volume a more useful one. Finally I wish to thank my friend Mr. J. L. Kirby, Librarian of the History Faculty Library, Oxford, for his many kindnesses to me throughout the preparation of this book.

PIERRE CHAPLAIS

Wadham College
Oxford

CONTENTS

LIST OF PLATES

ABBREVIATIONS AND REFERENCES

Unless otherwise stated, all the documents reproduced on the plates and all the manuscripts cited are preserved in the Public Record Office, London

Arch. Nat.: Archives Nationales, Paris
Brit. Mus.: British Museum, London
Cal.: *Calendar*
Calendar of Chancery Warrants, i (H.M.S.O., London, 1927)
C.Ch.R.: *Calendar of Charter Rolls* (1226–1516), 6 vols. (H.M.S.O., London, 1903–27)
C.C.R.: *Calendar of Close Rolls* (from A.D. 1272) (H.M.S.O., London)
C.F.R.: *Calendar of Fine Rolls* (from A.D. 1272) (H.M.S.O., London)
C.P.R.: *Calendar of Patent Rolls* (from A.D. 1232) (H.M.S.O., London)
Curia Regis Rolls (H.M.S.O., London)
Déprez (Eugène), *Études de diplomatique anglaise de l'avènement d'Édouard Ier à celui de Henri VII* (Paris, 1908)
Diplomatic Documents, ed. Pierre Chaplais, i (H.M.S.O., London, 1964)
English Hist. Rev.: *English Historical Review*
Facs. of Nat. MSS.: *Facsimiles of National Manuscripts, England*, 4 parts (Ordnance Survey, 1865–9)
Hall (Hubert), *Formula Book*: *A Formula Book of English Official Historical Documents*
  i: Part I: *Diplomatic Documents* (Cambridge Univ. Press, 1908)
  ii: Part II: *Ministerial and Judicial Records* (1909)
Hector (L. C.), *The Handwriting of English Documents* (London, 1958)
Jenkinson (H.), *The Later Court Hands in England* (Cambridge, 1927)
Johnson (C.) and Jenkinson (H.): *English Court Hand, A.D. 1066 to 1500* (Oxford, 1915)
K.R.: King's Remembrancer
L.T.R.: Lord Treasurer's Remembrancer
Maxwell-Lyte (Sir H. C.): *Historical Notes on the Use of the Great Seal of England* (H.M.S.O., London, 1926)
Mich.: Michaelmas
Otway-Ruthven (J.), *The King's Secretary and the Signet Office in the XVth Century* (Cambridge Univ. Press, 1939)
Patent Rolls (1216–32), 2 vols. (H.M.S.O., London, 1901–3)
Regesta: *Regesta Regum Anglo-Normannorum, 1066–1154*
  vol. I: *Regesta Willelmi Conquestoris et Willelmi Rufi, 1066–1100*, ed. H. W. C. Davis, with the assistance of R. J. Whitwell (Oxford, 1913)
  vol. II: *Regesta Henrici Primi, 1100–1135*, ed. C. Johnson and H. A. Cronne (Oxford, 1956)
  vol. III: *Regesta Regis Stephani ac Mathildis Imperatricis . . ., 1135–1154*, ed. H. A. Cronne and R. H. C. Davis (Oxford, 1968)
Rôles Gascons: vols. II and III, ed. C. Bémont (*Documents inédits*, Paris, 1900–1906)
  vol. IV, ed. Y. Renouard (*Documents inédits* and H.M.S.O., Paris/London, 1962)
Rot. Chart.: *Rotuli Chartarum* (1199–1216), ed. T. D. Hardy (Record Commission, London, 1837)

Rotuli de Oblatis et Finibus (reign of King John), ed. T. D. Hardy (Record Commission, London, 1835)

Rot. Litt. Pat.: *Rotuli Litterarum Patentium* (1201–16), ed. T. D. Hardy (Record Commission, London, 1835)

Rotuli Scotiae (Edward I–Henry VIII), ed. D. Macpherson and others, 2 vols. (Record Commission, London, 1814–19)

Rymer, *Foedera*: *Foedera, Conventiones, Literae* . . . (to A.D. 1383), ed. T. Rymer, 4 vols. in 7 parts (Record Commission, London, 1816–69)

Selden Soc., vol. 57: *Select Cases in the Court of King's Bench*, ed. G. O. Sayles, vol. II (Edward I)
vol. 82: *Select Cases in the Court of King's Bench*, ed. G. O. Sayles, vol. VI (Edward III)

Tout (T. F.), *Chapters*: *Chapters in the Administrative History of Mediaeval England*, 6 vols. (Manchester Univ. Press, 1920–33)

T.R.: Treasury of the Receipt

Trin.: Trinity

W.A.M.: Westminster Abbey Muniments

Wilkinson (B.), *The Chancery under Edward III* (Manchester Univ. Press, 1929)

INTRODUCTION

THE purpose of this book is to illustrate the palaeography and diplomatic of English royal documents from King John to Henry VI. To a large extent the choice of plates has been dictated by the format of the volume and its permissible length. As it was essential that all reproductions should be in actual or near-actual size, such large items as the charters of the fourteenth and fifteenth centuries had to be left out. For the same reason the enrolments of the chancery and exchequer, which in any case are well represented in *English Court Hand*, *A.D. 1066–1500*, edited by C. Johnson and H. Jenkinson, have been excluded. The margins of some of the larger documents have also had to be trimmed. More regrettable is the omission of seals and their attachments, although the most common sealing methods used in royal departments are illustrated on Plates **25–7**.

Throughout the book the emphasis has been placed on originals. For purposes of comparison a few drafts have also been included (Plates **7*c***, **11*b***, **17*a***, **23*c***), as well as extracts from two royal books, one a wardrobe account-book of Richard II's reign (Plate **17*b***), the other a cartulary of 1354 relating to Gascony (Plate **15**): the latter, which names the royal scribes who copied it, is of particular interest.

Although the vast majority of the documents which have been selected for reproduction come from one single repository, the Public Record Office, they were produced by different royal departments. Within each of those departments the documents issued varied considerably from one another in the purpose which they were designed to serve and in their diplomatic form. It is to the discussion of these problems that the greater part of this Introduction will be devoted. An attempt will be made in the following pages to outline the methods by which royal documents were produced in the main departments of state and to give a brief account of the diplomatic of each type of document. In the history of royal documents the reign of King John—the starting-point of this volume—is an important landmark, but because its importance cannot be fully understood without some knowledge of what happened before, this survey will, as necessary, intrude into the previous reigns.

I. THE GREAT SEAL AND CHANCERY

When King John came to the throne in 1199 the English royal chancery was, by continental standards, a comparatively recent institution. It had started only some 150 years before, in Edward the Confessor's reign.[1] From the embryonic office of King Edward's days—a royal seal and its keeper—it had developed into a secretariat no less sophisticated than the Capetian chancery, which had a much longer history behind it. King John's chancery

[1] For diverging views on the origin of the royal chancery, see F. E. Harmer, *Anglo-Saxon Writs* (Manchester Univ. Press, 1952), pp. 57–61; P. Chaplais, 'The Anglo-Saxon Chancery: From the Diploma to the Writ', *Journal Soc. Archivists*, iii. 4 (Oct. 1966), pp. 160–76.

still revolved around a royal seal, but this seal now deserved to be called a *magnum sigillum*,[1] not so much on account of its large size (3·8 inches in diameter) as because the king had by this time acquired another, smaller, seal which he also used for official business, a *sigillum parvum* or *privatum*.[2]

The seal of Edward the Confessor, from which all the later great seals of English kings were derived, was circular and double-sided, with a diameter of about three inches. Both sides were seals of majesty, representing the king enthroned and holding in his hands insignia of royal power: on one side a sceptre topped with a trefoil in his right hand and an orb topped with a cross in his left, on the other side a *virga* topped with an eagle in his right hand and a sword in his left. On each side the design (*imago*[3]) was surrounded by the same legend (*inscriptio*[4] or *circumscriptio*[5]): +SIGILLVM EADVVARDI ANGLORVM BASILEI.[6] Also circular and double-sided, but slightly larger, the seal of William the Conqueror portrayed the king in majesty on one side only: there William, sitting on a throne, held a sword in his right hand and an orb surmounted by a cross in his left. The other side was equestrian, representing William riding from left to right. The hexametric legend read, on the equestrian side, +HOC NORMANNORVM WILLELMVM NOSCE PATRONVM SI, continuing, on the majesty side, +HOC ANGLIS REGEM SIGNO FATEARIS EVNDEM, thus suggesting that each side was meant to represent the Conqueror in a different capacity: on the majesty (or royal) side he was king of the English; on the equestrian (or baronial) side he was duke of the Normans. Since the legend began on the equestrian side—presumably because William was already duke of Normandy when he acquired England—it seems reasonable to regard that side as the obverse (or face) of the seal and the majesty side as the reverse.[7]

The design of both sides of William the Conqueror's seal was retained by all his successors on the English throne until early modern times. After the Conqueror's death not one medieval English king failed to use a [great] seal which had a majesty side and an equestrian side, whether or not he held or claimed a baronial title independently of the English crown.[8] From the reign of William Rufus onwards one has to examine the legend of the equestrian side—now undoubtedly the reverse of the seal—before deciding what significance, if any, should be attached to that side. The equestrian side of William Rufus's seal had no particular meaning, since Rufus had no claim to the duchy of Normandy, and this was emphasized in the legend of the seal, which read on both sides: +WILLELMVS DEI GRATIA REX ANGLORVM.[9] The same is true of the first two seals of Henry I (the so-called 'second' seal, 1100–6, and 'third' seal, 1107–20), both of which had the same legend on both sides, +HENRICVS DEI GRATIA REX ANGLORVM, but not of his third seal (the so-called 'fourth' seal, 1121–35), which, while retaining the old

[1] Maxwell-Lyte, p. 20.

[2] Ibid., pp. 20–1.

[3] *Dialogus de Scaccario*, ed. C. Johnson (Nelson's Medieval Classics, 1950), p. 62.

[4] Ibid.

[5] Maxwell-Lyte, p. 41; P. Chaplais, 'The Chancery of Guyenne, 1289–1453', *Studies Presented to Sir Hilary Jenkinson*, ed. J. Conway Davies (London, 1957), p. 88, n. 8.

[6] Harmer, *Anglo-Saxon Writs*, p. 94. For reproductions of the English great seals, see A. B. and A. Wyon, *The Great Seals of England* (London, 1887).

[7] See *Journal Soc. Archivists*, iii. 4 (Oct. 1966), p. 161.

[8] *Guide to Seals in the Public Record Office* (H.M.S.O., 1954), p. 24. Empress Matilda's seal was one-sided.

[9] *Facs. of English Royal Writs to A.D. 1100 presented to V. H. Galbraith*, ed. T. A. M. Bishop and P. Chaplais (Oxford, 1957), plate xxx.

legend on the majesty side, changed that of the equestrian side to +HENRICVS DEI GRATIA DUX NORMANNORVM.[1] Stephen also called himself duke of the Normans on the reverse of his two successive seals. In the eyes of Henry II, Richard I, John, and Henry III (until 1259) the equestrian side represented all the baronial titles which they held on the Continent, those of duke of Normandy, duke of Aquitaine and count of Anjou; the majesty side represented the title of king of England under Henry II and Richard I, and the titles of king of England and lord of Ireland under John and Henry III. With the treaty of Paris of 1259, by which Henry III renounced his claims to all the former continental possessions of his predecessors except Aquitaine, began the practice of using on both sides of the great seal an identical legend, which enumerated all the king's titles.[2] The assumption of the title of king of France by Edward III and his successors, from 1340 onwards, did not bring about any major changes in the design of the great seal: the equestrian side remained, although one might have expected it to be replaced by a second side of majesty.

In John's reign the titular custodian of the great seal was styled *cancellarius* as he had been ever since 1069 at the latest,[3] but this office, filled under the Norman kings by a succession of mere royal chaplains, was now regarded as fit for a bishop or an archbishop to hold. Bishop William Longchamp of Ely had been chancellor under Richard I. Now it was the turn of Archbishop Hubert Walter to enhance the stature of the office. In the day-to-day running of his department the chancellor leaned heavily on two deputies: one, the vice-chancellor (*vicecancellarius*), was the real keeper of the seal (*sigillifer*), while the other, the protonotary (*protonotarius*), who had succeeded the *magister scriptorii* of Henry I and Henry II, supervised the clerical staff of the chancery in their writing duties.[4]

The surviving records of the period suggest that the volume of business transacted, and the number of clerks employed, in the royal chancery were, under John, much larger than they had been under his predecessors. Each document issued under John's name and sealed with his great seal was the occasion of a great deal of work for the chancery. First a draft (*forma*, *nota*, or *transcriptum*)[5] had to be prepared. Once the draft had been checked and corrected, the actual document which was to be presented to the seal—the 'original' or engrossment (*originale; originales littere*)[6]—had to be written in a fair hand. Finally, and this appears to have been an innovation of John's reign, the drafts were sorted out at intervals and some of them copied on rolls (*rotuli cancellarie*) for future reference. By 1201 three major series of chancery rolls had been created for the enrolment of royal documents sealed with the great seal, one for charters (*rotuli cartarum*: charter rolls), a

[1] P. Chaplais, 'The Seals and Original Charters of Henry I', *English Hist. Rev.* lxxv (1960), pp. 262–5.

[2] P. Chaplais, 'The Making of the Treaty of Paris (1259) and the Royal Style', *English Hist. Rev.* lxvii (1952), pp. 248–51.

[3] Ordnance Survey, *Facs. of Anglo-Saxon MSS.* (1878–84), II, Exeter xvi.

[4] Rymer, *Foedera* (Rec. Comm.), I. i. 75–6; *Dialogus de Scaccario*, ed. C. Johnson (Nelson's Medieval Classics, 1950), p. 129; Tout, *Chapters*, i, pp. 127–35.

[5] *Diplomatic Documents*, ed. P. Chaplais, i, nos. 29, 32, 40; Maxwell-Lyte, pp. 51–2, 359–60; H. G. Richardson in *Memoranda Roll 1 John* (Pipe Roll Soc., N.S. 21), pp. xlix–l; cf. P. Chaplais, 'Privy Seal Drafts, Rolls and Registers (Edward I–Edward II)', *English Hist. Rev.* lxxiii, pp. 270–2.

[6] *Dialogus de Scaccario*, ed. cit., p. 74; *Epistolae Cantuarienses*, ed. W. Stubbs (Rolls Series, 1865), p. 96; *Close Rolls, 1251–1253*, p. 205; Chancery Warrants (C. 81), 1329/99.

second for letters patent (*rotuli litterarum patentium*: patent rolls), and a third for letters close (*rotuli litterarum clausarum*: close rolls).[1]

'CARTA' AND 'BREVE'

There is abundant evidence that royal chancery instruments were in 1199 already classified in *carte*, *littere patentes*, and *littere clause*, the threefold division which was still in use at the end of the Middle Ages. That the classification existed before 1199 is likely, but the date of its introduction is hard to fix within narrow limits. Charters, letters patent, and letters close were all derived from a common ancestor, the Latin writ of William the Conqueror, itself the direct descendant of Edward the Confessor's writ in Old English. Judging from the examples still extant, it seems that every Old-English writ was a declaration under the king's name that he had made or confirmed a grant of land or a grant of rights on land. It was cast in the form of an open letter authenticated by the royal seal and addressed to the officials and suitors (i.e. the bishop, earl, and thegns) of the court of the shire in which the land granted was situated; if, as in confirmations of previous grants, the lands or rights granted covered more than one shire, the writ was addressed to all the shire-courts involved.[2] The first of the following writs, for the abbey of Westminster, is an example of the first type; the second, for Abbot Leofstan of Bury St Edmunds, is an example of the second type:

1. +Eadweard cyngc gret Leofwine b*isceop* 7 Eadwine eorl 7 ealle mi[ne þe]gnas on Stæffordscire freondlice. 7 ic kyþe eow *þæt* ic habbe gegifan Criste 7 S*anct*e Petre into [Wes]tmynstre *þæt* land æt Pertune 7 ælc þæra þinga þæs þe þær inn to herð on wuda 7 on felda mid saca [7] mid socne swa full 7 swa forð swa hit mesylfan on handa stod on eallan þingan þan abbude [to b]igleofan 7 þam gebroþran þe binnan þam mynstre wuniað. 7 ic nylle nane men geþafian *þæt* þær geutige ænig þæra þinga þæs þe þær [mid rihte] in to gebyrað.[3]
2. +Eadweard cyngc gret mine bisceopas 7 mine eorlas 7 ealle mine þegnas on þam sciren þær S*anct*e Eadmund hafað land inne freondlice. 7 ic cyðe eow *þæt* ic wylle *þæt* Leofstan abb' 7 ealle þa gebroðra on Eadmundes byrig beon heora sake 7 heora socne wurðe ofer ealle heora agene menn ægðer ge binnan burh ge butan. 7 ic nelle geðafian *þæt* heom ænig man ænig woh beode.[4]

It was the grantee, for whose protection the writ had been invented, who caused it to be written, apparently by one of his own scribes, presented it to the king for sealing, and took it to the shire-court where it was read aloud. Then the writ was handed back to the grantee who preserved it with his other muniments as evidence of title.[5]

For a few years after the Conquest writs in Old English continued to be issued in the same form as before and for the same purpose, namely for notifications of grants of land and grants of rights on land. The first significant change in the form of the writ seems to have been made in 1070, when Old English was almost entirely superseded by Latin,

[1] The charter rolls begin in the first year of John's reign. The close rolls may have begun at the same time, but the earliest close roll extant (incomplete) belongs to 2 John. Letters patent of 1–2 John are enrolled on the charter rolls; the series of patent rolls does not start until 3 John. For a short account of these and other chancery enrolments, see *Guide to the Contents of the Public Record Office*, i (H.M.S.O., 1963), pp. 14–26.

[2] Harmer, *Anglo-Saxon Writs*, pp. 45–54; *Facs. of English Royal Writs*, p. x.

[3] Ibid., no. 25; Harmer, op. cit., no. 96 (P).

[4] *Facs. of English Royal Writs*, no. 1; Harmer, op. cit., no. 11.

[5] Ibid., pp. 45–6.

and the peculiar structure of the Old-English letter replaced by the current form of the Latin *epistola*. This innovation was probably the result of the Normanization of the English Church, whose dignitaries appear to have always been the main beneficiaries of the writs and whose scribes had until then penned most—if not all—of them.[1] Other changes took place during the Conqueror's reign. One was the secularization of the writ, notably the disappearance of such religious or ecclesiastical features as the initial cross and the final anathema and valediction (*God eow gehealde*) occasionally found in Old-English writs. Perhaps this was due to the gradual involvement of royal scribes in the drafting and writing of the writs. Between 1070 and 1087 two new clauses were inserted at the end of the document: one was a list of witnesses (*T*[*estibus*] *A.*, *B.* etc.) and the other a mention of the place of issue (*Apud N.*), both of which clauses, however, are sometimes absent even from writs issued at the end of William I's reign, for example from the following original of 1087:

W. rex Anglor*um* H. de Portu et omnibus fidelibus suis francigenis et anglicis, salutem. Sciatis me dedisse Sancto Petro de Westmonasterio decimam de Rotelanda. Et tu, Hugo de Portu, inde eum saisias.[2]

It will be noticed that in this writ, the work of a royal scribe, the only addressee mentioned by name is the sheriff (Hugh de Port), now the main official of the shire-court, and that the rest of the address is much more general than it was before 1066, since it goes beyond the suitors of the shire-court to include all the king's lieges. It is also worth noting that this writ is more than a notification; its last clause is a specific order to the sheriff to give seisin to the grantee. Perhaps for new grants of land the writ had always implied a tacit order for livery of seisin. Perhaps also the use of the writ as a means of conveying an explicit injunction to the addressees in a sort of postscript to the notification of a grant was not entirely unknown in Anglo-Saxon times, although it certainly was rare.[3] But the use of the writ for injunctions pure and simple, as in the following example of William I's reign, appears to have been a post-Conquest development:

[W]illelmus rex Anglor*um* W. vicecomiti, salutem. Mando et precipio tibi ut abbatem Ailsi facias habere Isham sicut ipse eam dirationavit in Hamptona et sicut testimoniata est et jurata ad opus sancti. T*este* R. Bigot.[4]

Ephemeral injunctions of this kind, addressed to one or several named individuals and requiring them to perform one single action only, were not uncommon in William I's reign[5] and their number increased under William II. By that time there had also come into being another variety of writ which may be described as a hybrid between the notification and the injunction. Writs of exemption from toll and writs of protection belong to this category: like the notifications, they conferred permanent rights on their beneficiaries and had a more or less general address, but they were cast, like the injunctions,

[1] *Journal Soc. Archivists*, iii. 4, pp. 175–6.

[2] *Facs. of English Royal Writs*, no. 27.

[3] See Harmer, op. cit., no. 17, if authentic; compare C. R. Hart, *Early Charters of Eastern England* (Leicester Univ. Press, 1966), pp. 86–91.

[4] Oxford, Bodleian Lib., Rawlinson MS. B. 333, fol. 36v: *Regesta*, i, no. 288b.

[5] *Liber Eliensis*, ed. E. O. Blake (Royal Hist. Soc., Camden Third Series, xcii), pp. 203–7.

in the form of an order or prohibition; their text was normally introduced, not by *Sciatis*, but by a word of command such as *Precipio*. The following exemption from toll was granted to the abbot of Thorney by William II:

> W. rex Angl*orum* omnibus vicecomitibus suis et ministris tocius regni Angliȩ, salutem. Precipio vobis ut dimittatis abbaciam de Torneio quietam et solutam omnino ab omni theloneo et ab omni alia consuetudine de rebus illis quas monachi predictȩ abbaciȩ emunt ad proprium victum suum et ad vestimentum et ad cooperturam ȩcclesiȩ suȩ, sicuti meȩ aliȩ abbaciȩ quietȩ sunt et solutȩ de theloneo et aliis consuetudinibus. Et si quis supra hoc predictȩ abbatiȩ aliquam injuriam fecerit de hac re, volo ut mihi graviter emendet. T*este* W. cancellario apud Pontem Arcar' in proxima die post festum sancti Martini.[1]

In many respects notifications and injunctions were treated alike both by the king and by the beneficiary. All types of writ were regarded as title-deeds, irrespective of their outwardly ephemeral or lasting value. It was the beneficiary, either in person or through someone else's good offices (for example *per Turaldum abbatem de Burgo*[2]), who procured the required writ from the king and presented it to the appropriate persons for information or execution; once this had been done, notifications and injunctions were returned to the beneficiary, who preserved them with great care among his title-deeds. Because they were meant to be kept as evidence of title, writs of all kinds were sealed 'patent', that is to say 'open'; the seal authenticated the document without closing it up. From the time of Edward the Confessor this had been achieved by sealing the writ on a tongue. Two narrow and parallel strips of parchment were partially cut off the foot of the document, below the writing, the cuts starting on the right, then running parallel to the lower edge, to stop at a distance of one or two inches from the left margin.[3] The middle part (or the loose end) of one of the strips, normally the upper one, later known as *simplex cauda* ('tongue'), was imbedded in wax (*cum cera involutum*), which was then pressed between the two jaws of the double matrix of the royal seal. The document was folded several times vertically and, if required, also horizontally to form a small package, around which the second strip ('wrapping-tie') was wrapped and looped through itself or knotted, the tongue remaining free and pendent. Thus the writ could be read by unfastening the wrapping-tie, without damaging the seal or its attachment.

Whatever its object, until some time in Henry I's reign every writ was described as a *breve* in the terminology of the royal chancery, the word *carta* being, with a few exceptions, reserved for the diploma.[4] The latter type of document, which had never been widely used by the Norman kings outside their continental dominions except for ecclesiastical foundation-charters,[5] lost more and more ground to the writ after 1100. It was from about that time that the royal chancery began to refer to some writs as *carte* and to others as *brevia*, a classification which became more systematic and meaningful from *c.* 1120. The new terminology was not simply the result of a gradual shift in Latin usage.

[1] *Facs. of Early Charters from Northamptonshire Collections* (Northants Rec. Soc., iv), ed. F. M. Stenton, plate i (*b*); *Facs. of English Royal Writs*, no. 23.

[2] *Regesta*, i, nos. 330–2.

[3] *Facs. of English Royal Writs*, e.g. plates xxi–xxiv.

[4] *Regesta*, i, no. 315, a diploma: '. . . Confirmatio autem hujus chartȩ facta est apud Doveram . . .'; compare T. A. M. Bishop, *Scriptores Regis* (Oxford, 1961), plate ix (*b*): '. . . sicuti testantur brevia regis Edwardi et patris mei et mea . . .'. See also *Regesta*, ii, nos. 660, 666, 1122, etc.

[5] e.g. ibid. i, no. 315; ii, nos. 919–20.

It reflected a deliberate effort to differentiate, in name as well as in form and object, one type of writ from another, the notification from the injunction. By 1120 at the latest the notification had come to be known by the name of *carta*, while the injunction retained the name of *breve*. By then the address of the *carta* had become even more general than before, and its list of witnesses was normally longer than that of the *breve*, which often consisted of one single name.[1]

Even a cursory survey of sample writs issued between *c.* 1120 and *c.* 1160 clearly shows that during that period the classification in *carte* and *brevia* was far from rigid. The writ of exemption from toll, for example, is sometimes self-styled *breve*, sometimes quoted as *carta* in a confirmation.[2] Such a writ might be suitably described as a 'lesser *carta*' or a 'greater *breve*', a description which would be equally fitting for writs of protection.[3] It is clear also that the word *carta* was not infrequently used in a loose sense to describe any type of written evidence, sealed or unsealed, the writ-mandate as well as the writ-charter,[4] and even Domesday Book.[5] The word *breve* itself was before Henry I occasionally given the same loose meanings.[6] Several factors contributed to the confusion between *carta* and *breve*: on the one hand the *carta* resembled the *breve* in that it normally contained an incidental injunction or prohibition of some kind; on the other the *breve*, like the *carta*, was, as we have seen, treated as a title-deed by the beneficiary.

'BREVE PATENS' AND 'BREVE CLAUSUM'

By the 1160s it was no longer assumed that all writs had to be sealed patent: only those which had a general address and recorded a grant, that is to say the *carte* and some *brevia*, could not be sealed in any other way. Henry II's famous writ of inquisition on fees of 1166 and the baronial answers to it state that every tenant-in-chief had been ordered by the king to make his return by sealed letters patent (*per literas . . . extra sigillum pendentes*;[7] *per breve . . . sigillatum et apertum*;[8] etc.). Similarly in 1184 a writ of Henry II ordered the prior of Rochester and the twelve monks summoned with him to Westminster, ready to elect a new bishop, to bring along with them *literas de capitulo vestro patentes de ratihabitione illius eleccionis*.[9] These references to letters or 'writs' sealed patent or open, with a pendent seal, imply that the contemporaries were acquainted with some other sealing method. Perhaps it was even expected by the chancery officials that, unless specifically ordered to do otherwise, the barons in 1166 and the chapter of Rochester in 1184 would have complied with the king's command by sending letters close. This interpretation is

[1] Compare Bishop, *Scriptores Regis*, plate xiv, and *Northants Rec. Soc.* iv, plate iv (*a–b*).

[2] *Regesta*, ii, no. 1820 (and p. 381: 'super hoc breve meum'); iii, no. 214 ('sicut rex Henricus eis concessit per cartam suam').

[3] Compare Bishop, *Scriptores Regis*, plate xiii (*a*): 'sicut pater meus melius precipit per cartam suam et ego per meam'; *Regesta*, iii, no. 562: 'sicut testantur karte W. regis et H. regis'.

[4] In *Pipe Roll 31 Henry I* (Reprint, Pipe Roll Soc., 1929), p. 66, 'secundum carthas ęcclesię suę', the word *carthas* presumably refers to title-deeds of any kind. See also the endorsement written at Fécamp, probably in the late-twelfth century, on what is undoubtedly a writ-mandate: 'Carta Willelmi regis Anglorum' (*Facs. of English Royal Writs*, plate xii (*b*)).

[5] V. H. Galbraith, *The Making of Domesday Book* (Oxford, 1961), p. 210.

[6] Ibid., pp. 129–32, 207–10.

[7] Hall, *Formula Book*, ii, p. 38, no. 24. See V. H. Galbraith, *Studies in the Public Records* (Nelson, 1948), p. 73.

[8] *Red Book of the Exchequer*, ed. H. Hall (Rolls Series, 1896), i, p. 248.

[9] *Memoranda Roll 1 John*, p. lxxii; cf. ibid., p. lxx: 'breve capituli vestri extra pendens'.

confirmed by two passages from the *Dialogus de Scaccario*, written between 1176 and 1179. In the first the author, Richard son of Nigel, remarks that the pipe roll shared one feature with the *carte* and other 'writings patent' (*cum cartis et aliis scriptis patentibus*): like them, it had to be free from erasures.[1] In the second passage Richard returns to the problem of erasures, this time in connection with the exchequer *breve* of summons: because this *breve* was a *scriptum patens*, sent open to the sheriff, if a mistake was found in it while it was checked, the offending passage had to be thoroughly obliterated, so that it could not be read by anyone.[2] Here again the implication is that, whereas the *breve* of summons, like the *carta*, was sealed patent, there were other *brevia* which could not be read so easily, because they were closed up by the seal.

Several other texts prove conclusively that writs close were commonly issued by Henry II's chancery from the 1160s onwards. The pipe roll of the second year of Richard I's reign refers to a *breve* of the king's father which had come *clausum* to the exchequer.[3] More interesting still is the account given by Master David of London of various documents, among them several *littere incluse*, that is to say writs (or letters) close,[4] which were issued on his behalf in 1170 by Henry II, who was then in France:

Cum ad dominum Cant' . . . divertissem, durissimam mihi retulit controversiam super benefitio quod a domino rege acceperam. Unde propter hoc . . . illud mihi mutare feci in proprium dominium domini regis, qui illud carta sua mihi confirmavit; aliam etiam cartam confirmationis de benefitio, quod dominus meus Lond' in me contulit, mihi fecit. Mandat autem domino regi filio suo per litteras suas inclusas, ut suam et domini episcopi donationem, juxta tenorem cartarum illarum, mihi per similes suas confirmet. Precipit per litteras suas inclusas Rann' de Broc ut singulis annis statutis terminis xv libras mihi solvat, ita ut de cetero nec aliud breve nec aliud mandatum domini regis super hoc a me exigat. In eundem modum scribit domino London' pro v libris, et has litteras domino London' porrexi. Vicecomitibus de Middelsex' mandat per aliud breve ne has v libras a domino episcopo ulterius exigant. Baronibus de scaccario quoddam breve mittit, in quo precipit eis ut computent Rann' del Broc xv libras et episcopo London' v libras, et ut de cetero ab eis aliud breve non exigant. Transcriptum illius, et transcriptum ejus quod mittitur Rann', ad cautelam ne quandoque malignari possint sigillari feci, que penes vos retinebitis cum cartis meis . . .[5]

On this occasion Henry II had issued two *carte* obviously sealed patent, one writ close addressed to the young king Henry Court Mantel, one writ close [of *computabitur*] to Ranulf de Broc, one writ close [of *computabitur*] to the bishop of London, one writ probably close to the sheriffs of Middlesex, another probably close of *computate* to the barons of the exchequer, and two writs patent which were duplicates of the writs close to Ranulf

[1] *Dialogus de Scaccario* (Nelson's Medieval Classics), p. 31.

[2] Ibid., p. 74.

[3] *Pipe Roll 2 Richard I* (Pipe Roll Soc., N.S. 1), p. 155: 'Et in camera domini regis patris . . . per breve ipsius regis quod clausum venit ad scaccarium.' See Maxwell-Lyte, p. 302.

[4] In the contemporary terminology of the papal chancery the expressions *littere incluse* and *littere clause* were synonymous: *Chronica Rogeri de Hoveden*, ed. W. Stubbs (Rolls Series, 1868–71), iii, p. 281 ('. . . illud . . . ad nos sub sigillis vestris transmittatis inclusum . . .'); *Acta Pontificum Romanorum Inedita*, ed. J. v. Pflugk-Harttung, iii (1886), p. 268, no. 282 ('. . . depositiones . . . sub sigillo tuo clausas nobis transmittas . . .'). See also *Epistolae Cantuarienses*, p. 241: 'Aliis sigillo inclusis et paratis procedere, supervenerunt et vestrae.' See also Galbraith, *Studies in the Public Records*, pp. 73–4.

[5] Z. N. Brooke, 'The Register of Master David of London . . .', *Essays in History presented to R. L. Poole* (Oxford, 1927), p. 240 (cf. *Memoranda Roll 1 John*, p. lxxx). I am very grateful to Professor C. N. L. Brooke for permission to reprint this text and for the loan of his photographs of the Vatican manuscript.

de Broc and to the barons of the exchequer. It should be noted that a writ of King Stephen to Queen Matilda, similar to Henry II's writ close to Henry Court Mantel, was sealed patent since it has been copied in the cartulary of the beneficiary, the abbey of Arrouaise;[1] a writ of *computate* of Matilda the empress in favour of the canons of Oseney, which has survived in the original with its seal almost intact among the Oseney archives, is sealed patent.[2] Although it is likely that the writs patent for Arrouaise and Oseney were the only ones issued on both occasions, the possibility that they were only duplicates of writs close sent to the addressees, as in the case of Master David, cannot be entirely ruled out. It seems certain, however, that some writs which had previously been sent patent were replaced by writs close from the 1160s, probably as a result of the tightening of royal administration which took place in Henry II's reign, the king now relying less on the willingness of his subjects to carry out his orders than on the constraining power of his officials, particularly the sheriffs. The introduction of 'returnable' common-law writs, some time in Henry II's reign, was a step in that direction. There is no doubt that these writs, whose text ends with the characteristic clause *Et habeas ibi . . . hoc breve*, were sent close to the sheriff to whom they were addressed.[3]

A letter of Henry II to the convent of Christ Church, Canterbury, drafted by Hubert Walter on 3 February 1189 at Le Mans, was also a letter close since, when Archbishop Baldwin insisted on reading it before dispatch, the seal had to be broken to enable him to do so.[4] The majority of informal letters, as opposed to administrative writs, sent by Henry II to the pope and others were likewise certainly sealed close;[5] informal letters of earlier reigns may also have been sent close, but the evidence on this point is lacking.

How can we determine with reasonable certainty whether an extant original of Henry II should be identified as a writ close rather than as a writ patent? The absence of seal or seal-attachment, although it might be thought an essential condition, is not a reliable test by itself, since many writs undeniably sealed patent have accidentally lost both their seal and its attachment; conversely, the recipients of letters close sometimes succeeded in preserving almost intact the seal and its attachment (Plate **25*e***). One should in addition ensure that the writ was preserved in the archives of the addressee, not in those of the beneficiary, and, for further safety, that the order which the writ conveyed required the addressee to take one single action only, not a recurrent one as in the case of the writs of *computabitur* mentioned by Master David of London: although in that particular instance we know that the writs were issued close, we might have reasonably expected them to be sealed patent. To my knowledge only one extant original of Henry II, a writ of *liberate* preserved in the Public Record Office, meets all the requirements mentioned above and deserves to be regarded as a writ close:

H. Dei gratia rex Angl*orum* et dux Norm*annorum* et Aquit*annorum* et comes And*egavorum* R. thesaurario et Willelmo Malduit et Warino filio Giroldi camerariis suis, salutem. Liberate de th[esau]ro

[1] *Regesta*, iii, no. 25.

[2] Ibid., no. 628.

[3] See Doris M. Stenton, *English Justice between the Norman Conquest and the Great Charter* (London, 1965), pp. 32–3; *Pleas before the King or his Justices, 1198–1202*, i (Selden Soc. 67), p. 28.

[4] *Epistolae Cantuarienses*, pp. 282–3. The letter, as amended by Baldwin, is printed ibid., pp. 544–5.

[5] As no original is extant, the point cannot be proved.

meo xxv marcas fratribus Cartusie de illis L marcis quas do eis annuatim per cartam meam. T*este* Willelmo de Sancte Marie Ecclesia apud Westmoster.[1]

The *carta*, certainly sealed patent, to which the writ refers, is lost, but its text can be reconstructed from Richard I's confirmation.[2] Another writ close of *liberate* of Henry II's reign is extant in the Public Record Office, but it was issued under the name of Ranulf Glanville as justiciar, not under the king's name.[3]

In size and physical appearance Henry II's original *liberate* writ bears a close resemblance to the justiciar's writs of King John's reign,[4] and it is obvious that it was closed up and sealed by the same method as they were, the 'plying and sealing' method consistently used for all great-seal writs close in the medieval and early-modern periods.[5] Whereas writs patent had a tongue and a wrapping-tie, writs meant to be sealed close had no wrapping-tie, and their tongue, although cut in much the same way as in writs patent, was narrower (one-eighth of an inch in width in the case of Henry II's *liberate* writ). The tongue served as a wrapping-tie and as a support for the seal as well: once the writ had been folded into a small package, the tongue was wrapped round it and looped through itself to prevent unfolding; then the loose part of the tongue, close to the loop, was placed between two cakes of wax, which were joined together by pressing them between the two jaws of the matrix of the great seal.[6] Although the most important writs (and letters) close may have borne a full impression of the great seal, those of a routine character were sealed with only a fragment of the seal (one-half or less); this fragmentary impression was described in medieval times as the 'foot of the seal' (*pes sigilli*).[7] By the fourteenth century the tongue of writs and letters close was shaped like an elongated wedge, broader at its loose end than at its root; the reason for this was presumably to make more room for the address, which was written on the tongue between its loose end and the seal (Plate **25***e*). The writ close was normally opened either by breaking the seal or by severing the tongue near its root (see, however, Plate **25***e*). The short stub which remains in the bottom left-hand corner of Henry II's *liberate* writ is the only evidence that it once had a tongue.

One writ of Empress Matilda and two writs of Henry II were thought by Delisle and Tout to have been issued close;[8] in fact the three documents display several of the characteristics of writs patent: not only is their tongue too wide for writs close, but also they show, below the tongue, the remains of a wrapping-tie. A writ which bears traces of two parallel strips (one, usually the upper one, wider than the other), partially cut off the lower edge of the parchment, cannot be anything but a writ patent. In a few originals clearly sealed patent there is no obvious sign of a wrapping-tie;[9] in these cases either the

[1] Exchequer of Receipt, Warrants for Issues (E. 404), 1/1: Hall, *Formula Book*, i, p. 83, no. 77.

[2] *C.P.R., 1338–40*, p. 453: 'Ricardus . . . Sciatis nos . . . concessisse et presenti carta confirmasse Deo et priori et fratribus de Chartusa quinquaginta marcas argenti recipiendas singulis annis ad scaccarium nostrum Anglie his terminis, in termino Pasche xxv marcas, in termino Sancti Michaelis xxv marcas, quas dominus rex Henricus, pater noster, eis dedit et confirmavit ad eosdem terminos percipiendas . . .'

[3] *Memoranda Roll 1 John*, p. lxxii.

[4] See the plates in *Pleas before the King or his Justices, 1198–1202*, ed. Doris M. Stenton, i (Selden Soc. 67).

[5] Maxwell-Lyte, pp. 302–5 and plate (frontispiece); below, Plate **25***d*.

[6] Maxwell-Lyte, p. 303.

[7] Ibid., pp. 305–9.

[8] Tout, *Chapters*, i, p. 137, n. 1.

[9] R. C. Van Caenegem, *Royal Writs in England from the Conquest to Glanvill* (Selden Soc. 77), p. 165 and n. 2.

wrapping-tie was dispensed with or, perhaps more plausibly, it was so neatly cut off by the beneficiary as to leave no trace of its former existence. Empress Matilda's writ claimed by Delisle to have been sent close bears an address on its tongue. This was one of the distinguishing features of writs and letters close from the thirteenth century onwards, but it is not certain that it was already so in Henry II's time: another writ of Henry II, preserved in the archives of the dean and chapter of Lincoln, has a similar address on its tongue, although it may have been sent patent.[1]

The method of sealing patent on a tongue and fastening with a wrapping-tie, the only one used for Edward the Confessor's writs and for all types of Anglo-Norman writs from 1066 to 1100, was also the most commonly used for the *breve*, as distinct from the *carta*, from 1100 × 1120 to *c.* 1160, and for the *breve patens*, as opposed to the *breve clausum*, from *c.* 1160 until the end of the Middle Ages.

Soon after the Conquest other ways of sealing patent had been devised, but they were at first reserved for the diploma[2] and for other large and solemn documents in non-epistolary form: in one of them, apparently a unique example in England, the seal, which is now detached, was formerly applied to the surface of the parchment; in others the seal is appended to a projecting tongue, to a tag of parchment or leather, or to silk cords. The 'applied seal' method, which was used for the authentication of the record of the council of Windsor (Whit Sunday 1072),[3] a document written by a Canterbury scribe, was imitated from the practice adopted for sealing diplomas by the royal Merovingian, Carolingian, and early-Capetian chanceries: a circular hole of approximately one inch in diameter was cut out of the parchment near the lower right-hand corner; the impression of the seal was obtained by placing this corner of the parchment, after face and dorse—on and around the hole—had been lined with a thick layer of softened wax, between the two jaws of the double matrix of William I's seal. It was also from continental practice that the system used for sealing William's diploma af 1085 for the abbey of Fécamp, a document written by a royal scribe, was probably derived.[4] Here the royal seal was appended to a tongue projecting at right angles from the foot of the parchment; for this a sheet much taller than required for the writing was used; the blank portion below the writing was cut out except for the tongue, a vertical strip about one-inch wide, which was left in the centre. Compared with the tongue of Anglo-Saxon origin, the projecting one had the advantage of being less easily torn off under the weight of the seal, but a great deal of parchment was wasted. The practice of sealing on a tag, used for diplomas of William I and Henry I,[5] was much more satisfactory: it consisted of inserting a tag (*duplex cauda*), that is to say a loose strip of parchment or leather, through one or several horizontal slits made at the foot of the document; the two ends of the tag were joined

[1] *Registrum Antiquissimum*, i (Lincoln Rec. Soc. 27, ed. C. W. Foster), plate xvi, no. 195. As the document is not copied in a cartulary, it is impossible to tell whether Lincoln was its original home.

[2] Among other features which differentiated it from the writ, the diploma of Anglo-Norman type was not in epistolary form; the grantor was normally made to speak in the present ('Ego . . . concedo . . .'), and the marks of authentication consisted essentially of subscriptions or *signa*, to which the grantor's seal could be added.

[3] See *Facs. of English Royal Writs*, plate xxix and note.

[4] P. Chaplais, 'Une charte originale de Guillaume le Conquérant pour l'abbaye de Fécamp: la donation de Steyning et de Bury (1085)', *L'abbaye bénédictine de Fécamp*, i (Fécamp, 1959), plate facing p. 94.

[5] *Regesta*, i, no. 232; ii, nos. 735 (*a*) and 920; *Facs. of English Royal Writs*, plate xxviii and note.

together by sandwiching them between two cakes of softened wax, which were then pressed between the two jaws of the seal matrix. When, as was often the case, the parchment of the document was folded over at the foot for reinforcement, additional slits had to be made through the turn-up (*plica*) for insertion of the tag. In the foundation-charters of the sees of Bath (A.D. 1091)[1] and Ely (A.D. 1109),[2] both written by royal scribes, silk cords were used instead of a tag. The cords were attached to the diploma (with or without a turn-up) in the same way as a tag except that they were inserted through eyelets, not through slits.

It was to be expected that sooner or later the sealing methods used for the diploma would spread to the writ-charter. As early as 1100 some bilingual writs of Henry I for the archbishop of Canterbury and the convent of Christ Church were sealed on a horizontal tongue, projecting from the left margin of the document.[3] These writs, however, were the products of the Canterbury scriptorium, where for the greater part of the twelfth century the horizontal projecting tongue, a variant of the vertical one, was a favoured type of seal-attachment.[4] For royal *carte* written by royal scribes the tongue of Anglo-Saxon type remained the most common seal-attachment until the latter part of Henry II's reign, although examples of projecting tongues, either vertical or horizontal, have survived for the reign of Henry I, the earliest on a royal writ of 1105 for the abbey of Ely.[5] The tag, rarely used by Henry I's chancery,[6] occurs more frequently under Stephen,[7] during whose reign silk cords are also found on particularly important *carte*.[8] Towards the end of Henry II's reign, by which time fewer royal documents appear to have been written outside the chancery, the majority of *carte* were sealed either on a tag or on silk cords; for *brevia* patent the tongue of Anglo-Saxon type was still the rule, although some of the more important *brevia* were sometimes sealed on a tag or, rarely, on silk cords.[9]

'CARTE', 'LITTERE PATENTES', AND 'LITTERE CLAUSE'

During the reign of Henry II the word *littere*, perhaps borrowed from the vocabulary of ecclesiastical scribes, began to be used to describe royal documents. This general and non-technical term became increasingly popular during Richard I's reign, perhaps because it had the advantage of covering a wider range of documents than the words *carta* and *breve*, which were then beginning to acquire the restrictive meaning of grant in perpetuity (*carta perpetua*) and administrative order (i.e. writ *stricto sensu*) respectively. It seems that under Richard I any document in epistolary form which was not a *carta*

[1] *Regesta*, i, no. 315.

[2] Ibid. ii, no. 919.

[3] Ibid., no. 840; see *English Hist. Rev.* lxxv, pp. 264, 271.

[4] Brit. Mus., Campbell ch. vii. 5; *English Hist. Rev.* lxxv, p. 268 and notes 4–5.

[5] *Regesta*, ii, no. 684; see also ibid., nos. 1493, 1723, 1746; Bishop, *Scriptores Regis*, nos. 186, 248, 345, 412.

[6] *Regesta*, ii, no. 1875; Bishop, op. cit., no. 761 and plate xiv.

[7] *Regesta*, iii, nos. 114, 273, 317, 379, 504, 690, etc.

[8] Ibid., nos. 103 (self-styled *carta*), 276, 495. For the use of silk cords in William II's reign, see *Facs. of English Royal Writs*, plates xix–xx.

[9] See the plates in L. Delisle, *Recueil des actes de Henri II: Atlas* (Paris, 1909). For self-styled *carte*, see Bishop, *Scriptores Regis*, nos. 286, 328, 676, 689 (all sealed on silk cords); nos. 259, 261–2, 271–2, 281, 677, 688, 696 (all sealed on a tag); no. 275 (on a tongue). For *brevia* patent sealed on a tongue, see ibid., nos. 114, 242–4, 318, 604 and 724 (both exemptions from toll), 769; on a tag, see ibid., nos. 570, 754 (the latter an exemption from toll); on silk cords, see ibid., no. 607 (exemption from toll).

could be called *littere*. When royal justices stated that a royal order given by word of mouth was to be preferred to another sent by 'letter' (. . . *magis ratum habetur quod dominus rex ore precipit quam quod per literas mandavit*),[1] the type of letter which they had in mind was undoubtedly a *breve*. As early as 1188 a safe-conduct issued by the bishop of Chichester and others in their own name, but on behalf of Henry II and the archbishop of Canterbury (*ex parte domini regis et domini archiepiscopi*), was self-styled *littere patentes*;[2] similarly Richard I's promise to ratify what William Longchamp and his follow ambassadors to France would conclude on his behalf is described as *littere patentes* in the English version of the treaty of Mantes (9 July 1193).[3] Since the pipe roll for 1190 refers, as we have seen, to a *breve* sent *clausum* to the exchequer,[4] it is likely that Richard I's chancery and exchequer also knew the term *littere clause* and used it to describe writs close as well as informal letters close.

Under Richard I the form of chancery documents underwent important changes, due perhaps to the influence of William Longchamp, bishop of Ely and Richard's first chancellor. From 1066 to 1189 English kings had used the first person singular to refer to themselves in all documents except in a few diplomas. Richard had adopted the same practice as count of Poitou and even in charters issued by him as *dominus Anglorum*, between Henry II's death and his own coronation.[5] From Richard's coronation onwards, however, the royal chancery used the plural of majesty in all documents issued under the king's name, thus following a practice which had been current for some time in other royal European chanceries and in English episcopal chanceries.[6]

It was also under Richard I that in most respects the charter assumed its definitive form. The following extracts come from a typical charter of the reign:

[*A. Protocol* (*superscriptio*): (*a*) *king's name and style* (*intitulatio*)] Ricardus Dei gratia rex Angl*orum*, dux Norm*annorum*, Aquit*annorum*, comes Andeg*avorum*, [(*b*) *address* (*inscriptio*)] archiepiscopis, episcopis, abbatibus, comitibus, baronibus, justic*iis*, vicecomitibus et omnibus baillivis et fidelibus suis, [(*c*) *greeting* (*salutatio*)] salutem. [*B. Text*: (*a*) *dispositive clause* (*dispositio*) *in the form of a notification*] Sciatis nos concessisse et presenti carta nostra confirmasse . . . [(*b*) *injunction*] Quare volumus et firmiter precipimus . . . [*C. List of witnesses*] Testibus . . . [*D. Dating-clause*] Data per manum E. Elyensis episcopi cancellarii nostri apud Bellum Castrum de Rupe Andel' xv die junii, anno regni nostri nono.[7]

The protocol is very similar to that of Henry II's later *carte*. In the royal style the formula *Dei gratia*, which regularly appeared in the legend of the royal seal from William II's reign onwards, had been introduced in the protocol of chancery documents under Henry II, apparently in May 1172;[8] the style *rex Anglorum* . . . does not seem to have been altered to *rex Anglie* . . . until John's reign, if the legend of the great seals is to be trusted.[9]

[1] *Rotuli Curiae Regis*, ed. F. Palgrave (Rec. Comm., 1835), i, p. 47.

[2] *Epistolae Cantuarienses*, p. 168.

[3] Rymer, *Foedera* (Rec. Comm.), I. i. 61.

[4] Above, p. 8, n. 3.

[5] *Ancient Charters*, ed. J. H. Round (Pipe Roll Soc., O.S. 10), no. 55.

[6] See, for example, *Cartae Antiquae Rolls 11–20* (Pipe Roll Soc., N.S. 33), nos. 458 (where singular and plural are mixed), 503, 560–1, 611–12, etc. For the use of singular and plural in English episcopal chanceries, see C. R. Cheney, *English Bishops' Chanceries, 1100–1250* (Manchester Univ. Press, 1950), pp. 58–9.

[7] Duchy of Lancaster, Royal Charters (D.L. 10), no. 47; Lionel Landon, *The Itinerary of King Richard I* (Pipe Roll Soc., N.S. 13), p. 129, no. 500; see also p. 170.

[8] See Delisle, *Recueil des actes de Henri II: Introduction*, pp. 12–38; *Memoranda Roll 1 John*, p. xii, n. 7.

[9] A. B. and A. Wyon, *The Great Seals of England*: compare the legends on nos. 35–8 and 39–40.

The address is found in identical form in a whole group of *carte*, including at least one original, issued in the latter part of Henry II's reign;[1] it also occurs in charters of King John, sometimes with the addition of *prepositis* or *ministris* or both after *vicecomitibus* (Plate **1***b*);[2] with the addition of these two words, the further insertion of *prioribus* after *abbatibus* (in Henry III's reign) and the substitution of *justiciariis* for *justiciis*, it became the address characteristic of charters for the rest of the Middle Ages (Plate **4***b*).[3]

The general structure of the text, and the introductory words of the *dispositio* and injunction are the same as in some *carte* of Stephen, in many *carte* of Henry II (which read, of course, *me*, *mea*, etc. instead of *nos*, *nostra*, etc.), and in most later royal charters until the end of the Middle Ages. From John's reign, however, the words *presenti carta* were gradually replaced by *hac carta* (Plate **4***b*). Under John also began the practice of defining in two separate clauses of the *dispositio* of grants of land (*a*) the type of tenure under which the land was to be held (*Habend' et tenend'* . . .), (*b*) the services, rent, etc., owed by the grantee (*Reddendo* (or *faciendo*) *inde* . . .).

The list of witnesses is introduced, as under Henry II, by the word *Testibus*. From Henry III onwards *Hiis testibus* became the rule (Plate **4***b*).

The only new feature of Richard's charter concerns its dating-clause. Before the death of Henry II the vast majority of *carte* and *brevia* ended with a 'place-date' (*Apud N.*), which immediately followed the list of witnesses. It is true that for every reign between 1066 and 1189 a few writs have survived which give an actual date of issue by reference to a saint's day or religious festival,[4] to an important political event[5] or to the year of the Incarnation,[6] but these are anomalies, probably due to the particular habits of individual scribes. The same could be said of the formula *per manum Stephani capellani* (or *scriptoris*) inserted between the list of witnesses and the place-date of seven *carte* of Henry II, all of which seem to have been drafted, and some written, by the royal scribe and chaplain, Stephen of Fougères.[7] From the accession of Richard I the formula *Apud N.* was replaced by an elaborate dating-clause which gave the place of issue, the name of the chancery official who executed the charter (the chancellor or his deputy) and a full date consisting of the day of the month and regnal year (Plate **1***b*). The clause, an adaptation of the dating formula of papal solemn privileges, was used for royal charters from the beginning of Richard's reign, even before his coronation,[8] until August 1238, when, after the removal of the great seal from the custody of the chancellor, Ralph de Neville, the words *per manum* followed by the name of a datary were replaced by *per manum nostram*, i.e. by the king's hand (Plate **4***b*).[9] The clause in this modified form remained the normal dating-clause of royal charters until the end of the Middle Ages. It had already been used between 1189 and 1238 for charters issued in exceptional circumstances, sometimes during the absence of the normal datary or between his death or retirement and the

[1] Bishop, *Scriptores Regis*, no. 611.

[2] See also Johnson and Jenkinson, plate ix (*b–c*).

[3] Cf. ibid., plates xxv (lines 44 ff.), xxviii (*b*), xxxiv.

[4] *Facs. of English Royal Writs*, plates v (*b*), xvi, xxii; Bishop, *Scriptores Regis*, plates ix (*b*), x (*a–b*).

[5] Ibid., plate xii (*a*); *Regesta*, ii, nos. 499, 1280.

[6] Ibid., nos. 1742, 1746, 1764, 1892, etc.

[7] See V. H. Galbraith, 'Seven Charters of Henry II at Lincoln Cathedral', *Antiquaries Journal*, xii. 3, p. 274.

[8] Round, *Ancient Charters*, no. 55; Bishop, *Scriptores Regis*, plates xxxvii (*b*), xl (*b*), etc. See Cheney, *English Bishops' Chanceries*, pp. 83–9.

[9] See L. B. Dibben, 'Chancellor and Keeper of the Seal under Henry III', *English Hist. Rev.* xxvii, pp. 39–51.

appointment of his successor, and also when the charter was in favour of the chancellor or datary.[1] It was also, it seems, owing to special circumstances of the same kind that the older formula (*per manum* followed by a datary's name) reappeared for brief periods in charters issued by Henry III after 1238[2] and, even more surprisingly, in letters patent and close of the first ten years of Edward I.[3]

From the reign of King John until the end of the Middle Ages, English royal charters —like the *carte perpetue* issued by the kings of France—were normally sealed with the great seal in green wax (*cera viridis*) appended on twisted or plaited cords of silk strands (usually of two colours, red and green being the most common combination).[4] There are, however, exceptions to the rule: some charters issued between 1199 and 1461 are sealed with the great seal in white (i.e. natural; *cera alba*) wax appended on a tag.[5] White wax, often covered with a brown varnish, had been used for all chancery documents until the end of Henry I's reign.[6] Green wax made its appearance under Stephen[7] and, after a period of uncertainty during which red wax was also used, green wax gained in popularity under Henry II and Richard I eventually to become the accepted sealing-wax for perpetuities.[8] By the early part of the thirteenth century sealing in white wax was generally reserved for great-seal documents of ephemeral or temporary value (letters close and patent), while red wax (*cera rubea*)—with very few exceptions—was restricted to the smaller royal seals (privy seal until 1312; privy seal, secret seal, and signet after 1312).

By the fifteenth century the number of charters had dwindled considerably and consisted mostly of confirmations and exemplifications of earlier charters, and of grants of free warren, fairs, markets, and view of frankpledge.[9] Most other royal grants were made by letters patent.

It is broadly true to say that all the chancery documents of Richard I's reign which neither call themselves 'charters' nor display the distinctive dating-clause of charters should be classified under the general heading of 'letters'. The *brevia* of Henry II ended with an attestation-clause normally mentioning one witness only and followed by a place-date (*Apud N.*). The letters of Richard I are also usually attested by a single witness, but this witness is often, although not always, the king himself (*Teste me ipso*), and the place-date is followed by a time-date consisting of the day of the month, to which is occasionally added the regnal year. The formula *Teste me ipso*, which evidently dates from a period when the king was not yet using the plural of majesty, is found in charters issued by

[1] Landon, *The Itinerary of King Richard I*, pp. 116, 125–7 (cf. pp. 168–9), nos. 472–4, 485, 488–90; *Rot. Chart.*, pp. xxxi, 83, 127, 129, 167; *C.Ch.R.* iii, p. 142; *Cartae Antiquae Rolls 1–10* (Pipe Roll Soc., N.S. 17), p. 138; Cheney, op. cit., p. 88, n. 6; Dibben, art. cit., p. 41; Galbraith, *Studies in the Public Records*, pp. 127–30.

[2] Dibben, art. cit., p. 50.

[3] Maxwell-Lyte, p. 242.

[4] For facsimiles of charters sealed on silk cords, see *Facs. of Royal and Other Charters in the British Museum*, ed. G. F. Warner and H. J. Ellis (London, 1903), plate l, no. 77 (Richard I); *Northants Rec. Soc.* iv, plates xvi–xvii (King John); Maxwell-Lyte, frontispiece, no. 4 (Edward I).

[5] e.g. below, Plate **4***b*.

[6] See *Facs. of English Royal Writs*, pp. xix–xxii; *English Hist. Rev.* lxxv, pp. 271–5. For an exception, a seal of orange-red wax, see ibid., p. 274, no. 16.

[7] *Regesta*, iii, no. 206.

[8] Maxwell-Lyte, pp. 302, 310; Tout, *Chapters*, ii, p. 69, n. 2; v, pp. 130–1. For the use of red wax on great-seal letters to the king of Sicily in 1283, see Maxwell-Lyte, p. 309, and on a charter of King John, see *Northants Rec. Soc.* iv, plate xvi.

[9] Examples of these types of charters are given in Hall, *Formula Book*, i, p. 33, no. 23 (grant of market); pp. 33–4, no. 24 (grant of fair); p. 35, no. 26 (grant of free warren). See also *C.Ch.R.*, *passim*.

Richard as count of Poitou,[1] and a similar phrase, *Teste rege ipso*, occurs in a *breve* of Henry II, apparently authentic, but written outside the chancery.[2] From the reign of Richard I until about 1240 royal letters continued to be attested either by the king himself or by someone else (compare Plate **2***a* and Plates **1***a*, *c* and **2***c–d*). From about 1240 until the end of the Middle Ages all royal letters close and patent under the great seal were attested *Teste me ipso* while the king was in England (Plates **5***a*, **8***a*, **9***a*, *c*, **13***b*, **16***b*, **18***b*, **20***b–c*, **21***c*, **23***a*). Letters close and patent issued by the king, while he was abroad, were still attested *Teste me ipso*; on the other hand, those which were issued in England during his absence were attested by the regent, but their protocol still began with the king's name and titles (Plate **6***a*).[3]

Although it would be interesting to find out who was entitled to attest letters close and patent until the 1240s, no definite pattern emerges from a close examination of the chancery enrolments. In John's reign writs of interest to the chamber are often attested by clerks of the chamber,[4] while writs with a judicial import are sometimes attested by the justiciar or some other person connected with the administration of justice.[5] Examples of this kind suggest an occasional link between the subject-matter of the documents and their attestation, but this cannot be regarded as a general rule.

The exact significance of the formula *Teste me ipso* is also very difficult to ascertain. It seems that until the 1240s the formula was used when the draft of the letter had been read in the king's presence. This may have been the case in Richard I's reign. At any rate, this interpretation would make some sense of Archbishop Hubert Walter's enigmatic remark in a letter which he wrote in 1198 to the convent of Christ Church, Canterbury, on the question of a possible joint appeal to Rome:

> . . . solemniter nobiscum appelletis, teste me ipso, qui venturi estis Londonias ad nos;[6]

conversely, in Henry II's reign a royal letter to the same convent, drafted, apparently without the king's knowledge, by Hubert Walter as dean of York on 3 February 1189 at Le Mans, ends with the clause *Teste Huberto decano Eboracensi apud Cenomanniam.*[7] If the use of the formula *Teste me ipso* was restricted to letters read before the king, at least in draft, one can understand why, for example, one letter of King John is attested by the king himself, while another, dealing with similar matters and issued on the same day and from the same place, is attested by someone else;[8] the same interpretation would also help to understand why two letters of King John, which according to the chancery rolls were drawn up on the king's oral instructions or 'immediate warrant' (*per ipsum regem*), could be attested one by the king himself and the other by someone else:[9] whoever attested would have been actually present when the draft was read. The most difficult problem

[1] See Hilda Prescott, 'The Early Use of *Teste me ipso*', *English Hist. Rev.* xxxv, pp. 214–17.

[2] Canterbury, Dean and Chapter Lib., Ch. Ant. C. 8: Bishop, *Scriptores Regis*, no. 96.

[3] See Maxwell-Lyte, p. 168.

[4] e.g. Philip de Lucy, *Rot. Litt. Claus.* i, pp. 75a, 76a, 77b.

[5] For two writs attested by Simon de Pateshull, see ibid., pp. 70a, 70b.

[6] *Epistolae Cantuarienses*, pp. 429–30.

[7] Ibid., pp. 544–5 (cf. pp. 282–3).

[8] Compare two writs of *computate* for Hugh de Neville, issued at Portsmouth on 7 June 1205 and attested one by the king himself and the other by Peter de Stokes (*Rot. Litt. Claus.* i, p. 37a).

[9] Ibid., p. 65a: two writs issued at York on 13 February 1206 and attested one by the king himself and the other by Geoffrey fitzPeter.

concerns the great-seal letters of King John which are said to have been issued in pursuance of a written warrant sealed with the king's privy seal (*per breve* or *litteras . . . de parvo sigillo*). It is perplexing to find, for example, that of two chancery writs, both warranted by a privy-seal writ or letter and both dated 15 February 1208, one is attested by the bishop of Bath at Westminster and the other by the king himself at Winchester;[1] the great seal cannot have been in both places on the same day. The available evidence suggests that under John and Henry III it was only when the king was some distance away from the great seal and chancery that the issue of great-seal letters was ordered by a privy-seal writ. The following table, compiled from King John's *rotulus misae*, *rotulus litterarum clausarum*, and *rotulus litterarum patentium* of his fourteenth year, shows how the places of issue of letters sealed with the privy seal and of those sealed with the great seal compare with the king's known itinerary from 4 to 30 May 1212:[2]

DATE	KING AND WARDROBE	PRIVY-SEAL LETTERS	GREAT-SEAL LETTERS (*Teste me ipso*)	GREAT-SEAL LETTERS (*Teste*: other than king)
4	Lambeth	..	Lambeth; London	Lambeth
5	Lambeth; Odiham	..	London	..
7	Odiham	Odiham	..	..
8	Freemantle	..	..	London (*per breve de parvo sigillo*)
9	Freemantle; Winchester	Winchester	..	Westminster (*per breve de parvo sigillo*)
10	Winchester; Odiham	..	Odiham	Westminster (*per breve de parvo sigillo*)
11	Odiham	Odiham	Odiham	Westminster
12	Odiham; Guildford	Odiham	Odiham; Havering	Westminster
13	Guildford	..	Guildford	..
14	Ditton	..	..	..
15	Lambeth	..	Lambeth	Westminster (*per breve domini regis sigillatum sigillo Willelmi Brigwerr'*)
16	Lambeth	..	Lambeth	..
17	Lambeth	..	..	Westminster (*per breve de parvo sigillo*)
18–19	Tower of L.[3]	..	..	..
20	Tower of L.	..	Tower of L.	Tower of L.
21	Havering	..	..	Westminster
23	Lambeth	..	Lambeth	..
24	Lambeth	..	Lambeth; London	London
25	..	..	Lambeth	..
26	..	..	Woolmer	Westminster (*per breve de parvo sigillo*)
29	Winchester	..	..	Westminster (*per . . . breve de parvo sigillo*)
30	Odiham	..	Odiham	Westminster

[1] Ibid., pp. 103a and 105a.

[2] See *Documents Illustrative of English Hist. in the Thirteenth and Fourteenth Centuries*, ed. H. Cole (London, 1844), pp. 231–2; *Rot. Litt. Claus.* i, and *Rot. Litt. Pat.* under dates.

[3] i.e. Tower of London.

This table plainly shows that during the period considered (1) the places of issue of the great-seal letters attested by the king agree exactly with the royal itinerary, whereas those attested by others than the king do not and obviously represent the itinerary of the great seal and chancery; (2) when the great seal was with the king, some letters were attested by him and others were not; (3) when the great seal was away from the king, the latter sometimes sent to his chancellor written orders under his privy seal for the issue of great-seal letters, in which case the chancery, without any apparent logic, chose between two systems of dating: either the letters patent and close under the great seal simply reproduced the final clause of the privy-seal warrant, including its formula *Teste me ipso* and its place and date of issue; or they were attested by someone who was present in chancery at the time, and this attestation was followed by the real place and date of issue. The latter system was still in use in 1230. An original privy-seal warrant of that year ordering the issue of letters under the great seal ends with the clause:

> Teste me ipso apud Hamsted' ij die decembris. Has litteras privato sigillo nostro fecimus sigillari,[1]

while the resulting letters close under the great seal read:

> Teste J. Bathoniensi episcopo apud Westm' iij die decembris.[2]

By the 1240s, as already stated, all letters patent and close under the great seal were attested by the king himself except those which were drawn up under the king's name during a period of regency, for example when the king was abroad. This uniformity, however, did not extend to the place and date of issue. In 1272 Henry III still claimed that if letters patent bore a place and date which did not agree with his itinerary they were undoubtedly forged:

> Nec eciam die et anno predictis nec ante per quadriennium nec eciam hactenus post datam predictam fuimus apud Cantuar', quod inter cetera manifestum est indicium falsitatis littere supradicte.[3]

But this had ceased to be true by 1290 when Ralph de Hengham, chief justice of the king's bench, said of the practice of the chancery of his own day:

> . . . si clerici ignorabant de ponendo rectam datam, propter hoc non fuerunt brevia viciosa, quia in cancellaria et alibi in uno et eodem die unus clericus ponit unam datam et alius aliam.[4]

Although Hengham's remark should perhaps not be taken too literally, lack of consistency in the dating practice of the chancery persisted throughout the fourteenth century. It is true that great-seal letters which were warranted by writs of privy seal usually bore the same date and place as the originating warrants, but they sometimes bore the same place and a different date. Sometimes their date and place were those of the delivery of the warrant to the chancery, which practice was eventually made compulsory for all letters patent by an Act of parliament of 1439.[5] When after that year a chancery clerk

[1] Chancery Warrants (C. 81), 1/1.

[2] *Close Rolls, 1227–1231*, pp. 460–1.

[3] *Diplomatic Documents*, i, no. 434.

[4] *State Trials of the Reign of Edward I, 1289–1293*, ed. T. F. Tout and Hilda Johnstone (Royal Hist Soc., Camden Third Series, ix), p. 35.

[5] Maxwell-Lyte, pp. 258–61. A memorandum, giving the date on which the warrant was received by the chancery, was sometimes written on the warrant itself. Notes of this kind (livery clause) occur from the reign of Edward III (ibid.). For an example of deliberate back-dating, see below, Plates **6***b* and **7***a*.

noted that some particular letters patent had been issued *de data predicta auctoritate parliamenti*, he simply meant that he had faithfully observed the provisions of the Act of 1439.[1]

Letters patent were always less solemn and less costly than charters.[2] Both types of document were used for royal grants, but grants made by letters patent were, more often than not, of a temporary nature, whereas charters normally recorded grants in perpetuity. Commissions, for example, grants of offices to be held during the king's pleasure, safe-conducts, and protections were made by letters patent. In many cases, however, the difference of purpose between charters and letters patent was very tenuous. Licences to acquire land in mortmain, granted by letters patent, were perpetuities in the sense that the lands acquired within the limits of the licence were exempt for ever from the provisions of the statute of mortmain; for that reason they were often sealed with the great seal in green wax appended on silk cords, instead of being sealed, like most letters patent, with the great seal in white wax appended on a tag or tongue.[3] The evidence suggests that, by and large, letters patent which were sealed with the great seal in green wax appended on silk cords (e.g. royal ratification of a treaty of peace or alliance) were more important and more lasting than those sealed in white wax on a tag (e.g. royal ratification of a truce), and in turn the latter were more important and more lasting than letters patent sealed in white wax on a tongue (e.g. commissions to ambassadors).

From the reign of King John to the end of the Middle Ages, letters and writs patent had, as a rule, a general address (Plates **2***d*, **5***a*, **6***a*, **13***b*, **20***c*, **23***a*) and contrasted with letters and writs close, which had a special address (Plates **1***c*, **2***c*, **8***a*, **9***a–b*, **16***b*, **18***b*, **20***b*, **21***c*). From the thirteenth century onwards the most common address of letters patent was *Omnibus ad quos presentes littere pervenerint* (Plates **2***d*, **6***a*, **13***b*, **20***c*, **23***a*). There are, however, countless exceptions, notably among the various classes of writs patent (Plates **1***a*, **2***a*, **9***c*, **10***c*), for example the writs *de intendendo*, some of which are addressed to a single individual[4] and others to groups of royal officials and subjects.[5] In most of their other formulae writs patent are more closely related to letters close than to letters patent.

From the beginning of John's reign a corroboration-clause, stating that the letters were sent patent, was often placed between the text of the letters and their attestation, e.g.

> Et in hujus rei testimonium has litteras nostras patentes fecimus (*or* . . . patentes vobis mittimus, *or* . . . patentes fieri fecimus). (Plate **1***a*)[6]

By the next reign this corroboration-clause had become one of the characteristic features of letters patent and had reached its definitive form:

[1] See Johnson and Jenkinson, plates xl (*b*), xli (*a*).

[2] Maxwell-Lyte, pp. 332, 334; Rymer, *Foedera* (Rec. Comm.), I. i. 75–6.

[3] Below, Plate **13***b*; Johnson and Jenkinson, plate xxx (*a*). Duplicates were sometimes sealed in different ways: e.g. Oxford, Balliol College, Deeds B. 1. 102 (great seal in green wax on silk cords) and D. 5. 14 (great seal in white wax on silk cords); Oriel College, Deeds 404 and 405 (one with the great seal in green wax on silk cords, the other with the great seal in white wax on a tag). For letters patent sealed on a tongue, see below, Plate **25***b*, and Maxwell-Lyte, frontispiece, nos. 1–2; for letters patent sealed on a tag, see below, Plate **25***c*, and Maxwell-Lyte, frontispiece, no. 3.

[4] Duchy of Lancaster, Royal Charters (D.L. 10), 128, addressed 'dilecto et fideli suo Henrico de Lacy'.

[5] Duchy of Lancaster, Royal Charters, no. 133, addressed 'omnibus tenentibus de manerio Novi Castri subtus Limam'.

[6] See Johnson and Jenkinson, plate x, line 40.

In cujus rei testimonium has litteras nostras fieri fecimus patentes. (Plates **5*a*, 6*a*, 9*c*, 13*b*, 20*c*, 23*a***)[1]

By then it had become usual for all chancery documents to be dated, not only by the day and month, but also by the regnal year.

THE CHANCERY STAFF

From the constitution of 7 June 1199, which regulated the scale of chancery fees, we gather that the personnel of King John's chancery was headed by a chancellor, assisted by a vice-chancellor, who acted as keeper of the great seal, and by a protonotary, who supervised the writing of chancery documents. It is worth noting that the constitution is a document of unusual form: amongst other peculiarities it has an anathema, which suggests an ecclesiastical draftsman, perhaps Hubert Walter himself.[2] We may wonder therefore whether the titles *vicecancellarius* and *protonotarius* were used as commonly in the royal chancery as the document implies. They are not found in any royal document of later date, although it is certain that the chancery of King John continued for some time to have two officials who performed the duties associated with these two titles.[3] Of the large staff which worked under the chancellor and his two assistants the constitution says nothing. The first authoritative account of the clerical organization of the royal chancery comes from a chapter of *Fleta* (II. xiii: *De cancellaria*), a legal treatise written towards the end of Edward I's reign.[4] This account is unfortunately incomplete, with a legal slant: what the author set out to do was not to describe the organization of the chancery in detail, but to comment on the duties of such chancery clerks as were concerned with the production of 'original' writs. According to him there were two main groups of chancery clerks. The first group consisted of *superiores clerici* of unspecified number, close associates of the chancellor. Among these higher clerks (*a*) the *preceptores* ordered the issue of the writs *de precepto*, (*b*) the *prenotarii* wrote them, and (*c*) others, whom perhaps one might call *examinatores*, were legal experts who examined the form and substance of all writs before they were presented to the seal. The second group consisted of junior clerks whose duty it was to write the writs *de cursu* under the responsibility of the higher clerks. *Fleta* adds that every writ had to bear the name of the scribe who wrote it, so as to engage the scribe's responsibility towards the purchaser of the writ.

A chancery ordinance which purports to have been made in the twelfth year of Richard II's reign is more explicit than *Fleta*.[5] It divides the clerical staff of Richard's chancery into three groups: (*a*) twelve clerks of the first bench (*clerici de prima forma*), (*b*) twelve clerks of the second bench (*clerici de secunda forma*), and (*c*) twenty-four *cursitores*.

The clerks of the first bench, the successors of *Fleta*'s *superiores clerici* and of the

[1] See also Johnson and Jenkinson, plates xxx (*a*), xl (*b*). In French the general address varies slightly from period to period: 'a touz ceux qi cestes presentes lettres verront ou orront', 'a touz ceux qi cestes lettres verront ou orront', 'a touz ceux qi cestes lettres verront', 'a touz ceux as queux cestes lettres vendront'; the corroboration-clause often reads: 'En tesmoignance de queu chose nous avoms fait faire cestes nos lettres overtes (*or* patentes)'. See *Treaty Rolls*, i, ed. P. Chaplais (H.M.S.O.), nos. 394 and 660; *Rôles gascons*, iv, pp. 541 (XII) and 542 (XIV); Treaty Rolls (C. 76), no. 40, m. 8, and no. 44, mm. 6 and 11, etc.

[2] Rymer, *Foedera* (Rec. Comm.), I. i. 75–6.

[3] *Memoranda Roll 1 John*, pp. xxxv–xxxviii, and lxii, n. 3. For Walter Merton as protonotary *temp.* Henry III, see Holdsworth, *Hist. Eng. Law*, ii. 615 (14).

[4] *Selden Soc.*, vol. 72, ed. H. G. Richardson and G. O. Sayles, pp. 123–6.

[5] Wilkinson, *The Chancery under Edward III*, pp. 214–23.

'chancellor's clerks residing in the chancery' mentioned in a wardrobe account of 1299–1300,[1] were already twelve in number by the end of Edward II's reign.[2] From about 1370 onwards they were often styled 'chancery masters' (*magistri cancellarie* or *magistri de cancellaria*).[3] By that time one of the masters, styled 'keeper of the chancery rolls' (*custos rotulorum cancellarie*), an office already in existence in 1215,[4] had risen to a status equal to that of the protonotary of 1199 and assumed pre-eminence over his eleven colleagues: not only was he responsible for the custody of the chancery rolls once they had been compiled, but he also supervised the work of enrolment as well as the drafting and writing of the chancery engrossments themselves.[5] Two of the other eleven masters acted as *preceptores*, whose duties were approximately the same as those of *Fleta*'s *preceptores*, and six were *examinatores*, checking the documents written by the cursitors and some of the documents written by the clerks of the second bench. From 1336 one of the masters, styled *notarius regis in cancellaria sua*, was entrusted with the writing and enrolling of documents of international character. During our period this post, which required special qualifications, was generally given to a notary by apostolic authority or to a clerk holding a degree in canon or civil law. After 1413 he was styled *notarius* (or *prothonotarius*) *regis in cancellaria sua*. Although he was awarded an additional fee for these special duties, the medieval notary or protonotary in chancery does not appear to have been very actively engaged in writing or enrolling documents of an international nature except during the tenure of Master John de Branketre (1355–75).[6] Each of the chancery masters had a staff of three clerks, except the keeper of the chancery rolls, whose staff was increased from three to six by Richard II's ordinance. None of the masters' assistants belonged to either of the two benches or to the cursitors' class, and each wrote to the great seal under the name of his master.

The clerks of the second bench were of lower status than the chancery masters. They included the two clerks of the crown (*clerici de corona*), who wrote the 'writs of the crown', the commissions of gaol delivery and some writs connected with the needs of the royal household (Plate 9*b*, note);[7] the clerks of the petty bag (*clerici de parva baga*), who wrote the writs of *diem clausit extremum* ordering escheators to hold an 'inquisition *post mortem*';[8] the clerk in charge of searches through the chancery rolls, and the clerk who read the records and pleas of chancery. Every clerk of the second bench was allowed one clerk to assist him in his work, except the clerks of the crown, who were entitled to two assistants each.

The twenty-four cursitors wrote the writs of course (*brevia de cursu*), the writs *ad quod dampnum*,[9] and apparently some charters and letters patent, but all the documents written by them had to be examined by the *examinatores* of the first bench before they could be

[1] *Liber Quotidianus Contrarotulatoris Garderobae* . . . (London, Soc. of Antiquaries, 1787), p. 358: '. . . cancellario regis . . . nomine expensarum et robarum suarum et clericorum suorum in comitiva sua in cancellaria commorancium.'

[2] Maxwell-Lyte, p. 4.

[3] Tout, *Chapters*, iii, p. 211, n. 1; *Studies presented to Sir Hilary Jenkinson*, p. 88, n. 8.

[4] Galbraith, *Studies in the Public Records*, p. 80.

[5] Wilkinson, *The Chancery under Edward III*, pp. 72–3.

[6] Maxwell-Lyte, pp. 274–5; *Catalogue of an Exhibition of Treaties at the Public Record Office* (H.M.S.O., 1948), pp. 13–14. A study of Branketre's work will be published in *Journal Soc. Archivists*, April 1971.

[7] Wilkinson, op. cit., pp. 84–6.

[8] Maxwell-Lyte, pp. 273–4 (also p. 218). For an example of a writ of *diem clausit extremum*, see Hall, *Formula Book*, ii, p. 71, no. 37.

[9] Maxwell-Lyte, p. 217. A writ *ad quod dampnum* is printed in Hall, op. cit. ii, p. 89, no. 50.

presented to the seal.[1] Every cursitor had to write his documents himself unless he was incapacitated through old age or illness, in which case he might be allowed to employ a clerk who would write under his (the cursitor's) name.

Although Richard II's ordinance makes only a passing allusion to the keeper of the hanaper of the chancery (*custos hanaperii cancellarie*), this official played an important part in the running of the department from about 1244 onwards.[2] Normally a clerk (sometimes he was also styled *clericus hanaperii*), but not necessarily a clerk of the first bench, the keeper of the hanaper was responsible for collecting the fines and great-seal fees owed by the beneficiaries of charters, letters patent, and writs. Not until these fines and fees had been paid up did he deliver the sealed documents to their intended recipients; while waiting for payment he kept the documents stored in the special chest (*hanaperium*) or chests which had given his office its name. When, as a special royal favour, some fees were remitted, their amount was allowed to the keeper of the hanaper in his account (Plate **16***b–c*). Out of the money which he collected the keeper paid the yearly allowance due to the chancellor and the wages of some chancery employees (e.g. the spigurnel, chafe-wax, and portejoye), and purchased the wax and parchment needed by the chancery. For these receipts and expenses he accounted once a year to the crown, in the king's wardrobe until 1324 and at the exchequer thereafter.

The exaction of great-seal fees for the issue of chancery documents was probably as old as the great seal itself, but until the latter part of Henry III's reign these fees had normally been collected for the sole benefit of the chancellor and his senior colleagues in the chancery. Only during the brief periods of vacancy of the chancellor's office did the fees accrue to the king: for example, from the death of Hubert Walter (13 July 1205) until the appointment of Walter de Gray, his successor as chancellor (2 October 1205), the great-seal fees were collected on the king's behalf by Adam of Essex.[3] For the privilege of appropriating the fees, the chancellor undertook, on entering office, to pay the king a very large sum of money (from £3,000 to 5,000 marks).[4] This system was still in operation at the time of issue of the constitution of 7 June 1199, which fixed once and for all the fees of the great seal.[5] According to the constitution, 12 marks and 5 shillings were to be charged for a charter of new enfeoffment (10 marks for the chancellor, 1 mark for the vice-chancellor, 1 mark for the protonotary, and 5 shillings for the wax), 18*s*. 4*d*. for the confirmation of an earlier charter (1 mark for the chancellor, 2 shillings for the vice-chancellor, 2 shillings for the protonotary, and 1 shilling for the wax) and 2 shillings for letters patent of simple protection. This scale of fees was apparently the same as it had been in Henry II's time and one-ninth of the exorbitant rates which had been charged in the last years of Richard I's reign.

The farming of the great seal came to an end in 1244, on the death of Ralph de Neville,

[1] The note 'Examinatur per A. (*or* per A. et B.)' found on the turn-up of many royal confirmations and exemplifications of previous grants seems to refer to the checking of the new text against that of the original grant. Whether the clerks said to have done the checking were necessarily the 'official' *examinatores* of the first bench is uncertain. See Wilkinson, *The Chancery under Edward III*, p. 76 and n. 3; *New Pal. Soc.* i. 250c; below, Plate **25***c*.

[2] Maxwell-Lyte, pp. 283–6, 345, 414; Wilkinson, op. cit., p. 59.

[3] *Rot. Litt. Pat.* i, p. 70. See also *Rot. Litt. Claus.* i, p. 48b, 49b.

[4] Maxwell-Lyte, p. 328.

[5] Rymer, *Foedera*, I. i. 75–6.

who had been appointed chancellor for life in 1227. After 1244, except for short periods, for example during the chancellorship of Robert Burnell (1274–92) who collected the great-seal fees for his own use, the fees were collected for the benefit of the crown. It was the need for a permanent official who could be entrusted with the collection of those fees which led to the creation of the office of keeper of the hanaper, some time between 1244 and 1257.[1] Once the fees had been transferred to the king's use, a new system of remuneration for the chancellor had to be devised. This was done in 1260 when Nicholas of Ely, the new chancellor, was given a fixed allowance of 400 marks a year. This figure was raised to 500 marks in 1265, and after a further increase which brought the allowance up to £500, it remained unchanged until the early nineteenth century. Out of his allowance the chancellor had to provide for the maintenance and robes of the chancery clerks, those at least who resided in the chancery, that is to say the clerks of the first bench. In addition to his fixed allowance the chancellor still received a share of the great-seal fees, but this share was now very small. Out of 12 marks 5 shillings, normally charged for what the hanaper called a *carta de magno feodo*, that is to say a charter proper recording a grant in perpetuity, the king received 11 marks 5 shillings and the chancellor 1 mark; out of 18*s.* 4*d.* charged for a *carta de parvo feodo* (i.e. most letters patent, including those which recorded grants for life, licences to alienate in mortmain, etc.), 16*s.* 4*d.* went to the king and 2 shillings to the chancellor. The accounts of the hanaper show that the fees exacted for one particular type of document could vary slightly, but on the whole the scale fixed by the constitution of 1199 was still in force at the end of the Middle Ages.[2]

Besides the chancellor, clerks of the two benches, cursitors, and keeper of the hanaper, the chancery staff included a number of other employees, who, menial though the tasks of some of them were, all contributed to the smooth running of the office. The spigurnel (*spigurnellus*, also called *consignator brevium*), whose office was hereditary until the thirteenth century, performed the manual work involved in the actual sealing of documents. His official title of *spigurnellus* was possibly derived from the original name (apparently unattested) of the 'sealing-staff'—a sort of rolling-pin with a silver tip—which he used for pressing the matrix on to the wax.[3] His assistant, the chafe-wax (*chaufecire* in French; *calefactor cere* in Latin) heated the wax before it could be used for sealing.[4] The portejoye, also called *custos summariorum* (or *portitor*) *rotulorum cancellarie*, in addition to his chief duties consisting of looking after the pack-horses which carried the chancery rolls, supplied the ink for the enrolling work and saw to the repair of the chancery rolls and bags.[5]

II. THE PRIVY SEAL, SECRET SEAL, AND SIGNET

THE PRIVY SEAL

Although Henry II may have had a privy seal, no conclusive evidence has yet come to light to prove that he did.[6] The first English king of whom we can say with reasonable confidence that he had such a seal is Richard I. In 1191 he had taken his great seal with

[1] Wilkinson, op. cit., pp. 7, 59.
[2] Maxwell-Lyte, pp. 4–5, 8, 327–59.
[3] Ibid., pp. 287–91, 311–12. [4] Ibid., pp. 291–2.
[5] Ibid., pp. 293–5 and references.
[6] Tout, *Chapters*, i, p. 147 and n. 2; J. Boussard, *Le Gouvernement d'Henri II Plantegenêt* (Paris, 1956), p. 347 (and n. 1); see also p. 548; *English Hist. Rev.* lxxx, pp. 343–4.

him to Sicily. His exchequer seal had been left in England, where, in its normal home, the exchequer, it remained at the disposal of William Longchamp, Richard's chancellor, who had also stayed behind to rule the kingdom in the king's absence.[1] It was this exchequer seal which Gervase of Canterbury described as a *sigillum parvum, regia tamen majestate signatum.*[2] Whether or not Gervase really meant by those curious words that the seal depicted the king enthroned in majesty, as we might be inclined to believe, at least he wanted his readers to know that this was no ordinary small seal: there was something in it which identified it as a royal official seal. Perhaps he insisted on this point because Richard I had another small seal which was not *regia majestate signatum*, in other words a private seal. According to Gerald of Wales, Richard had in fact with him in Messina a small seal as well as his great seal. Gerald tells us that, when the archbishop of Rouen came back to England from Messina in the summer of 1191, he brought with him a royal writ (*mandatum*), which was in effect a commission appointing him justiciar in place of Longchamp; this writ was sealed with both royal seals, the great seal and the small seal (*una cum regio mandato utroque sigillo, tam majore scilicet quam minore, munito . . .*).[3] It has been suggested that the small seal was the exchequer seal, which may have been appended to a covering writ once the archbishop was in England, but this interpretation seems unnecessarily complicated and even implausible.[4] On the other hand, there were good reasons for a writ which concerned the chancellor and justiciar to be sealed not only with the great seal, of which the chancellor was technically still the custodian, but also with a royal privy seal, as the addition of the latter would show that the writ represented the king's personal will. A century later the kings of France often used their *sceau du secret* in addition to their great seal on documents issued in the chancellor's favour.[5] If Richard I had a privy seal, it is likely that it consisted of an antique intaglio gem mounted in a finger-ring. It has been claimed that such a ring, now in the British Museum, belonged to Richard, but its legend makes this identification most improbable.[6]

Although the privy seal eventually came to be regarded as a minor seal of state, there is little doubt that it began as a royal private seal, which the king could use for his personal and secret correspondence. Perhaps the small seal which King John used as count of Mortain, before his accession to the throne, served that purpose as well as that of a counterseal to his single-sided great seal. The word *secretum* of its legend (SECRETVM IOHANNIS) may at that early date have still retained its etymological meaning; its matrix, an antique intaglio gem set in a finger-ring, also suggests that it had been originally designed for private rather than official use.[7]

After his accession John certainly had a privy seal, which is described as a *parvum* or *privatum sigillum* in the records of the reign. Whether or not this seal, of which we have

[1] Tout, *Chapters*, i, p. 148; Landon, *The Itinerary of King Richard I*, pp. 173–5.

[2] Tout, *Chapters*, pp. 148, n. 1, and 149, n. 2.

[3] *Giraldi Cambrensis Opera*, ed. J. S. Brewer, iv (Rolls Series, 1873), p. 426.

[4] Landon, op. cit., p. 174.

[5] G. Tessier, *Diplomatique royale française* (Paris, 1962), p. 204, n. 4.

[6] Peter E. Lasko, 'The Signet Ring of King Richard I of England', *Journal Soc. Archivists*, ii (1960–64), pp. 333–5 and plate. The legend seems to read 'S' RICHARD (?) RE . . . P', which Mr. Lasko proposes to expand to 'S[IGILLUM] RICHARD[I ?] REG[IS] P[RIVATUM]': the word *privatum* occurs in no other medieval royal seal in England.

[7] Tout, *Chapters*, v, pp. 133–4; C. H. Hunter Blair, 'Durham Seals', *Archaeologia Aeliana*, Third Series, xiii, pp. 122–3.

no wax impression, was the *secretum* which John had used as count of Mortain is a matter for speculation. Its existence is only known to us from the many references to it which are recorded on the chancery rolls of the reign. These references make it clear that John often used his privy seal for official business, for example when the great seal was not with him: (1) either the chancery writs and letters, which should normally have been sealed with the great seal, were authenticated by the privy seal as a substitute;[1] (2) or the king sent under his privy seal a writ to the chancellor, ordering him to issue the required document under the great seal.[2] Because the privy seal was small, a letter sealed with it was easier to conceal than another sealed with the great seal. For that reason, when the roads were regarded as unsafe (*propter viarum pericula*), chancery documents were occasionally sealed with the privy seal.[3] Other references testify to the close association between the privy seal and the king and his chamber: for example, several writs connected with the collection of debts are said to have been sealed with the privy seal, because the king wanted the money to be paid into his chamber; had he wanted it paid into the exchequer, he would have used his great seal.[4] A curious note in an early register of writs suggests that in John's reign the writ *ne vexes contra libertates* might also have been issued under the privy seal rather than the great seal:

Istud breve non est in curia, set fit per graciam ex camera domini regis et non cancellarii.[5]

It is possible, however, although perhaps less likely, that the writ was issued under the great seal, on a warrant from the chamber.

The form of King John's privy-seal letters is the same as that of his great-seal letters, except that they are invariably attested by the king himself (*Teste me ipso*) and that they often contain a clause specifying that they were issued under the privy seal (e.g. *Has litteras privato sigillo nostro sigillari fecimus*).[6]

Henry III also had a privy seal, at least from 1230. No wax impression of it has so far been found, but it seems that it represented the royal arms on a shield,[7] like all the royal privy seals extant from Edward I onwards. At least five originals formerly sealed with Henry III's privy seal are still in existence, all of which seem to be warrants to the chancellor for the issue of letters under the great seal.[8] Diplomatically they closely resemble the privy-seal letters of King John, differing, like them, only in small details from contemporary letters under the great seal: they end with the clause *Teste me ipso*, followed by a place-date (*apud N.*), a time-date (day of the month and sometimes regnal year), and a reference to the use of the privy seal (sometimes in a form similar to that of a warranting note, *per privatum sigillum nostrum*).[9] Diplomatic similarities between great-seal and

[1] e.g. *Rot. Litt. Claus.* i, p. 152a: 'Et quia magnum sigillum nostrum nobiscum non habuimus, has literas privato sigillo nostro fecimus sigillari.' See also ibid., p. 114b. Compare, for Edward I's reign, Maxwell-Lyte, p. 35, and for Edward II's reign, *Rôles gascons*, iv, nos. 981–1039, etc.

[2] *Rot. Litt. Claus.* i, p. 102a: 'per breve regis de parvo sigillo'; p. 102b: 'per litteras regis de parvo sigillo'.

[3] *Rot. Litt. Pat.*, p. 155a.

[4] *Rot. Litt. Claus.* i, p. 115; Maxwell-Lyte, p. 20.

[5] Cambridge, Corpus Christi College, MS. 297, fol. 121^{v}. I owe this reference to the kindness of Mr. G. D. G. Hall.

[6] e.g. *Rot. Litt. Claus.* i, pp. 120b, 177, 214a.

[7] Maxwell-Lyte, p. 41; Tout, *Chapters*, i, p. 210.

[8] Chancery Warrants (C. 81), 1/1, 1/1B, 1/1C, 1/1D; Ancient Correspondence (S.C. 1), vol. 62, no. 90. See Maxwell-Lyte, pp. 49–50, 59.

[9] Ibid., pp. 49–50; Tout, *Chapters*, i, p. 211 and n. 2. The note *per privatum sigillum nostrum* occurs on Chancery Warrants 1/1B, 1/1D, and Ancient Correspondence, vol. 62, no. 90.

privy-seal letters are not surprising, since it was as a substitute for the great seal that the privy seal began to be used in matters of state. Nevertheless the organization which surrounded the privy seal was quite separate from the chancery and was, in normal circumstances, not subject to the chancellor's authority. From 1230 until 1312 all matters connected with the privy seal were in the hands of officials of the king's wardrobe, who seem to have inherited these functions from the chamber clerks of King John. From 1232 to 1234 Peter des Rivaux, keeper of Henry III's wardrobe, had the custody of the privy seal;[1] it was also in the wardrobe that the privy-seal letters of Henry III were written, by confidential clerks who obviously had no connection with the chancery, since in September 1238 they wrote a whole group of letters against the chancellor, Ralph de Neville, *clericis de cancellaria domini regis ea ignorantibus* (Plate **3***a*).[2]

In the early years of Edward I's reign, the keeper of the wardrobe may have retained control of the privy-seal organization (custody of the seal and its archives, and supervision of the writing of documents sealed with it), but he was already assisted in this task by the controller of the wardrobe.[3] There are indications that Walter Langton, keeper of the wardrobe from 1290 to 1295, was in charge of the privy seal during his term of office,[4] but when he relinquished the keepership on 20 November 1295, the privy seal passed into the hands of the controller, John Benstead.[5] This was the beginning of a short-lived association between the custody of the privy seal and the controllership of the wardrobe. This association continued under Robert of Cottingham, Benstead's successor as controller (1305–7), and during the first five years of the tenure of William of Melton, the next controller (1307–14); it stopped early in 1312 when, as a result of the ordinances of 1311, Melton, the first wardrobe clerk to be given the official title of *custos privati sigilli*, was relieved of his privy-seal duties to be replaced by an independent keeper of the privy seal, Roger of Northburgh.[6] The ordinances had stipulated that a suitable clerk should be appointed to keep the privy seal and that this appointment, like that of the chancellor, should be made by the king in parliament, on the advice of his barons and with their approval. The privy seal had ceased to be the seal of the king and his wardrobe to become, in effect, the seal of the council; instead of following the king around the country, it was often away from him for long periods at a time. A new department of state had been created, the privy-seal office, whose permanent staff consisted, as early as 1312, of a keeper of the seal assisted by four clerks.[7] Compared with the large body of chancery clerks, this was indeed a very small staff, and it is not surprising that in times of stress casual clerks had to be brought in from other departments, notably from the chancery.[8] By the late fourteenth century the number of clerks working for the privy seal was still nominally restricted to four, but by then the four clerks, one of whom had been given the

[1] Tout, *Chapters*, i, pp. 217–25.

[2] See ibid., p. 287.

[3] Four letters connected with Anglo-Castilian relations were delivered to Thomas de Gunneys, [controller], at Cirencester in the tenth year of Edward I's reign, to be kept in the wardrobe (*Treaty Rolls*, i, p. 68, n. 4).

[4] See *Treaty Rolls*, i, no. 254: 'Ista littera postmodum mutata fuit per W. de Langeton', custodem garderobe regis'; see also ibid., nos. 397–8, and compare Tout, *Chapters*, ii, p. 282 and n. 2; Maxwell-Lyte, pp. 364–5.

[5] Tout, *Chapters*, ii, p. 37.

[6] Ibid., pp. 70, 283–7.

[7] Ibid., pp. 287–8 and notes.

[8] Ibid., p. 280 and n. 3.

honorific title of *secundarius privati sigilli*,[1] had become senior clerks, each of them having one or more junior clerks to assist him in his work.[2]

During the first twenty years of Edward I's reign the steady growth of the wardrobe as a department of state as well as the increasing interest taken by the king in the government of the realm resulted in a spectacular rise in the importance of the privy seal as an independent official seal; this rise is particularly conspicuous from 1290 onwards, that is to say from the beginning of Walter Langton's keepership of the wardrobe. The form of privy-seal letters moved gradually away from that of chancery letters. As late as 1280 the dating-clause of great-seal letters, *Teste me ipso apud N.* followed by the day of the month and regnal year, still occurs in privy-seal letters, sometimes with the words *sub sigillo nostro privato* inserted after the place of issue (Plate **5***b*).[3] By then, however, this type of dating-clause had been virtually superseded by another formula, which was already in evidence in 1275[4] and soon became characteristic of privy-seal letters:

Dat*um* sub privato sigillo nostro apud N., followed by the day of the month and regnal year. (Plate **5***c*)

In great-seal letters sent to foreign rulers, many of which are known to have been drafted in the wardrobe, the formula *Teste me ipso* had also been replaced by the word *Datum* before 1280;[5] the *Datum* formula also occurs in some great-seal letters sent to Gascony (Plate **10***c*). Whether this departure from chancery usage was due to the influence of wardrobe draftsmen or rather to the desire to conform to continental—and particularly French—practice is uncertain, since the replacement of *Teste me ipso* by *Datum* in diplomatic correspondence under the great seal was accompanied by the substitution of the year of grace to the regnal year, a change which did not take place in privy-seal letters. At any rate the chancery clerks soon became used to these peculiar features of diplomatic letters, although as late as September 1311 one of them was not sure whether he ought to use *Teste me ipso* or *Datum* (*Utrum 'Datum' vel 'Teste' poni debeat*) and the regnal year or the year of grace in letters patent appointing English commissioners to treat with the French.[6]

From 1290 not only do we notice a sharp increase in the number of extant privy-seal letters, but also French is now the predominant language of the privy seal, while Latin, which until then had normally been used for privy-seal and great-seal letters alike, remains the language of the chancery. After 1290 privy-seal letters in Latin consist mostly of documents of a routine character, for example letters to the exchequer concerning respites or pardons, warrants to the chancellor connected with presentations to benefices, with ecclesiastical elections or grants in charter-form.[7] This linguistic specialization of the wardrobe and chancery was so real that, when the king wished some particularly important

[1] Ibid. v, p. 104.

[2] Ibid., pp. 78–81.

[3] See also Chancery Warrants (C. 81), 1/39A.

[4] e.g. Chancery Warrants 1/2 (26 Aug. 1275). In these early letters the place-date (*apud N.*) is sometimes found between *Dat'* and *sub privato sigillo nostro*.

[5] See *Treaty Rolls*, i, nos. 134–51, 155, 159–60, 166–8, etc. (but see ibid., no. 169).

[6] *Rôles gascons*, iv, p. 133. By the latter part of the fourteenth century, great-seal letters connected with foreign relations had acquired other distinctive features: they often mentioned, either in the corroboration-clause or in the dating-clause, that it was the great seal which was used, e.g. 'Donne par tesmoignance de nostre grant seal'; at the same time, the place of issue was often given as 'palacium nostrum Westmonasterii' instead of 'Westmonasterium', etc.

[7] Tout, *Chapters*, v, p. 116; J. Conway Davies, *Studies presented to Sir Hilary Jenkinson*, p. 141.

and confidential letters to be sent in Latin under the great seal, they were first drafted in French by a wardrobe clerk and then forwarded to the chancery for translation.[1] Perhaps because French had the advantage of being more readily understood than Latin by the king and laity, it remained the current language of the privy seal throughout the Middle Ages: French retained the first place, and Latin second place, even after the introduction of English into privy-seal documents at the end of Henry V's reign.[2]

Under Edward I the number and variety of documents sealed with the privy seal increased considerably. They included numerous warrants to the chancellor for the issue of great-seal documents; letters and writs dealing with diplomatic, financial, judicial, and military matters; as well as the king's private correspondence. According to their form the privy-seal documents of Edward I's reign fall into four main categories: letters and writs close; letters and writs patent; bills; indentures.

(A) *Letters and writs close.* These can be subdivided into several types, which are illustrated by the following examples, arranged in descending order of formality:

(*a*) Administrative writs close in Latin and French

1. Edwardus Dei gracia rex Anglie, dominus Hibernie et dux Aquitannie, dilecto clerico et fideli nostro magistro Willelmo de Grenefeld, cancellario nostro, salutem. Cum . . . [*writ ordering the issue of a great-seal document* (*grant of free warren*)]. Dat*um* sub privato sigillo nostro apud villam Sancti Andree primo die aprilis, anno regni nostri xxxij. (*1 April 1304*)[3]
2. Edward par la grace de Dieu roy Dengleterre, seigneur Dirlaunde et ducs Daquitaine, a nostre cher clerk' et foial maistre Williame de Genefeud', nostre chancellier, saluz. Nous vous mandoms que . . . [*writ ordering the issue of great-seal letters in Latin according to the French draft enclosed*]. Don*e* souz nostre prive seal a Thresk' le xxvj jour daveril, lan de nostre regne xxxj°. (*26 April 1303*)[4]

(*b*) Draft 'littere de statu' (concerning the health of the correspondents) to Philip IV, king of France

A treshaut, tresnoble et trespuissant nostre treschier et tresame seignour et cousin Ph. par la grace de Dieu roi de France, Edward etc., saluz et touz honours. Treschier sire, nous vous mercioms . . . Nostre Sire vous eit en sa garde. [*The full dating-clause is not given, but a brief note of the place and date of issue is given in Latin at the foot of the parchment, which contains two other drafts*: Douary x die aprilis]. (*10 April 1304*)[5]

(*c*) Draft letter to Edward of Carnarvon, prince of Wales

Edward par la grace de Dieu roy Dengleterre, seigneur Dirlaunde et ducs Daquitaine, a Edward nostre chier filz, prince de Gales, conte de Cestre, de Pontif' et de Moustroill', saluz ove nostre beneizon. Chier filz, tot ausint come nous vous feismes nad guerres savoir que vous feussiez a nous a Cambuskyneth icest mardy precheinement avenir, uncore vous feisoms assaver que nostre volunte \`est´ que vous y soiez meisme le mardy a houre de tierce au plus tard por parler a nous. Don*e* souz nostre prive seal a Inverkethyn le xv jour daveril, lan de nostre regne trentisme secund. (*15 April 1304*)[6]

[1] Maxwell-Lyte, pp. 51–2.

[2] Ibid., pp. 52–3.

[3] Ancient Correspondence (S.C. 1), vol. 61, no. 24: corrected engrossment (*littere rescribende* or *rescripte*). See Exch., K.R., Accounts Various (E. 101), 354/11/80 (last document in a file), endorsed: 'Bille et littere rescripte in garderoba' (29 Edw. I).

[4] Chancery Warrants (C. 81), 32/3207: original engrossment.

[5] Ancient Correspondence, vol. 13, no. 206.

[6] Chancery Miscellanea (C. 47), 22/7/13.

(*d*) Original letter of Edward I to his wife, Queen Margaret

Chiere .. cousine. Pur ce que nous avoms entendu que leglise de Lugwardyn pres de Hereford, que est de nostre donoison, est ja voide par la mort Wautier de Redmarle qui en feut persone, si voloms que vous vous avisez le quel de vos clerks vous volez qui eit meisme cele eglise. Et sur ce nous vous enveoms nos lettres escrites a Johan de Langeton', nostre chauncellier, par les queles nous li mandoms qil presente de par nous a la dite eglise tiel de vos clerks come vous li nomerez par vos lettres. Don*e* souz nostre prive seal a Linliscu le xxvij jour de decembre, lan de nostre regne trentisme. (*27 December 1301*)[1]

All these types of writs and letters close were still current in the fifteenth century, although the use that was made of them varied slightly from one period to another. Type (*a*), in its Latin and French versions, remained the most popular for orders to royal officials (chancellor; treasurer, barons, and chamberlains of the exchequer; sheriffs etc.). In these privy-seal writs the unabbreviated protocol was the same as in great-seal writs, except on a small point: from about 1290 the addressee of privy-seal writs was normally referred to as *nostro* in Latin and *nostre* in French ('cancellario *nostro*', '*nostre* chancellier'; 'fideli *nostro*', '*nostre* feal'), whereas the chancery always preferred *suo*. Types (*b*) and (*c*), with their more courteous and friendly greeting, often followed by a short address in the vocative resembling an apostrophe (*Treschier sire*; *Chier filz*), and their occasional valediction (*Nostre Sire vous eit en sa garde*), were often used for letters to foreign rulers and to the king's kinsmen:[2] in letters to other kings and to the pope, the address came before the king's name and title, a practice which was also followed by the English chancery and indeed by all other royal chanceries in Europe. Type (*d*), the most informal, with no protocol but only an apostrophe, was commonly used, in the late-thirteenth century, by persons of all ranks, particularly for news-letters, but only two letters of this kind sent under Edward I's privy seal have so far been noticed: both were sent to Queen Margaret, addressed in each as *Chiere cousine*.[3] Some of Edward II's letters to Queen Isabella simply begin with the apostrophe *Tresdouz cuer*,[4] while others have a short protocol, made up of an address and a greeting and followed by an apostrophe: *A nostre treschere et tresamee compaigne, saluz come a nostre cuer demeisn. Treschere et tresamee compaigne* . . .[5] From the reign of Edward II until the end of the Middle Ages type (*d*), generally in French but sometimes in Latin, was often used for informal correspondence with foreign rulers (Plate **12**)[6] and, from Edward III onwards, for administrative letters to the chancellor and

[1] Chancery Warrants 27/2663. Compare Maxwell-Lyte, pp. 172–3, a letter sent by Edward III to the duke of Cornwall and beginning 'Trescher fils'.

[2] See Ancient Correspondence, vol. 13, no. 30; *The Diplomatic Correspondence of Richard II*, ed. E. Perroy (Royal Hist. Soc., Camden Third Series, xlviii), nos. 109, 157, 169, 228; J. Conway Davies, *The Baronial Opposition to Edward II* (Cambridge Univ. Press, 1918), p. 595; *Facs. of Nat. MSS.* I. xxvii.

[3] See P. Chaplais, 'Some Private Letters of Edward I', *English Hist. Rev.* lxxvii, p. 84 (draft).

[4] Exch. Miscellanea (E. 163), 4/11/15 (draft).

[5] Exch. Miscellanea 4/11/37 (draft).

[6] See also *The War of Saint-Sardos*, ed. P. Chaplais (Royal Hist. Soc., Camden Third Series, lxxxvii), no. 20 (draft; 8 Feb. 1324), and pp. 176–8, 179–80, 181, 192; Paris, Arch. Nat., J. 655, no. 38, a letter of Edward II to Charles IV of France (10 March 1322): 'Treschier et tresamez frere. Nous avoms receu et bien entenduz voz lettres . . . Treschier et tresamez frere, Nostre Seignur vous eit en sa garde. Don*e* souz nostre prive seal a Birton' sur Trente le x jour de marz, lan de nostre regne xvme'; *The Diplomatic Correspondence of Richard II*, nos. 13, 16, 17, 29, 40, 123, 142, 206. Some of Richard II's privy-seal letters to foreign rulers are preceded or followed by *Rex Anglie et Francie* (ibid., nos. 29, 123), *Ricardus* (with or without *Dei gracia*) *rex Anglie et Francie* (ibid., nos. 6, 16) or *Per regem Anglie et Francie* (ibid., nos. 40, 216), the last form being apparently rarely used in letters to kings.

other royal officials. Administrative letters of this type had, as an additional feature, the heading *Depar le roi* or *Per regem*,[1] like the letters under the secret seal and signet:

Depar le roi

Reverent piere en Dieu. Nous vous envoions close deinz cestes une peticion . . . Don*e* souz n*o*stre prive seal a nostre chastel de Wyndesore le xxvj jour de marz. (*26 March* [*1365*])[2]

This diplomatic form, with the heading *Depar le roi*, is almost certainly of French origin. As early as 1311 the heading *Depar la reyne* or *Depar la reyne Dangleterre* was inserted at the beginning of letters of Queen Isabella, apparently sealed with her privy seal and written in a hand unmistakably French.[3] One of these letters, whose sealing method—also French and adopted by Edward III after 1345—will be discussed later, reads as follows:

Depar la reyne Dangleterre

Chier cousin. Savoir vous faisons que, Dieu merci, nous estiens en bonne sante quant ces lettres furent faites, laquelle chose nous desirrons toujours oir de vous. Si vous prions, biau cousin, que le plus souvent que vous pourrez bonnement nous en rescrivez la certeinete aveuc vostre volente, que nous feriens volenters et de cueur. Chier cousin, nous vous prions cherement que des besoingnes que nostre ame P. Aug*er*, vallet nostre s*ire* le roy, a affaire en Gascoingne vueillez pour lamour de nous estre par raison gracieus et favorables insint quil se puisse aparcevoir de noz prieres. Nostre S*ire* vous gart. Donn*e* a Berewik' le xxvj jour de Fevr*ier*. (*26 February* [*1311*])[4]

A number of letters close of Edward III ordering the chancellor to issue great-seal letters have the heading *Depar le roi* or *Per regem*, but no apostrophe or protocol of any kind:

Per regem

Cum dederimus et concesserimus dilecto clerico nostro . . . Dat*um* sub privato sigillo nostro apud Clarendon' vicesimo quinto die julii, anno regni nostri Anglie decimo septimo, regni vero nostri Francie quarto. (*25 July 1343*)[5]

Letters of type (*d*) are usually dated by the day and month only.

Because the great seal was large and double-sided, any method of closing up letters with it which consisted of impressing the seal on the actual surface of the main parchment was impracticable, but this did not apply to the privy seal, which was small and one-sided. It seems that throughout the medieval period privy-seal letters and writs close were closed up by applying the seal to the dorse of the documents over a tongue. A narrow strip (tongue) was partially cut off the foot of the document, below the writing, from right to left, the cut stopping at a distance of one inch or less from the left margin; sometimes the tongue was made broader at its loose end by trimming the left portion of its lower edge. Then the document was folded two or three times vertically and sometimes also horizontally (once or twice) to form a small package approximately square, around which the tongue was wrapped once and then looped through itself at a point situated well below the centre of the square and to its left. The seal was applied over the loop, thus securing

[1] Maxwell-Lyte, pp. 57–8; E. Déprez, *Études de diplomatique anglaise*, pp. 54–6.

[2] Chancery Warrants (C. 81), 908/19.

[3] Ancient Correspondence (S.C. 1), vol. 63, nos. 186 and 187.

[4] Ancient Correspondence, vol. 63, no. 187.

[5] Chancery Warrants 908/1: Maxwell-Lyte, p. 57. See also Déprez, op. cit., pp. 51–4.

together the tongue and main parchment (see below, drawings 1–4, and Plate **26***a*–*b*).[1] This method was used until May 1345, when it was superseded by another of French origin. According to the new method, once the letter had been folded, a cut was made through all the layers of the package and the tongue inserted through the slits thus provided. On the exit side of the tongue (corresponding to the section of the document which bore the root of the tongue) the seal was applied over tongue and slit, close to the right-hand margin of the dorse (see below, drawings 5–8, and Plate **26***c*–*d*).[2] There are isolated

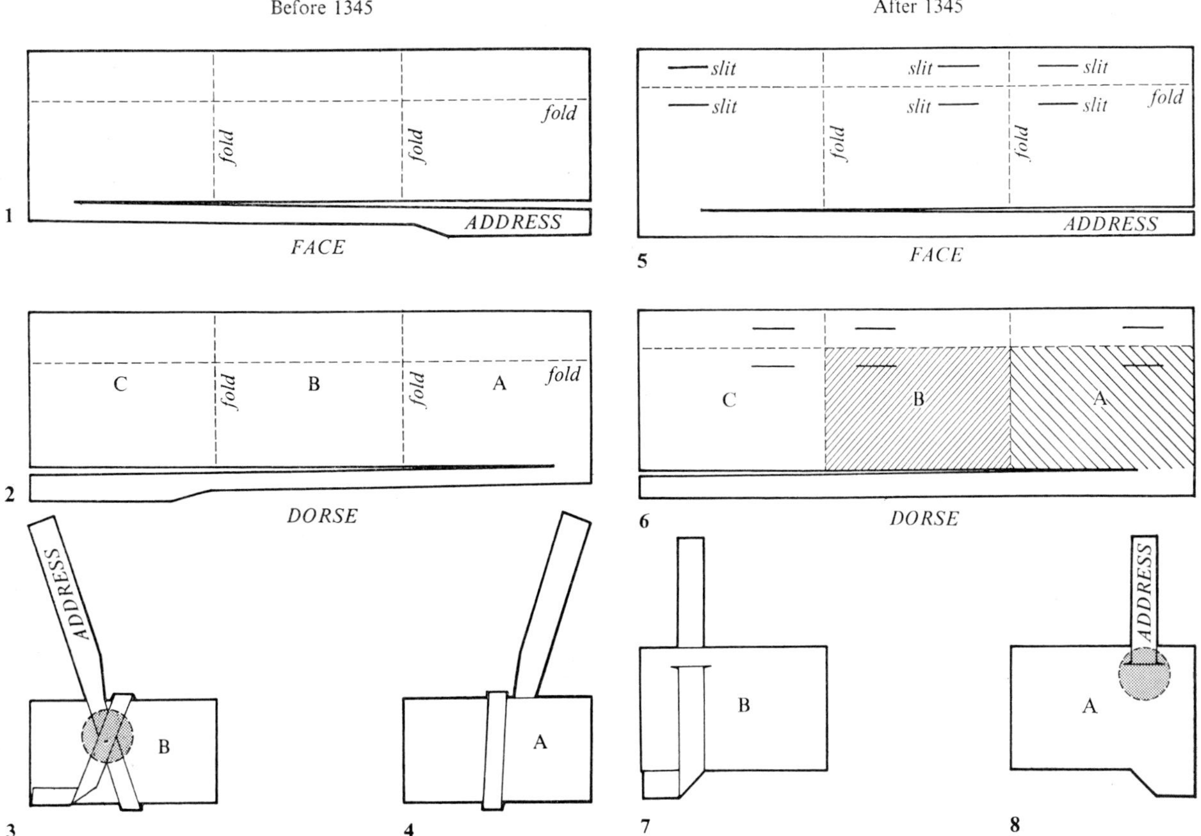

examples of the royal privy seal being applied in this way or in a similar one between 1337 and May 1345, but in May 1345 the new practice seems to have superseded all others.[3] Although the method was new in the royal privy-seal office, it had been used by the privy-seal clerks of Queen Isabella as early as 1311,[4] and later by those of Queen Philippa. Whichever method was used, the address of the letter was written lengthways on the portion of the tongue which was to remain free after sealing. In a letter of Henry V to the duke of Burgundy (29 June 1414) the address is, exceptionally, on the dorse of the document, and the privy seal was formerly applied, not over a tongue and slit, but over a thong

[1] See also Tout, *Chapters*, v, p. 118 (slightly different reconstruction).

[2] Ibid., p. 119; the reconstruction is erroneous in my view.

[3] Maxwell-Lyte, p. 49; Tout, *Chapters*, v, pp. 118–20.

[4] Ancient Correspondence, vol. 63, nos. 186 and 187. See also Tout, *Chapters*, v, p. 120, n. 6, and p. 288.

as in signet letters; here, however, probably because the privy seal was a much larger seal than the signet, the cross of red wax, at the centre of which the signet was applied, was dispensed with.[1]

(B) *Letters patent.* The form of letters patent under the privy seal is in most respects similar to that of letters patent under the great seal. Letters patent proper (commissions to some royal officers, receipts, acknowledgements of debts, etc.) have a general address, which is frequently in the form *Omnibus ad quos presentes littere pervenerint*,[2] or *A touz ceux qui ces lettres verront* (Plate **19***a*),[3] or *A touz ceux a queux cestes lettres vendront.*[4] Their dating-clause, which is identical to that of administrative writs close of type (*a*), is generally (but not always) preceded by a corroboration-clause, *In cujus rei testimonium has litteras nostras fieri fecimus patentes*,[5] or its French equivalent, *En tesmoignance de quele chose nous avons fait faire cestes noz lettres patentes.*[6] Some letters of protection and safeguard issued under Edward I's privy seal are addressed *a touz nos foialx et loialx ministres et autres a queux cestes lettres vendront* and have a time-limit clause: *En tesmoignance de queu chose nous avoms fait faire cestes nos lettres overtes a durer nostre volunte.*[7]

A large number of writs addressed to individual officials and couched in the same terms as writs close were sealed patent when it was expected that they would have to be produced at some later date with their seal intact.[8] This applied in particular to writs ordering the collection and delivery of money or victuals needed by the household, although writs of this kind were sometimes sent close.

Letters and writs patent were sealed with the privy seal pendent, either on a tongue (normally accompanied by a wrapping-tie; Plate **27***a*: the small step in the bottom left-hand corner, below the tongue, is not shown on the plate) or on a tag (inserted through a turn-up).

(C) *Bills.* Privy-seal bills, like letters patent, were sealed open, but, instead of being appended to a tongue or tag, the seal was applied to the surface of the document itself, either on the face or on the dorse. Curt administrative orders without protocol or address, and normally written in the third person of the subjunctive, the bills were used especially as warrants to the chancellor for the issue of routine documents under the great seal, for

[1] Brit. Mus., Add. MS. 14820 (A).

[2] Déprez, *Études de diplomatique anglaise*, p. 48; Exch., K.R., Accounts Various (E. 101), 684/60/8 (dated at Peebles, 10 Aug. 1301; with tongue and wrapping-tie).

[3] See also Conway Davies, *The Baronial Opposition to Edward II*, p. 563, no. 39, and p. 597, no. 136; Exch., T.R., Ancient Deeds, Series A (E. 40), 15105 (below, Plate **27***a*).

[4] Déprez, op. cit., p. 50; Chancery Miscellanea (C. 47), 22/9/36.

[5] Déprez, op. cit., p. 49.

[6] Exch., T.R., Ancient Deeds, Series A (E. 40), 15105 (below, Plate **27***a*); Conway Davies, op. cit., p. 563, no. 39, and p. 597, no. 136.

[7] Chancery Miscellanea 22/7/12 and 15; 22/9/124. For other privy-seal letters patent, see Maxwell-Lyte, pp. 389–90.

[8] The same could be said of some letters connected with foreign relations, e.g. the following letter of Richard II to Charles VI: 'A treshaut et puissaunt prince C. par la grace de Dieu nostre trescher et tresame piere de France, R. par icelle mesme grace roy Dengleterre, etc[a], salut et entierre dileccion. Come en le traitee de ceste mariage . . . En tesmoignaunce de ce nous avons fait faire cestes noz lettres patentes. Donne souz nostre prive seal a nostre palois de Westmouster le xiiij jour de may, lan de nostre regne dis et noefisme' (Paris, Arch. Nat., J. 643, no. 8; with the privy seal on a tongue and with a wrapping-tie): *Diplomatic Correspondence of Richard II*, no. 228. Note Richard's abbreviated style: had he used his full, usual, style 'King of England and France . . .', Richard would have offended Charles VI; but similar letters patent, addressed generally, have his full style (Plate **19***a*).

example commissions, protections, and safe-conducts. Most of them begin with the words *Fiat* or *Soit faite* (*Fiat proteccio cum clausula volumus pro* . . . (Plate **17***c*);[1] *Soient faites lettres de sauf' conduyt' pur* . . .,[2] etc.), but others, including some of the earliest, begin *Dominus rex concessit* . . .,[3] *Le roi ad done congie* . . .,[4] etc. They have no corroboration-clause, and until about 1350 many have either no date or a date which is short and mentions neither the privy seal nor the king's regnal year, e.g. *Done a Westm' le xx jour daugst'*.[5] By the end of Edward III's reign they have the same dating-clause as the privy-seal writs of type (*a*) (Plate **27***b*), and some of them are headed *Depar le roi*,[6] possibly in order to distinguish the bills authorized by the king himself (when the privy seal was with him) from those authorized by the king's council. The ten privy-seal bills copied in the fifteenth-century formulary of Thomas Hoccleve, all in the form *Fiat* . . . or *Soient faictes* . . ., are described in a heading as: *Au chanceller: sauf conduytz, commissions, proteccions et autres garranz overtes issanz souz le prive seal nient faisantz mencion de le stile de chanceller*.[7]

Although the earliest extant bills which are known to have been sealed with the privy seal (*c*. 1300) are in fact petitions bearing on the dorse a note of assent together with an impression of the privy seal (e.g. *Fiat ei perdonacio* . . .),[8] already in 1286 the wardrobe sent self-contained bills to the chancellor in the form *Fiat littera domini regis de aquietancia* . . .[9]

(D) *Indentures*. The most important documents in this class consist of bipartite agreements for military service between the king and a retainer. The terms of the contract were copied twice on the same piece of parchment, a blank space being left between the two texts. The two halves were then separated by cutting through the blank along a wavy or indented line: one part, sealed with the king's privy seal, was handed over to the retainer, and the other, sealed with the retainer's seal, was kept by the king. Edward I used this system to recruit custodians of castles during his Scottish wars:

Fait a remembrer que covenancez est a mons' Patrik' de Dombar, conte de la Marche, quil demoerge gardein du chastel et de la contee de Are . . . [*Then follow the terms of the contract, conditions, and duration of service*] . . . En tesmoignance de queu chose feust ceste endenture faite a Bothevill' le xx jour de septembre, lan du regne nostre seigneur le roi Edward xxix, dont lune partie sealee du prive seal le roi demoert devers le dit conte et lautre partie demoert en la garderobe le roi sealee du seal le conte avantdit. (*20 Sept. 1301*)[10]

Although the conditions of indented service changed considerably from one reign to the next, the diplomatic form of the indentures remained fairly constant. They retained the form of a memorandum ending with a corroboration-clause which usually stated that the two parts of the indenture had been sealed *alternatim* or *entrechangeablement*. Under Edward II military indentures still began *Fait a remembrer qe* . . .,[11] as they did in the early

[1] Maxwell-Lyte, pp. 55–6; Déprez, op. cit., pp. 58–62.

[2] Chancery Warrants (C. 81), 909/9; Maxwell-Lyte, pp. 54–5; Déprez, op. cit., pp. 65–7.

[3] Maxwell-Lyte, p. 54.

[4] Ibid., p. 55; Déprez, op. cit., p. 70.

[5] Chancery Warrants 909/9.

[6] Déprez, op. cit., p. 65.

[7] Brit. Mus., Add. MS. 24062, fol. 33^{v}.

[8] Maxwell-Lyte, p. 53.

[9] Chancery Warrants 1762/43.

[10] Exch., K.R., Accounts Various (E. 101), 68/1/27.

[11] Conway Davies, *The Baronial Opposition to Edward II*, pp. 566–7, nos. 46–7.

part of Edward III's reign, by which time, however, the great seal was sometimes used instead of the privy seal.[1] By the mid fourteenth century their opening words had altered slightly:

> Ceste endenture tesmoigne qe mons' Johan de Beauchamp', frere au counte de Warr', est demoere capitan de Caleys . . . En tesmoignance de quele chose a lune partie de ceste endenture demurrante envers le dit Johan nostre seignur le roi ad fait mettre son grant seal en absence de son prive seal et a lautre partie de ceste endenture demurrant envers le roi le dit mons' Johan ad mys son seal. Done a Westm' le x jour de feverer, lan du regne nostre dit seignur le roi Dengleterre trentisme et de France disseptisme. (*10 Feb. 1356*)[2]

Indentures of Richard II's and later reigns normally begin *Ceste endenture faite parentre nostre seignur le roy . . ., dune part, et . . ., dautre part, tesmoigne que . . .*,[3] or, in Latin, *Hec indentura facta inter . . . regem Anglie . . ., ex una parte, et . . ., ex altera, testatur quod . . .*[4] Throughout the medieval period the seals of military indentures were appended sometimes to a tongue, more often to a tag.

The colour of the wax used for the privy seal was always red.

In the latter part of Edward I's reign, and possibly as early as 1284, privy-seal letters and writs were regularly transcribed on wardrobe rolls and registers, in which were also copied some great-seal letters which were too confidential to be entered on the chancery enrolments. All these rolls and registers, however, appear to have been lost except for a damaged leaf from the register for 1301.[5] The enrolling practice may have continued for a while under Edward II, at least until 1312, but it certainly stopped long before 1385, in which year some privy-seal writs were enrolled on the close roll *pro eo quod registrum in dicto officio privati sigilli non habetur*.[6] The wardrobe and privy-seal office also kept their drafts of privy-seal documents. Under Edward I and Edward II those drafts were arranged in monthly files, a system which may have gone on uninterrupted throughout the fourteenth and fifteenth centuries. Only a small fraction of what was originally preserved in those files has survived.[7] The rest was either lost through neglect or burnt in the fire which destroyed the Banqueting House in Whitehall in January 1619.

THE SECRET SEAL AND SIGNET

Within a year of Roger of Northburgh's appointment as an independent keeper of the privy seal, Edward II had a new seal attached to his person, a secret seal. On 4 January 1313 some letters *sub sigillo regis secreto* were sent to Aymer de Valence, earl of Pembroke,[8] and another letter *souz nostre secre seal*, also addressed to the earl and dated 26 January

[1] R. Nicholson, *Edward III and the Scots* (Oxford Univ. Press, 1965), p. 243, no. 17 (under the great seal). See also Rymer, *Foedera* (Rec. Comm.), III. i. 324 (great seal *en absence de son prive seal*); III. i. 420.

[2] Treaty Roll (C. 76), no. 34, m. 18d.

[3] Hall, *Formula Book*, i, no. 146; *New Pal. Soc.* i. 249a.

[4] Rymer, *Foedera* (Original edition, London), x. 123–4.

[5] P. Chaplais, 'Privy Seal Drafts, Rolls and Registers (Edward I–Edward II)', *English Hist. Rev.* lxxiii, pp. 270–3, and plate facing p. 272.

[6] Maxwell-Lyte, p. 27.

[7] *English Hist. Rev.* lxxiii, pp. 270–3. For the fifteenth century most of the privy-seal drafts are preserved in Exch., T.R., Council and Privy Seal Files (E. 28).

[8] Exch., K.R., Accounts Various (E. 101), 375/8, fol. 42^{r}. Privy seals, secret seals, and signets are reproduced in Tout, *Chapters*, v, plates i–iv.

1313, has survived in the original.[1] The new seal was smaller than the privy seal; its legend read SIGILLVM SECRETVM DOMINI REGIS EDWARDI, whereas the legend of the privy seal read SECRETVM REGIS EDWARDI; the design on Edward II's secret seal portrayed a man on horseback, whereas the privy seal represented the three leopards of England on a shield.[2]

By the end of his reign, whether the privy seal was with him or not, Edward II sent under his secret seal his private and secret correspondence, and letters dealing with matters which he took especially to heart (*Et qe vous sachez qe nous avoms ceste busoigne a cuer, nous vous escrivoms souz nostre secre seal*).[3] When the privy seal was not with him, he used the secret seal as a substitute (*pur ce qe nostre prive seal ne feut mie pres de nous a la feissance de cestes*),[4] or to order the issue of documents under the privy seal or great seal.[5] During his reign, letters and writs under the secret seal were drawn up in the same form as those under the privy seal, apart from the replacement of *prive seal* and *privatum sigillum* by *secre seal* and *secretum sigillum* in the dating-clause (Plate **10***a*).[6] Indeed it seems that in September 1322 the same scribes wrote letters under both seals, since in drafts made in that month the word *secre* was struck out or erased to be replaced by *prive* (Plate **11***b*).[7]

Unlike his father, Edward III had, at least during two periods of his reign, more than one personal seal at a time. From 1329 to 1354 he had three secret seals for ordinary business in fairly rapid succession (first seal 1329–30; second seal *c.* 1331–8; third seal *c.* 1338–54), each of which was sometimes called 'signet', and in addition—from 1335 to 1354—another secret seal, the griffin seal, which he used for business connected with his chamber. His fourth and last 'ordinary' secret seal, one inch in diameter, in use from 1354 to 1367 (with the legend SIGNETVM REGIS ANGLIE ET FRANCIE), sometimes called 'signet' even in the dating-clause of documents, was for a period of seven years (1360–7) duplicated by a smaller seal, half an inch in diameter, the signet proper. In 1367 the use of the one-inch secret seal was discontinued, and from that year until the end of the reign only the half-inch signet remained. By that time the designation 'signet' had superseded that of 'secret seal'.[8] One signet of Richard II and all the signets of the fifteenth century represent the royal arms (France and England quarterly) on a shield. The wax used for the secret seal and signet was red.

(A) *Letters and writs close.* The vast majority of extant documents issued under the secret seal or signet consist of administrative orders, sent close not only to the chancellor and keeper of the privy seal, but also to a wide variety of royal officials. Until 1360 they assume various forms:

[1] Ancient Correspondence (S.C. 1), vol. 49, no. 21. See Maxwell-Lyte, p. 101.

[2] Ibid., p. 102.

[3] Exch., K.R., Memoranda Roll (E. 159), no. 97, m. 42d. Compare Rymer, *Foedera* (Rec. Comm.), II. i. 632 (27 June 1326): 'Et ut vobis constet premissa de certa nostra consciencia processisse, mittimus vobis presentes litteras nostras in gallico scriptas sub privato sigillo nostro, translatas insuper in latinum sub magno sigillo nostro consignatas.'

[4] Chancery Miscellanea (C. 47), 35/21/23; see also Chancery Warrants (C. 81), 1329/105. For the reign of Richard II, see Maxwell-Lyte, p. 112.

[5] Ibid., p. 76; Chancery Warrants 1329 (*passim*).

[6] Déprez, *Études de diplomatique anglaise*, pp. 74–7.

[7] See also Maxwell-Lyte, p. 102.

[8] Tout, *Chapters*, v, pp. 171–81; Maxwell-Lyte, pp. 106–7.

(*a*) Some are writs close similar in form to those of Edward II's reign, with a full protocol made up of the king's name and title, an address and a greeting (*saluz*), and with the dating-clause *Done souz nostre secre seal* [or *souz nostre signet*] *a*, followed by the place of issue, the day of the month, and regnal year:

Edward par la grace de Dieu roi Dengleterre, seignur Dirlaunde et ducs Daquitaine, al honurable piere en Dieu R. par la mesme grace evesqe de Cicestre, nostre chaunceller, salutz. Come . . . Don*e* souz nostre secre seal a Haveringges atte Bowre le x jour daveril, lan de nostre regne douzisme. (*10 April 1338*)[1]

After 1352 this type seems to have been mainly used for warrants to the chancellor, issued under the secret seal or signet in the absence of the privy seal.[2]

(*b*) In a second category, used in the first fifteen years or so of Edward III's reign, the protocol consists of a greeting only, *Saluz et bon amour* or *Saluz*. When there is a dating-clause it often omits the regnal year:

Saluz et bon amour. Nous vous signifioms qe . . . Don*e* souz nostre secre seal a Clipston' le v jour daugst. (*5 August* [*1331*])[3]

Salutz. Come nous soions tenuz a noz chers clercs Johan de Walingford . . . Don*e* souz nostre secre seal a Schotle le quint jour de juyn, lan de [nostre regne Dengleterre] qatorzisme et de France premer. (*5 June 1340*)[4]

(*c*) In a third category there is no protocol at all, but only the heading *Depar le roi* or *Per regem*. The mention of the regnal year in the dating-clause is exceptional:

Depar le roi

Nous avons grantez . . . Don*e* souz nostre signet a Clipston' le primer jour de septembre. (Plate **14***b*: *1 Sept.* [*1354*]; see also Plate **16***a*)[5]

(*d*) The fourth category also has the heading *Depar le roi*. It has no protocol, but only a short address in the form of an apostrophe, for example *Reverent piere en Dieu*. The regnal year is omitted in the dating-clause:

Depar le roi

Reverent piere en Dieu. Nous avons done . . . Don*e* souz nostre secre seal a Clarydon' le xxvij jour de juyl. (*27 July* [*1354*])[6]

After 1360 type (*d*) became the norm for letters close under the signet until the end of the Middle Ages (Plates **18***a*, **20***a*, **21***a*, **22***b*, **24***a*). Under Richard II the royal signature ('sign-manual') was sometimes added (*Le roy R S*: Plate **18***a*), a feature which became very common under Henry VI (*R H*).[7] Under Henry IV and Henry V the apostrophe was often followed by a greeting, which consisted not of one word (*saluz*) at the end of the protocol as in writs, but of several words at the beginning of the text, for example *Nous*

[1] Maxwell-Lyte, pp. 108–9.
[2] Ibid., p. 109; Déprez, op. cit., p. 93.
[3] Maxwell-Lyte, p. 103.
[4] Exch. of Receipt, Writs and Warrants for Issues (E. 404), 4/27.
[5] Maxwell-Lyte, p. 109.
[6] Ibid., pp. 105–6.
[7] See ibid., pp. 152–3; Otway-Ruthven, *The King's Secretary and the Signet Office in the XVth Century*, pp. 24–6 (also p. 39).

vous saluons tressovent et (*volons* . . . or *savoir vous faisons* . . .).[1] Until the reign of Henry V French was the normal language of the secret seal and signet, although Latin was occasionally used. From Henry V's reign French and Latin were superseded by English except for diplomatic correspondence, where the choice between French and Latin was determined according to the country to which the letters were dispatched.[2]

Signet letters to foreign rulers either were of type (*d*) or followed the pattern adopted for diplomatic correspondence under the privy seal. Letters of this kind were sometimes headed *Per regem Anglie et Francie*, *Rex Anglie et Francie*, *Le roi Dengleterre*, or *Le roy Dengleterre et de France*, but in letters to the pope and in many letters to foreign kings there was no heading at all. In a letter of type (*d*) sent by Edward III to King John of France the note *Le roi Dengleterre vostre frere* occurs, not as a heading, but as a sort of non-autograph subscription, and the dating-clause is preceded by a valediction, a common feature in diplomatic correspondence:

Trescher et tresame frere. Por ce que nous avons ordonne . . . Trescher et tresame frere, li Saint Espirit vous ait toutdis en sa garde. Don*e* souz le signet que vous savez a nostre manoir de Haverynge le xxx jour de juillet. (*30 July* [*1362*])

Le roi Dengleterre
vostre frere.[3]

The same features are found in two other letters of Edward III to the king of France, one under Edward III's secret seal and the other under his privy seal:

Trescher et tresame frere. Nous avons receu et entendu voz lettres . . . Et trescher et tresame frere, li Seint Espirit vous veulle touz jours garder. Don*e* souz nostre secree seal a nostre chastel de Wyndesore le xxiiij jour daverill'. (*24 April* [*1366*])

Vostre frere le
roi Dengleterre.[4]

Trescher et tresame frere. Come pur le present anee que se finera . . . Et trescher et tresame frere, lui Seint Espirit vous veulle touz jours garder. Don*e* souz nostre prive seal a nostre manoir de Shene le xxix jour doctobre. (*29 Oct.* [*1361*])

Vostre frere le roi
Dengleterre.[5]

Letters close under Edward III's four 'ordinary' secret seals were sealed in the same way as privy-seal letters close. Those under Edward III's signet proper (1360–77) and under all later signets were sealed, not over a tongue partially detached from the foot of the document, but over a thong completely loose, which—like a wide version of our modern staples—was inserted through two horizontal slits made in the folded letter. These slits were parallel, arranged like the opposite sides of a square, and about two inches apart. On one side of the package (side of exit of the thong), between the two slits, wax was smeared, in the shape of a cross with one bar forming a right angle with the slits. The two ends of the thong were then brought together and made to adhere lightly to the

[1] Déprez, op. cit., pp. 97–101.
[2] Otway-Ruthven, op. cit., pp. 28–9.
[3] Paris, Arch. Nat., J. 641, no. 13 (2).
[4] Paris, Arch. Nat., J. 642, no. 9 (3).
[5] Paris, Arch. Nat., J. 641, no. 12 (2). Cf. G. Tessier, *Diplomatique royale française*, p. 306, n. 3.

surface of the parchment or paper by pressing them against the cross of wax. Finally the signet was applied in the centre of the cross over the two ends of the thong (see the drawings below, and Plate **27***d*). Sometimes the signet was protected by surrounding it with a fender of twisted rush.[1] On the other side of the package (the side of entry of the thong) was written the address, e.g. *A nostre trescher et tresame frere le roi de France.*[2]

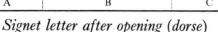

Signet letter after opening (dorse)

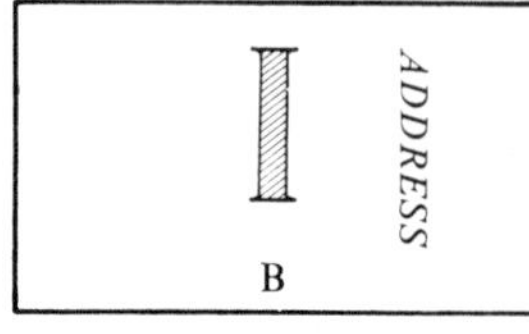

Closed (one side)

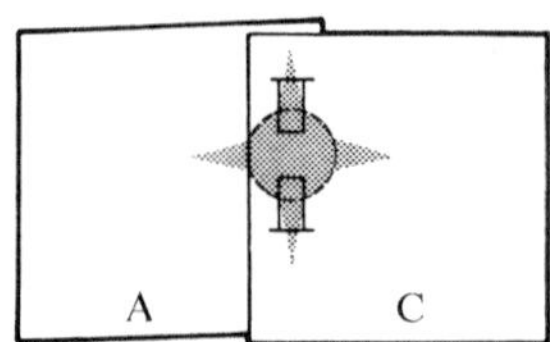

Closed (other side)

(B) *Bills and other documents sealed patent.* Signet warrants to the chancellor sometimes took the form of bills. Signet bills, like signet letters, were normally headed *Depar le roi* or *Per regem*; they were sealed patent, with the signet applied to the face or dorse of the document, in the centre of a cross of wax.[3] The following example, sealed with the signet in the absence of the privy seal, differs from a privy-seal bill only in its dating-clause and sealing:

Fiat proteccio cum clausula volumus pro dilecto nobis Galfrido de Seynt Quyntyn, qui in obsequium nostrum ad partes transmarinas profecturus est, ibidem in municione ville nostre Cales' moraturus, usque ad festum natalis Domini proximo futurum duratura. Dat*um* sub signeto anuli \`nostri′ in absencia privati sigilli nostri apud manerium nostrum de Kenyngton' viij die julii, anno regni nostri primo. (*8 July 1377*) (Plate **27***c*)

On other documents, for example on royal wills and on instructions to ambassadors, both of which classes were, from Richard II onwards, authenticated by the great seal, privy seal, and signet as well as by the sign-manual, the signet was appended on a tag.[4]

From 1377 the signet was kept by an official styled 'king's secretary', who also supervised the writing of signet documents. He was assisted in this task by a group of signet clerks: there were four of them in Henry IV's reign; their number increased in the following reigns, but it seems that there were never more than four senior clerks at a time, the others acting as their assistants.[5]

[1] Otway-Ruthven, op. cit., plate ii, facing p. 24.

[2] Paris, Arch. Nat., J. 641, no. 13 (2).

[3] Maxwell-Lyte, p. 109. Signet bills sent to the chancellor for the issue of great-seal documents also took the form of petitions bearing on their face a note of royal assent (e.g. *Le roy lad grantez par tesmoignance de son signet*) and on their dorse an impression of the signet and an address (e.g. *A lonurable piere en Dieu levesque de Seint David, nostre chanceller*): ibid., p. 108.

[4] See Royal Wills (E. 23), e.g. the will of Richard II; Exch., T.R., Scottish Documents (E. 39), 95/12 (4 April 1399).

[5] Otway-Ruthven, op. cit., pp. 109–13. For secret-seal clerks *c.* 1340, see Tout, *Chapters*, v, p. 180.

III. WARRANTS FOR THE GREAT SEAL AND PRIVY SEAL

(A) WARRANTS FOR THE GREAT SEAL

In King John's reign it was already the practice of the royal chancery to insert on the chancery rolls, after the enrolment of some charters, letters, and writs, a warranting-note stating on whose authority the originals had been issued (e.g. *per ipsum regem*; *per cancellarium*; *per breve de parvo sigillo*). The practice developed in the following reigns and, from the second half of the thirteenth century, similar notes were sometimes added at the foot, or on the dorse, of the originals themselves. The authorization of chancery documents is such a complex problem that only broad generalizations, which admit of many exceptions, can be attempted here.[1] One should be warned that, owing to constitutional, political, and administrative considerations, the warranting system varied from period to period and from one type of document to another, and also that in a given period one particular type of document could be authorized in several ways, by word of mouth or in writing, by the king and by others; royal authorization could be given of the king's own motion or in response to a request made by the interested party himself in an oral or written petition, or following the intervention of a third party, normally someone with influence at the royal court.

1. *Immediate royal warrants* (*Per ipsum regem*)*: orders by word of mouth or in writing under the secret seal and signet.* The king could authorize the issue of chancery documents by giving oral instructions to the chancellor. This was without doubt the earliest type of royal warrant and probably the only one used during the first century of the English chancery. From the time of King John the enrolment of great-seal documents authorized in this way was followed by the warranting-note *per ipsum regem* (Plates **10***c*, **16***b*).[2] Logically this note without further qualifications should have meant that the king had given his oral instructions to the chancellor in person, but it was sometimes used in a less restrictive sense to cover other eventualities. When, for example, the king's oral orders were relayed orally to the chancellor through an intermediary because the chancellor was away from the king, the warranting-note might simply read *per ipsum regem*, although the fuller and more correct note *per ipsum regem nunciante A.* occurs.[3] Similarly, when the intermediary, himself unable to find the chancellor, had to send him the king's oral message in writing, the full warranting-note should have read, as it sometimes did, *per ipsum regem nunciante A. per litteram suam*, but this cumbersome formula was often shortened to *per ipsum regem nunciante A.* or even *per ipsum regem.*[4]

The note *per ipsum regem* was not restricted to chancery instruments issued of the king's own motion. It is also found at the end of documents known to have been requested

[1] For further details, see Maxwell-Lyte, pp. 141–222; A. L. Brown, 'The Authorization of Letters under the Great Seal', *Bull. Inst. of Hist. Res.* xxxvii, pp. 125–56 and notes.

[2] See Maxwell-Lyte, pp. 141–67; Johnson and Jenkinson, plates xxiii (*a*), lines 25, 29, 34; xxxviii (*a*), line 18; xli (*a*), line 62; *Rôles gascons*, iv, nos. 156, 624–30.

[3] *New Pal. Soc.* i. 175c; *Rôles gascons*, iv, nos. 128, 159–60, 235–41, etc. In October 1319 Edward II instructed the chancellor to accept only two types of royal warrants, those he had received from the king's own mouth and those sent by writ of privy seal; great-seal letters were not to be issued at the request of an intermediary purporting to come with an oral warrant from the king. Those instructions, however, appear to have had little effect (Maxwell-Lyte, pp. 143–4).

[4] Ibid., pp. 142–7.

by the interested party in a written petition or by a third party who had intervened on his behalf. Details of this kind are given sometimes in the text of the great-seal letters, seldom in their warranting-notes, although such phrases as *per ipsum regem ad instanciam B.*, indicating a third party's intervention, occur from time to time.[1] When the chancery document was issued in answer to a petition (*peticio*; sometimes *billa* in Latin or *bille* in French) from the interested party, this was sometimes specified in the warranting-note, at least when the petition was presented to the king and council, for example *per ipsum regem et peticionem de consilio*,[2] but such mentions are comparatively rare. Although the enrolment of a writ of 1 April 1313 for Arnaud Barbiers, a Gascon, is simply followed by the note *per ipsum regem*, we know that in fact the writ had been requested by the beneficiary, whose extant petition bears a note of the royal assent (*Rex precepit ista negocia expedire*).[3] Presumably the king had given his assent orally in the chancellor's presence, as in the case of a petition of 1385, which has the following note: 'Ceste bille estoit grantee par le roy a Wyndesore venredy darrein passee en presence du chanceller et pour ce soit fait *per ipsum regem*.'[4] A grant of free warren, dated 20 July 1318, is followed on the charter roll by the note *per ipsum regem, nunciante magistro Thoma de Cherleton'*.[5] Here also the petition of the beneficiary, John de Whelnetham, is still extant:

> A nostre seignur le rei prie son bachelier Johan de Whelnetham qil de sa grace lui voille grauntier garenne en ses demeines terres de Grant Whelnetham, Petite Whelnetham, Bradefeld, Stanefeld et Alfeton' (*et du seal faire sa grace, struck out*) en contee de Suff'.

On the face of the petition another hand has made a note of the king's assent, *Ista peticio concessa est per regem*; in addition, traces of a small seal can still be seen, also on the face of the document.[6] There is every reason to believe that the seal was that of Master Thomas Charlton (controller of the wardrobe 7 July 1316–7 July 1318; keeper of the privy seal 7 July 1316–? January 1320), who took the petition to the chancery and, by adding his seal to it, assumed full responsibility for the statement that the king had approved the petition: in this case again the king had probably given his assent by word of mouth, but obviously not in the chancellor's presence.

Since by the mid fifteenth century the chancery clerks often specified that the chancellor had received his instructions from the king's own mouth (*per ipsum regem oretenus*),[7] it is evident that by then the note *per ipsum regem* on its own had lost this restrictive meaning. In the case of a grant by letters patent for Simon Marcheford, a canon of Windsor College (1 May 1412), the king's oral instructions had been conveyed to the chancery in writing: Marcheford's petition bears on its face Henry IV's sign-manual, accompanied by a note of assent in the king's own hand (*H R avons grante pour ly*).[8] Nevertheless the warranting-note on the patent roll simply reads *per ipsum regem*.[9] For a pardon to Richard Clerk of Salisbury, also said to have been warranted *per ipsum regem* (15 August 1416),[10]

[1] Maxwell-Lyte, pp. 151–2; *Rôles gascons*, iv, nos. 1618, 1620, 1620 *bis*.

[2] Ibid., no. 285.

[3] Ibid., no. 883 and note.

[4] Maxwell-Lyte, p. 148.

[5] Charter Roll (C. 53), no. 105, m. 18: *C.Ch.R.* iii, p. 389.

[6] Ancient Petitions (S.C. 8), 233/11619.

[7] Maxwell-Lyte, p. 157; *C.P.R., 1446–52*, p. 257.

[8] *Facs. of Nat. MSS.* I. xxxiii. See also ibid. xxxiv.

[9] *C.P.R., 1408–13*, p. 401 (1 May 1412).

[10] *C.P.R., 1416–22*, p. 42.

the king's authorization had also been notified to the chancery in writing, this time not in the king's own hand, but in the hand of Humphrey, duke of Gloucester, as chamberlain of England, whose autograph note and signature are found on the face of the grantee's petition:

A treshaut, tresexcellent et tresgracious
seignur nostre seignur le roy

Supplie humblement Richard' Clerk' de Salesbury, haberdassher en le counte de Wiltes', qe come il le vendredie proschein devaunt le dismenge en la passioun darrein passe soit enditez de ceo qil a Canterbury traiterousement trencha deux grosses et quatre deniers et une mail del money de vostre cune, issint qe le dit moneye par celle enchesoun est empeire et poise meyns par un denier et un ferlyng' dargent a tresgraund' damage de vous et en desceit de vostre poeple, pur la quelle chose le dit suppliant fuist pris et mys en prisone a Canterbury et la unqore il est, attendant la mercie de Dieu et le vostre. Qe please a vostre tresgracious seignurie de vostre grace especiale pardoner a dit suppliant la suyte de vostre pees qe a vous envers luy appartient pur la trencheure de la dite moneie et tout ceo qe a vous appartient ou purra apparteigner pur les choses avauntditz ou pur ascun dycelles pur Dieu et en oevere de charite. [*At the top*:] Le roy la grante. [*At the foot*:] H. chambellan Dengleterre.[1]

After 1312 the king sometimes used his secret seal or signet to authorize the issue of great-seal documents: either a writ close was sent to the chancellor, ordering him to issue the required instrument,[2] or, when the procedure had started with a petition, the secret seal or signet was applied to the face or dorse of the petition as a sign of royal approval and the sealed petition was forwarded patent to the chancery.[3] In such cases, until 1387 the chancery clerks noted that the great-seal documents had been warranted *per litteram* (or *breve*) *de secreto sigillo* (or *signeto*), or *per billam de signeto* in the case of a petition authenticated with the signet.[4] As early as 1343, however, great-seal writs issued on receipt of a royal writ sealed with the griffin seal were noted as having been warranted *per ipsum regem*.[5] After 1387 warranting-notes seldom mentioned the signet; chancery documents issued in pursuance of letters, writs, or bills under the signet were noted on the chancery rolls as having been warranted *per ipsum regem*.[6] In some cases, it is true, the signet document was simply a written reminder of an order received by the chancellor from the king's own mouth. This is clearly stated once in a signet letter of Richard II (14 August 1387) which ordered the chancellor to issue a safe-conduct *selonc ce qe nous vous chargeasmes par bouche a nostre citee de Wircestre*; the safe-conduct under the great seal, Richard's letter continued, should be made in haste *par vertue du garant 'per ipsum regem' tantsoulement*.[6]

2. *Warrants by writ or bill under the privy seal* (*per breve* or *billam de privato sigillo*). When the chancellor was away from the royal court, the king, instead of sending verbal instructions through an intermediary, could order the issue of chancery documents by addressing to the chancellor a writ close under his privy seal. Charters, letters, and writs authorized in this fashion were noted as warranted *per breve de privato sigillo*, a type of warranting-note which occurs regularly on the chancery rolls from John's reign onwards

[1] Ancient Petitions 230/11477.
[2] Maxwell-Lyte, pp. 103–5.
[3] Ibid., p. 108.
[4] Ibid., pp. 104, 105, 108, 113, 225; *Rôles gascons*, iv, no. 1108.
[5] Maxwell-Lyte, pp. 111–12.
[6] Ibid., p. 116.

(Plates **13***b*, **20***c*).[1] From 1199 until 1312 privy-seal warrants represented direct orders from the king, since during that period the privy seal was normally with the king. This was no longer true after 1312: in that year, as we have seen, the privy seal ceased to be the king's own seal and became the seal of a state department, controlled by the king's council rather than by the king himself.[2] From that time onwards, privy-seal warrants could only be regarded as representing the king's will when they themselves had been authorized by the king verbally or in a document sealed with his secret seal or signet.

By the early fourteenth century, documents under the great seal could be authorized by several kinds of writs of privy seal: (*a*) If the chancery document which was needed was of common form (e.g. presentation to a benefice, royal assent to an episcopal election, etc.), a writ of privy seal was sent on its own, ordering the chancellor to issue the required document 'in due form', and giving only the relevant particulars (Plate **5***b*). (*b*) If the chancery document had been requested by petition, the king might forward the petition to the chancellor with a covering note in writ-form ordering him to issue whatever document seemed appropriate. (*c*) Sometimes, because the king wished the chancery instrument to be drawn up in a form of his own choice, for example in matters of foreign policy, a draft was prepared in French by a clerk of the privy seal and sent to the chancellor with a covering writ ordering him to have the draft translated into Latin, engrossed and sealed with the great seal (Plates **6***b*, **7***a*).[3]

From Edward I's reign onwards a large number of chancery documents, particularly those of a routine character (protections, pardons, safe-conducts, etc.), were authorized, not by a writ of privy seal (*per breve de privato sigillo*), but by a bill under the same seal (*per billam de privato sigillo*: Plate **14***a*, note): *Fiant littere* . . ., *Fiat proteccio* . . ., etc. (Plate **17***c*).[4] Among the extant bills some are self-contained documents ending, like writs, with a dating-clause, and others, including the earliest, appear in the form of short notes written on the dorse of petitions:

> Fiat ei perdonacio sicut petit in forma debita sub sigillo regis in Anglia et sit quietus de feodo sigilli.[5]

Generally speaking, it seems that great-seal documents warranted by privy-seal writs were more important and more costly than those warranted by privy-seal bills: most documents warranted by a privy-seal bill seem to have been liable to a chancery fee of 2 shillings, whereas those warranted by a privy-seal writ cost from 18*s*. 4*d*. to 12 marks 5 shillings.[6]

3. *Ministerial warrants*. Besides the king there were many others who could authorize the issue of chancery documents. The royal council, often associated with the king in immediate warrants (e.g. *per ipsum regem et consilium*),[7] could on its sole responsibility

[1] See Maxwell-Lyte, pp. 49–53; *Pal. Soc.* i. 254a; Johnson and Jenkinson, plates xxvii, line 45, xxviii (*b*), line 40, xxxi, line 8, xl (*b*).

[2] Tout, *Chapters*, ii, pp. 286–91.

[3] For type (*a*) see Maxwell-Lyte, pp. 50–1; Hall, *Formula Book*, i, p. 104, no. 108. For type (*b*) see Chancery Warrants (C. 81), 63/591–2. For type (*c*) see Maxwell-Lyte, pp. 51–2.

[4] Ibid., pp. 53–6; *Rôles gascons*, iv, nos. 155, 157–8, 320, 343.

[5] Maxwell-Lyte, p. 53.

[6] Wilkinson, *The Chancery under Edward III*, p. 223.

[7] Maxwell-Lyte, p. 183; *Pal. Soc.* ii. 160; *Rôles gascons*, iv, nos. 725–6, 764, 923, 1300.

order the chancery to draw up documents under the great seal. Council warrants, which could take many forms, are recorded on chancery engrossments and enrolments in a variety of ways, for example *per consilium*,[1] *per peticionem de consilio* (Plate **8***a*),[2] etc. Some categories of royal officers, for example the treasurer, admiral, butler, and others, could also apply direct to the chancery for the issue of whatever documents they needed to carry out their official duties. These ministerial warrants often took the form of bills: the chancery ordinance of 12 Richard II refers to *littere patentes minoris feodi, per billas . . . thesaurario Anglie aut ejus deputatis seu aliis ex officio confiendas . . .*[3] The following document is a typical example of a treasurer's bill:

Fiant littere regis patentes Willelmo Asshe, uni hostiariorum camere regis, ad constituendum ipsum Willelmum camerarium et receptorem regis Suthwall' quamdiu regi placuerit, ita quod de exitibus et proficuis officii predicti que predictus Willelmus recipiet regi respondeat ad scaccarium suum de Kermerdyn, percipiendo in eodem officio feoda consueta per manus suas proprias quamdiu steterit in officio supradicto, cum clausula de intendendo.
Custodi magni sigilli [*traces of a signet at the centre of a cross of wax*] per thesaurarium Anglie.[4]

This bill led to the issue of letters patent under the great seal, dated 4 December 1395; their enrolment on the fine roll is followed by the warranting-note *per billam thesaurarii*.[5] The next example is an admiral's bill:

Fiat comissio Hugoni de Mitford' quod sit substitutus et deputatus Johannis de Bello Monte, admiralli in partibus borialibus ad intendendum officio predicti admiralli.
Domini regis cancellario [*traces of round seal*] per ipsum admirallum.[6]

The great-seal commission to Hugh de Mitford, dated 13 November 1389, is enrolled on the treaty roll with the warranting-note *per billam ipsius admiralli*.[7]

The practice of inserting at the end of the engrossment or enrolment of a chancery document a note of the warrant which had led to its issue had obvious administrative advantages, especially in the case of a written warrant. As written warrants were systematically filed in the *filacie cancellarie*, where they could be checked easily, the warranting-note served the purpose of a cross-reference to one particular file of warrants. Because, however, warranting-notes did not add anything to the authenticity of the documents to which they were appended, one should not be surprised to find that sometimes they were inaccurately made or even omitted altogether.[8] Omissions are particularly regrettable, because they make it impossible for us to draw up exhaustive lists of the chancery documents which could be issued without a warrant and of those which could not. It is certain,

1 Below, Plate **25***e*; Maxwell-Lyte, pp. 180–1; Johnson and Jenkinson, plate xvii (*a*), line 31; *Rôles gascons*, iv, nos. 244, 282, 298, 359.

2 Maxwell-Lyte, pp. 193–5; *Rôles gascons*, iv, nos. 33, 47, 72, 85, 106, etc.

3 Wilkinson, op. cit., p. 223.

4 Chancery Warrants (C. 81), 1550/48.

5 Fine Roll (C. 60), no. 199, m. 18: *C.F.R.* xi (1391–9), p. 169. See also *Pal. Soc.* i, 257*b*; Johnson and Jenkinson, plate xxxi, line 49; Maxwell-Lyte, pp. 200–2.

6 Chancery Warrants 1656/8.

7 Treaty Roll (C. 76), no. 74, m. 14. See also Maxwell-Lyte, pp. 209–10.

8 For examples of errors, see ibid., pp. 58, 102–4. On the fine roll of 19 Ric. II the great-seal appointment of William Ledes as *contrarotulator cunagii stannar' regis* in Devon and Cornwall is followed by no warranting-note, although the treasurer's bill which ordered the issue of the commission has survived (Chancery Warrants 1581/15; *C.F.R.* xi, p. 168).

however, that there were some writs for which no outside warrant was needed. The majority of them seem to have consisted of the so-called 'original writs', some of which were known as writs 'of course' (*brevia de cursu* or *brevia cursoria*) and others as writs *de precepto* (or *de comandement*; also called *brevia de gratia*, *remedialia*, or *magistralia*). (*a*) The writs *de cursu* were writs which were available as of right to all the king's subjects and whose form, fixed once for all, was entered in the chancery 'registers of original writs'. Because their form was fixed, they were cheap and easy to obtain. Any bona fide applicant could procure them, usually without a fine, by paying simply the standard fees for their writing (1*d*.) and sealing (6*d*.). The writs of course were normally written by the chancery clerks of the lowest rank, the cursitors (*cursitores* or *clerici de cursu*), without having to be authorized either by a warrant from outside the chancery or by a chancery clerk of the first form. (*b*) The writs *de precepto* could only be obtained by special grace of the chancellor or of one of the chancery *preceptores*; some of them were very similar in form to the writs of course and appear to have merely extended the application of the latter to cases outside their scope, whilst others, drawn up to fit each individual case, departed from the standard form of the writs of course to a much greater degree.[1] Although they could be drawn up without an outside warrant, they had to be authorized by the chancellor or by a chancery clerk of the first form, by a *preceptor*.[2] This authorization was recorded on the dorse of the writ in a note such as *per cancellarium* (Plates **9***b*, **20***b*) or *A. de B. precepit* (Plate **9***c*) or *C. de D. precepit ad instanciam E.*[3] Some writs *de cursu* and *de precepto* were granted on payment of a fine and others without a fine.[4] No writ of course and only a small proportion of the writs *de precepto* appear to have been enrolled on the chancery rolls.

(B) WARRANTS FOR THE PRIVY SEAL

It may be assumed that, as long as the privy seal remained under the king's direct control, that is until 1312, the issue of documents sealed with it was, as a rule, authorized by the king himself. Whether or not this rule suffered many exceptions is difficult to ascertain because during that period original engrossments under the privy seal, unlike those under the great seal, seldom bear a note stating on whose authority they were issued. The existence, however, of the note *per peticionem coram consilio* at the foot of a privy-seal writ issued at Durham on 7 November 1298[5] is a salutary reminder that some sort of association between the privy seal and the king's council was not unknown in Edward I's reign. It is also difficult to believe that the note *per regem*, found at the end of a warrant

[1] For the distinction between writs *de cursu* and writs *de precepto*, see T. Madox, *The Hist. and Antiquities of the Exchequer* (London, 1711), p. 49, note k; *Statutes of the Realm*, i, p. 306; *Fleta*, ed. H. G. Richardson and G. O. Sayles (Selden Soc. 72), p. 123; H. G. Richardson in *Law Quart. Rev.* lxviii, pp. 540–1.

[2] For the *preceptores*, see *Fleta*, ed. cit., p. 125; Wilkinson, *The Chancery under Edward III*, pp. 74–8, 218, 221.

[3] Wilkinson, op. cit., pp. 77–8; a writ of Edward II (Windsor, 16 March, 6 Edw. II) addressed to William de Brikhull, clerk, and giving him power to receive the attorneys of Vincent fitzJohn del Hull of Lichfield is endorsed *A. de Osgod' precepit ad instanciam domini Johannis de Sand'* (Chancery Miscellanea (C. 47), 138).

[4] Brit. Mus., Cotton MS. Julius D. II (Irish Register of Writs), fol. 147: one writ *justicies* for debt detinue to 40 shillings is noted as *sine dono*, while a writ of *justicies de plegio acquietando* beyond 40 shillings is *non sine dono*. I owe these references to the kindness of Mr. G. D. G. Hall.

[5] Miscellaneous Inquisitions (C. 145), 58/22.

to the chancellor (16 April 1282),[1] was merely stating the obvious. This note probably meant that the wardrobe clerk who kept the privy seal had received his order to issue the writ from the king's own mouth, whereas notes such as *nunciante R. de Manton'*, *nunciante J. Botetourte*, etc.[2] meant that the king's oral authorization had been relayed orally through an envoy, when the privy seal was not with the king. At any rate, since until 1312 the privy seal was seldom far away from the king, who in any case seems to have had no other seal of his own at the time, no royal warrant for the privy seal is likely to have been issued in writing before that date. Notes such as *Per regem ad instanciam Bertrani Assalit*, found on a privy-seal writ of Edward II, meant that the royal order had been issued at the request of a third party, normally an influential friend or protector of the beneficiary.[3]

When, in 1312, Edward II acquired a new personal seal, the secret seal, to replace the privy seal which he no longer controlled, the warranting system for the privy seal became as complicated and varied as it already was for the great seal. When the privy seal was with him, Edward II authorized the issue of privy-seal documents in person by word of mouth: on several drafts of privy-seal letters of September 1322, this is indicated by the warranting-note *per ipsum regem.*[4] When the privy seal was away from him, Edward conveyed his instructions to the keeper of the privy seal either orally through an envoy or in writing by a writ of secret seal: the former method is again attested by warranting-notes found at the foot of privy-seal drafts for September 1322 (*per ipsum regem, nunciante domino Roberto de Kendale*;[5] *nunciante Th. de Weston'*),[6] and the latter by extant writs under the secret seal.[7]

From the second half of the fourteenth century, by which time the term 'signet' had gradually replaced that of 'secret seal', privy-seal documents could be authorized by oral warrants from the king himself: perhaps the heading *Depar le roi* or *Per regem* represented an oral warrant. They could also be authorized by a written warrant under the king's signet in the form of a letter or in that of a bill, or by a ministerial warrant normally in the form of a bill.[8]

IV. DEPUTED CHANCERIES

Perhaps for a hundred years or so after the Conquest one single writing-office, the chancery, had successfully coped with all the writing requirements of the king. During that period, however, the volume and variety of business with which the chancellor's staff had to deal had gradually increased to such proportions that towards the middle of the twelfth century some measure of secretarial decentralization had to be introduced as a matter of expediency; as soon as some branches of the *curia regis* ceased to follow the king in his

[1] Chancery Warrants (C. 81), 1/40A.

[2] Exch., K.R., Memoranda Roll (E. 159), no. 75, mm. 4 and 4d; Maxwell-Lyte, p. 75.

[3] *Rôles gascons*, iv, no. 326, note.

[4] Exch. Miscellanea (E. 163), 4/11 *passim.*

[5] Exch. Miscellanea 4/11/11.

[6] Exch. Miscellanea 4/11/51 (3).

[7] e.g. Chancery Warrants 1329/59: Maxwell-Lyte, p. 76.

[8] Ibid., pp. 79 (letter under the signet), 78 (warranting-note *per billam de secreto sigillo* on a privy-seal writ), 85 (warranting-notes *per billam thesaurarii* on privy-seal writs), 86 (ministerial warrant to the keeper of the privy seal in the form of a bill).

travels, decentralization had even become a necessity. The first step in that direction had already been taken when—during or perhaps even before Henry II's reign—the exchequer was given a seal of its own. This new royal seal was apparently an exact replica of the chancery seal, but unlike the latter, which followed the king, chancellor, and itinerant court around the country, it was permanently kept in the exchequer. This was the position in Henry II's reign, as we learn from the *Dialogus de Scaccario.*[1] At that time, however, the exchequer was still far from being independent of the chancery. The official custodian of the exchequer seal was the chancellor, although he exercised this duty through a deputy, the *clericus cancellarii*; in the chancellor's absence no exchequer writ could be sealed. It was also the chancellor who appointed the scribe entrusted with the writing of exchequer writs, the *scriptor cancellarii.*[2] Except for the *scriptor thesaurarii*, who wrote the pipe roll and seems to have had no connection with the chancery,[3] the secretarial staff of Henry II's exchequer was little more than a branch of the chancery. If exchequer writs of Henry II had survived in the original, they would be unlikely to show different palaeographical characteristics from the extant chancery writs, although their diplomatic features would easily identify them as exchequer documents. According to the *Dialogus*, exchequer writs resembled chancery writs in that they began with the king's name and titles, but they differed from them in their final clauses: exchequer writs were always attested by two witnesses, one of whom had to be the justiciar as president of the exchequer court and the other the constable or some other baron of the exchequer; their place-date (*Apud N.*) was also followed by the words *ad scaccarium*,[4] a formula which occurs in extant copies of two writs of Henry II, one of which at least, a writ of *perdono*, is likely to have been issued under the exchequer seal.[5]

During the reign of Richard I the exchequer seems to have made considerable progress towards independence, although this progress is somewhat obscured by a new development. It had been decided that, while Richard was abroad with his chancery seal, chancery documents issued in England by the justiciar should be made out under the king's name and title (*Ricardus Dei gratia rex Anglorum*, etc.) and sealed with the exchequer seal;[6] of this seal we only know that it was smaller than the chancery seal or, as we may already call it, the 'great seal',[7] and that it was a seal of majesty. During the king's absence exchequer writs may also have been issued under the king's name and sealed with the exchequer seal, but there is no satisfactory evidence on this point.[8] At any rate some of the work previously done by chancery officials was now dealt with by exchequer clerks: for example, the summonses of the exchequer were no longer sealed by a deputy of the

[1] *Dialogus de Scaccario* (Nelson's Medieval Classics), p. 62: 'Expressam autem habet imaginem et inscriptionem cum deambulatorio curie sigillo, ut par cognoscatur utrobique jubentis auctoritas et reus similiter judicetur pro hoc ut pro illo qui secus egerit'; also p. 19.

[2] Ibid., pp. 17–19.

[3] Ibid., pp. 13, 17, 18, 29–31.

[4] Ibid., pp. 32–3, 70.

[5] *Recueil des actes de Henri II*, ed. L. Delisle and E. Berger, ii, no. dxlii (writ of *perdono*). *The Cartulary of Cirencester Abbey, Gloucestershire*, ed. C. D. Ross, i (London, 1964), no. 68 (writ of naifty).

[6] Landon, *The Itinerary of King Richard I*, pp. 173–5.

[7] Tout, *Chapters*, i, pp. 148–9 and notes.

[8] *Memoranda Roll 1 John*, p. lxiv: the writ issued at Westminster on 15 Oct. [1190] and attested *Teste Ricardo Londoniensi episcopo, thesaurario nostro* was undoubtedly sealed with the exchequer seal, as stated by Mr. H. G. Richardson, but it is difficult to be sure that it is an exchequer writ, since during the king's absence the exchequer seal was used for chancery business.

chancellor, but by clerks of the treasurer and chamberlains.[1] When in 1232 the justiciarship was abolished, the treasurer replaced the justiciar at the head of the exchequer. Henceforth exchequer writs were at all times drawn up under the king's name and attested by one witness only, not by two as in Henry II's reign; that witness was not, as in chancery documents, the king himself while the king was in England, or the regent while the king was abroad, but always the treasurer (or his lieutenant) or one of the barons of the exchequer (Plates **4***a*, **7***b*).[2] Some exchequer writs were already attested in this way in the 1220s.[3] Between 1232 and 1248 a new office had also been created, that of chancellor of the exchequer (*cancellarius scaccarii*), whose functions were those formerly discharged by the *clericus cancellarii*.[4] From then onwards the exchequer had a fully independent chancery, staffed by a chancellor and clerks of its own.

By the end of Edward I's reign a large number of writs, some of which were returnable (*brevia retornabilia*) and others were not (*brevia irretornabilia*), some close and others patent, were constantly issued under the exchequer seal for exchequer business; they were apparently written under the supervision of the *clericus brevium*.[5] Commissions to some particular classes of royal officers were also made out in the form of letters patent attested by the treasurer and sealed with the exchequer seal; for these letters patent the familiar corroboration-clause of letters patent under the great seal (*In cujus rei testimonium*, etc.) had been adopted. Before 1311 sheriffs and custodians of royal castles and manors were appointed in this way.[6] Exchequer writs and letters patent were regularly enrolled on the memoranda rolls of the exchequer by the remembrancers (*rememoratores scaccarii*).[7] The warranting-notes which are often found at the foot of the enrolled documents, and sometimes at the foot of the engrossments themselves, state on what authority the exchequer writs and letters patent were issued. This authority could be (*a*) a verbal order from the king relayed orally to the exchequer by the treasurer (*per ipsum regem nunciante ipso thesaurario*)[8] or a verbal order from the treasurer (or his lieutenant) given by him in person (*per ipsum thesaurarium*;[8] *per ipsum Johannem*, i.e. the treasurer's lieutenant, who attests the writ (Plate **7***b*); *per eundem thesaurarium et alios de consilio*)[9] or relayed orally through an intermediary (*per eundem thesaurarium nunciante R. de Heghham*);[10] (*b*) a written warrant from the king under the great seal (*per breve de magno sigillo inter communia de eodem anno*)[11] or under the privy seal (*per breve de privato sigillo*);[12] or simply one of the exchequer

[1] Tout, *Chapters*, i, p. 146, n. 1.

[2] Ibid. v, p. 163, n. 1: *sub sigillo secretarii nostri* should be corrected to *sub sigillo scaccarii nostri*.

[3] See, e.g., Exch., K.R., Memoranda Roll (E. 159), no. 3, m. 13: writs attested by William of Sainte-Mère-Église, bishop of London; no. 4, m. 9d: writ attested by Eustace of Fauconberg, bishop of London, [treasurer]. See also *The Memoranda Roll of the King's Remembrancer for Mich. 1230–Trin. 1231*, ed. Chalfant Robinson (Pipe Roll Soc., N.S. 11), pp. 33, 37, 51–2, 59, etc.

[4] Tout, *Chapters*, i, p. 146; Madox, *The Hist. and Antiquities of the Exchequer* (1711), p. 580.

[5] Ibid., p. 732.

[6] After the ordinances of 1311, which ordered that sheriffs should receive their commission under the great seal (and no longer under the exchequer seal), the appointments of sheriffs and custodians of castles and royal manors were enrolled on the fine rolls of the chancery. See Conway Davies, *The Baronial Opposition to Edward II*, pp. 518–19, 521–7.

[7] Madox, op. cit., pp. 714–16. See Conway Davies, 'The Memoranda Rolls of the Exchequer to 1307', *Studies presented to Sir Hilary Jenkinson*, pp. 97–154.

[8] Exch., L.T.R., Memoranda Roll (E. 368), no. 75, m. 72d.

[9] Ibid., m. 79d; Exch., K.R., Bille (E. 207), 5/16: 'per ipsum thesaurarium et alios de consilio'.

[10] Exch., L.T.R., Memoranda Roll no. 75, m. 72d.

[11] *Merton Muniments*, ed. P. S. Allen and H. W. Garrod (Oxford, 1928), plate xi (*a*).

[12] Exch., K.R., Accounts Various (E. 101), 12/6/2.

records themselves (the pipe roll: *per magnum rotulum de anno xxxij° in Wyltes*';[1] a memoranda roll: *per rotulum memorandorum de anno regni nostri tercio*;[2] or even a tally: *per unam talliam de scaccario*),[3] etc.

The earliest exchequer seal for which wax impressions are still extant is that of Henry III, a single-sided seal, representing the royal arms (the three leopards of England) on a shield (Plate **4***a*, note).[4] From Edward I's reign onwards it was double-sided like the great seal, but smaller: it had an equestrian obverse, representing the king on horseback, with a legend made up of the king's name and style; the reverse represented the royal arms on a shield, with the legend *Sigillum de scaccario domini regis*.[5] Apparently the exchequer always used green wax only, hence the title of 'chancellor of the green wax' occasionally given to the chancellor of the exchequer as early as the thirteenth century.[6]

By 1230 the privilege of issuing writs under the king's name had been extended to the justices of the royal courts. One royal writ, the 'original' writ (*breve originale*), so called because it initiated the action in the relevant court, always had to be obtained from the chancery: this writ, like all other chancery writs, was made out under the king's name and, from the 1240s, attested by the king himself. Once the original writ had been issued, numerous writs were required at various stages of the legal proceedings, but there was no need to apply to the chancery for them. Those writs, known as 'judicial' writs (*brevia de judicio* or *brevia judicialia*), were drawn up—under the king's name—by clerks of the court and attested by one of its justices (e.g. *Teste W. de Ralegh*).[7] The difference between original and judicial writs is clearly set out in the following comment made before the king's bench in 1293:

> . . . dicunt quod ipsi sunt ad communem legem et non debent predicto abbati inde respondere sine brevi regis originali ubi rex est testis. Et predictum breve per quod ipsi modo veniunt in curia est breve de judicio sub testimonio G. de Thornton', unde petunt judicium si abbati nunc per hujusmodi breve etc. inde debeant respondere.[8]

In theory the judicial writs were supposed to be sent under the justice's seal to the chancery, where—possibly after being examined by a chancery clerk—they should have received an impression of a portion of the great seal (*pes sigilli*). In practice, however, at least from the reign of Edward I, royal justices tended to regard their own seal as sufficient for the authentication of judicial writs and often omitted to forward the writs to the chancery.[9] This unsatisfactory state of affairs came to an end in 1344, when Edward III granted to each of the two courts of the king's bench and of common pleas a great seal of its own with which the judicial writs were to be sealed in future.[10]

When there is a warranting-note at the foot of a judicial writ, it is often confined to a reference to the membrane (*rotulus*) of the plea roll on which were recorded the court

[1] Exch., L.T.R., Memoranda Roll no. 75, m. 79d.
[2] Exch. Writs (E. 202), 1/3 (formerly 1/2/4).
[3] Exch. Writs 1/3 (formerly 1/9/3 (15)).
[4] See also Maxwell-Lyte, p. 41.
[5] H. Jenkinson, 'The Great Seal of England: Deputed or Departmental Seals', *Archaeologia*, lxxxv, pp. 296–8, and plate lxxxiv.
[6] Tout, *Chapters*, iii, p. 357, n. 2; v, p. 130, n. 3.
[7] *Curia Regis Rolls*, xiv, nos. 2474–5, 2477, 2480.
[8] *Select Cases in the Court of King's Bench under Edward I*, ed. G. O. Sayles (Selden Soc. 57), p. 146; see also p. lxxxix, n. 4.
[9] Ibid., pp. lxxxix–xci.
[10] B. Wilkinson, 'The Seals of the Two Benches under Edward III', *English Hist. Rev.*, xlii, pp. 397–401; *Archaeologia*, lxxxv, pp. 299–303, and plates lxxxv–lxxxvi.

proceedings which had led to the issue of the writ (e.g. *ro. Lij*: Plate **10***b*);[1] sometimes the name of the judge on whose authority the writ was issued was also given (e.g. *per J. de Mutford*: Plate **10***b*).[2]

The reduplication of the great seal and the setting up of departmental chanceries were such convenient administrative devices that they spread to other royal offices in the course of the thirteenth and fourteenth centuries. Before 1250 a separate royal chancery with another great seal was set up in Ireland, and in due course the Dublin exchequer and the Irish courts of the king's bench and of common pleas also acquired royal seals under which documents drawn up under the king's name were issued.[3] The following extracts come from two writs of *liberate*, one issued by the Irish chancery, the other by the Irish exchequer: the first is attested by the head of the Irish government at the time, the justiciar (this attestation corresponding to *Teste me ipso*—when the king was in England—or *Teste A. custode regni nostri*—when the king was abroad—in similar writs issued by the English chancery); the second is attested by one of the barons of the Dublin exchequer (instead of one of the barons of the English exchequer in exchequer writs of the same kind issued at Westminster):

(*a*) Edwardus Dei gracia rex Anglie et Francie et dominus Hibernie thesaurario et camerariis suis de scaccario Dublin', salutem. Liberate de thesauro nostro . . . Teste Waltero de Birmyngham, justiciario nostro Hibernie, apud Trym tercio die decembris, anno regni nostri Anglie vicesimo, regni vero nostri Francie septimo. (*3 Dec. 1346*)[4]

(*b*) Edwardus Dei gracia rex Anglie, dominus Hibernie et dux Aquitannie, thesaurario et camerariis ˋ suis ˊ de scaccario suo Dublin', salutem. Liberate de thesauro nostro . . . Teste W. de Moenes, barone scaccarii nostri predicti, xiiij° die augusti predicto, anno regni nostri quinto. (*14 Aug. 1311*)[5]

Other deputed chanceries were created, one for the administration of Scotland in Edward I's reign,[6] another for the administration of Calais in Edward III's reign,[7] and so on. According to *Fleta*, the keepers of all royal seals everywhere, except the keeper of the privy seal, were mere deputies of the chancellor.[8] Nevertheless they all had their separate writing-offices, staffed with their own scribes, whose professional training was not necessarily received in the central chancery.

[1] See also H. Jenkinson, *The Later Court Hands in England* (Cambridge, 1927), plate XLI. iii, vii, viii.

[2] Compare, for King John's reign, *Selden Soc.*, vol. 67, p. 381, no. 3506: a writ drawn up in the name of Geoffrey fitzPeter, justiciar, attested by Geoffrey of Buckland, and followed by the note *per magistrum Radulfum*.

[3] *Archaeologia*, lxxxv, pp. 314–23, and plates xci–xciv.

[4] Exch., K.R., Accounts Various (E. 101), 241/13.

[5] Ibid. 235/21/15. See also *Calendar of Ormond Deeds*, ed. E. Curtis, vols. i–ii (Irish MSS. Comm., Dublin, 1932 and 1934).

[6] *Archaeologia*, lxxxv, pp. 323–5, and plate xcv; H. Jenkinson, 'A Seal of Edward II for Scottish Affairs', *Antiquaries Journal*, xi, pp. 229–39.

[7] *Archaeologia*, lxxxv, pp. 308–9, and plate lxxxix, nos. 5–6; *Studies presented to Sir Hilary Jenkinson*, p. 73, n. 4.

[8] *Fleta*, ed. H. G. Richardson and G. O. Sayles (Selden Soc. 72), p. 123.

V. SCRIPTS AND SCRIBES

By the year 1200 the script of business documents written by English royal scribes (charters, letters, etc.) differed markedly from the script normally used in books. Not only was the business hand more natural, more current, more rounded, and less deliberate than the book hand, but also the two scripts contrasted in the shapes of some letters and in the execution of some particular combinations of letters. The professional scribes working in the royal departments of John's reign could not fail to be aware of these differences, if indeed they had not been trained to write both types of script. A hundred years later one of the scribes of the royal *registrum* known as 'Liber B' not only could differentiate the two scripts from one another, but also gave them a name, probably the current one in his time (*c.* 1300). This is how he described two books kept in the royal treasury:

> In cofro de D . . . Item unus liber de transcriptis cartarum Vasconie in grosso texto [*sic*]. Item alius liber de quibusdam litteris transcriptis de recognicionibus serviciorum et feodorum in partibus Vasconie regi debitorum sub manu curiali.[1]

It is clear that in this context the scribe gave the word *textus* the same meaning as his successors of the fifteenth century were to give it, the meaning of 'text hand', that is to say the book hand used in the transcription of what the contemporaries called *textus*, i.e. a gospel-book.[2] What the scribe meant by *manus curialis*, 'court hand', was the official business hand used at the time in all royal departments, a hand which had developed from the current writing practised by the royal scribes of the Norman period and which continued to evolve independently of the text hand throughout the Middle Ages.[3]

(A) *Documents sealed with the great seal and deputed seals.* We have already seen that the three categories of documents issued under the great seal, namely—in descending order of lasting value—charters, letters patent, and letters close, differed from one another in their diplomatic form and method of sealing. Charters, used for grants in perpetuity, had more solemn formulae and a more elaborate type of seal-attachment than letters patent, which were of temporary value; letters patent were themselves in some ways more solemn than the ephemeral letters close. These differences in formulae and methods of sealing were matched by corresponding differences in handwriting. Although the same type of script, the court hand, was used for charters as for letters patent and letters close, varying degrees of solemnity were achieved by greater or lesser currency, greater or lesser decoration of individual letters; the more solemn the document, the less abbreviated it was, and so on. In the latter part of Henry II's reign and under Richard I and John a more solemn effect was given to some charters by imitating some of the devices used by

[1] Exch., T.R., Misc. Books (E. 36), no. 275, fol. 22v. Although this manuscript is described in English sources of the fourteenth century as a register, it is in fact a cartulary. On the distinction between cartularies and registers, see A. Giry, *Manuel de diplomatique* (Paris, 1894), pp. 28–36.

[2] One of the books kept in the wardrobe towards the end of Edward I's reign is described in contemporary inventories as *unus liber qui vocatur textus, in uno casso de corio, super quem magnates jurare solebant* (Exch., K.R., Accounts Various, 354/28).

[3] See L. C. Hector, *The Handwriting of English Documents* (London, 1958), pp. 51–6. For the period before 1189, see Bishop, *Scriptores Regis*, Introduction.

the papal and episcopal chanceries: a looped tittle was sometimes used instead of a plain horizontal stroke as a mark of abbreviation;[1] sometimes the superscript sign for *us* was decorated with a coil-like tail;[2] when only a few words were left for the last line the line was often filled in by writing some of the words in capitals which were well spaced out and had exaggerated horizontal bars (e.g. in *N* of *NOSTRI*),[3] and by using stretched ligatures (e.g. *st* of *nostri*)[4] of the type used by the papal chancery in letters of grace. King John's charter of Plate **1***b*, although not particularly ornate, is nevertheless more decorated than the letters patent and writ reproduced on the same plate. Note in particular the *g* with its added tail in *gratia* of line 1, and the final *s* throughout.

From the reign of Henry III, the first line of charters had tall ascenders, sometimes decorated (Plate **4***b*), a feature which spread to letters patent when, with the gradual decline of charters in the fourteenth century, they tended to become the most solemn documents issued by the chancery (Plates **13***b*, **20***c*, **23***a*). Sometimes the scribes of charters and letters patent adopted some letter-forms which belonged to the text hand rather than to the court hand (Plate **8***b*).[5]

Once the exchequer, the courts of justice, and other royal offices had acquired independent secretariats staffed with scribes of their own, one might have expected the handwriting practised in each of these departments to develop in due course some characteristic features which would identify it with reasonable ease and differentiate it from the handwriting of the chancery. If distinctive features of this kind did in fact exist throughout our period, they are not at all obvious in the documents reproduced in this volume, at least until the mid fourteenth century. The exchequer writs of Plates **4***a* and **7***b* do not exhibit such marked differences with the chancery writs of the same period that one would unhesitatingly rule out their chancery origin on purely palaeographical grounds. To find a script which can be regarded as typical of the exchequer, we have to turn to the pipe rolls, documents with a much longer exchequer tradition behind them than the writs:[6] as early as Henry II's reign the pipe rolls were written by an exchequer scribe, the *scriptor thesaurarii*, whereas in the same reign the exchequer writs were still written by scribes on the chancellor's staff. Nor can we confidently say that the script of the judicial writs of Plates **3***b* and **10***b* is strikingly different from that of contemporary chancery writs. The judicial writ of Plate **21***b* has no punctuation at all, a feature characteristic of judicial writs in the late fourteenth and fifteenth centuries,[7] but care should be taken not to attach undue importance to the fact that the judicial writ of Plate **3***b*, issued in 1248, is punctuated by one solitary point, because this feature was not at all typical of judicial writs at that early date.

[1] *Facs. of Royal and Other Charters in the British Museum*, ed. G. F. Warner and H. J. Ellis (London, 1903), plates xlv and l. See Cheney, *English Bishops' Chanceries*, p. 54, n. 3.

[2] Warner and Ellis, op. cit., plate xlv (*Abbatibus*, line 1; *eius*, line 3). See also Duchy of Lancaster, Royal Charters (D.L. 10), nos. 47, 53, 54.

[3] Duchy of Lancaster, Royal Charters, no. 46.

[4] Duchy of Lancaster, Royal Charters, nos. 52, 54. In the 1160s the scribe Stephen of Fougères was already using some of these devices to fill in the last line (*Antiquaries Journal*, xii, plates xlvi–xlix; Bishop, *Scriptores Regis*, plate xxxi (*b*)).

[5] Oxford, Bodleian Lib., MS. DD Christ Church M. 86. On the use of text hand in charters, see Hector, op. cit., p. 53.

[6] See Johnson and Jenkinson, plates viii, xvi, etc.; Bishop, *Scriptores Regis*, pp. 28–9.

[7] Jenkinson, *The Later Court Hands in England*, plate xli.

(B) *Documents sealed with the privy seal and signet.* We might like to claim that by the end of Edward I's reign we can at least distinguish the script of privy-seal documents from that of great-seal documents. On further examination this confidence appears to be largely unjustified, induced perhaps by the linguistic, and palaeographically deceptive, contrast between the French of privy-seal documents and the Latin of analogous documents issued under the great seal.

It was only during the last years of Edward III's reign that the style of writing used for privy-seal and signet documents acquired some unmistakably distinctive features. But this was the result of a break-away from English writing traditions rather than the outcome of a gradual evolution. In 1372 or thereabout, for reasons which still have to be determined, the scribes of privy-seal and signet documents began to use a 'secretary' hand, apparently an angular and upright version of a writing style used in France for several generations.[1] The privy-seal writ reproduced on Plate **16***c* is an early example of the new script, but earlier ones exist.[2] The script was new, not only in its general appearance, but also in the shapes adopted for some letters, for instance *a*, *g*, *r*, and *s*. The evidence suggests that it was imported into England by English scribes who had worked in the privy-seal office of the Black Prince in Gascony. A privy-seal writ of the Black Prince, issued at Angoulême on 25 April 1370 and apparently written by John Fordham, is in the new script.[3] Fordham, secretary of the Black Prince, came back to England with his master in 1371 and, after the latter's death (8 June 1376), became keeper of the privy seal of Richard of Bordeaux, a position which he retained when Richard succeeded to the throne.[4] There is no proof, however, that between 1371 and 1376 Fordham worked for Edward III as well as for the Black Prince. Whether he or one of the English clerks who served under him in Gascony was personally responsible for introducing the new script into England must therefore remain an open question.

The new script made its appearance in documents issued under the signet as soon as it was introduced in the privy-seal office.

(C) *Individual scribes.* From the reign of Edward I onwards it is not uncommon to find the name of a clerk written in the bottom right-hand corner of some chancery documents (Plates **8***a–b*, **9***a–c*, **16***b*, **18***b*, **20***b–c*, **21***c*, **23***a*). The same practice was followed for privy-seal documents between 1360 and 1362 and after 1434,[5] and for signet documents during the reign of Richard II and from Henry V's reign onwards.[6] There is no doubt that it was the name of the clerk who assumed responsibility for the writing of the document, but it is in most cases impossible to tell whether he actually wrote the document himself or entrusted one of his assistants with the work. The identification of John Southwell, how-

[1] N. R. Ker, *Medieval Manuscripts in British Libraries*, i. *London* (Oxford, 1969), p. xii; M. B. Parkes, *English Cursive Book Hands, 1250–1500* (Oxford Palaeographical Handbooks, Oxford, 1969), p. xix.

[2] See Chancery Warrants (C. 81), 437/30138. See also ibid. 1336/35 (2 Sept. 1372, *souz le signet de nostre anel*). For the evolution of the new script from 1379 to 1476, see Jenkinson, *The Later Court Hands in England*, plate xxiii.

[3] *Facs. of Nat. MSS.* I. xxix. Compare Tessier, *Diplomatique royale française*, plate ix, facing p. 232. On 9 Aug. 1356 Branketre (above, p. 21, n. 6) wrote a document in the 'Avignon script'.

[4] Tout, *Chapters*, iii, p. 330; iv, pp. 189–90; v, pp. 379–81, etc.

[5] Ibid. v, p. 114 and note; Maxwell-Lyte, p. 34.

[6] Otway-Ruthven, *The King's Secretary and the Signet Office in the XVth Century*, pp. 26–7.

ever, as the writer of the documents reproduced on Plate **9***b* and *c*, and of Robert Fry as the writer of the documents reproduced on Plate **19** seems beyond question.

It has already been pointed out that in times of stress one particular royal department sometimes applied to another department for clerical assistance. One should therefore refrain from attributing too hastily the writing of a great-seal document to a chancery clerk or the writing of a privy-seal document to a privy-seal clerk. For example, the original engrossment of a commission issued under Edward III's great seal on 20 November 1361 (Dijon, Arch. Côte d'Or, B. 11924) is unlikely to have been written by a chancery clerk. The hand reappears in additions made in 1361–2 to a book which seems later to have formed part of the signet archives (formerly Yelverton MS. 5; now Brit. Mus., Add. MS. 48004), and a substantial number of these additions consist of transcripts of letters issued under the privy seal and signet.[1] The problem is further complicated by the fact that the great-seal commission is addressed to Thomas de Uvedale in connection with one of his missions to France, and that all the additions to Add. MS. 48004 appear to be connected with this and other missions entrusted to Uvedale himself and to the clerk Thomas de Donclent.

VI. EDITORIAL NOTE

The documents reproduced in facsimile (except the much-reduced ones of Plates **25–7**) have been transcribed in full, as faithfully as possible, including capitals and punctuation marks. Abbreviations, contractions, and suspensions have been expanded in italics, except for names of persons and places, which have been left unexpanded. Interlineations are indicated by the signs ` ′ and a change of line by a double oblique stroke, preceded by a superscript figure giving the number of the finished line. In documents cited, but not reproduced, and in those reproduced in reduced size on Plates **25–7**, the use of the letters *i* and *j*, *u* and *v*, as well as the punctuation and capitals have been modernized, and abbreviations, contractions, and suspensions have been expanded silently.

[1] Fols. 19v (2nd entry), 20r (2nd entry)–21r, 26v (2nd entry), 42v (entries 2–4), 47r (2nd entry)–48v, 51r–53v, 54v–57r, 58r–66r, 71r–72v. On fol. 75v there are various additions concerning the private affairs of John Lincoln of Grimesby; one of them reads: 'Fait a remembrer que le xxvj jour de juin lan du roi Richard xxme Johan Edmond', orfevre, me aporta primerement le seal qil me avoit fait de mes armes ove la circumscripcion S. Johannis Lincoln' de Grymesby clerici.' At the time, Lincoln was Richard II's secretary (Tout, *Chapters*, v, pp. 223–5). Extracts from Add. MS. 48004 are printed in P. Chaplais, *Some Documents regarding the Fulfilment and Interpretation of the Treaty of Brétigny, 1361–1369* (Royal Hist. Soc., Camden Miscellany XIX: Camden Third Series, lxxx, part i), pp. 9–45. (On p. 22, line 3, read *dont aucuns ont failiz devers li leur fois* (instead of . . . *leur fors*).)

1

a. Duchy of Lancaster, Royal Charters (D.L. 10), no. 67

WRIT PATENT of King John to Hugh de Neville, dated at Woodstock, 4 June [1207]. Parchment. Sealed with the great seal in natural wax (fragment only), appended on a tongue (*in simplici cauda*).

Enrolled on Patent Roll 9 John (C. 66/7), m. 6: *Rot. Litt. Pat.* I. i. 73a. See also *Rot. de Oblatis et Finibus*, pp. 372, 443–4.

. I . d*ei* g*ra*t*ia* Rex Angl*ie* . D*omi*n*us* Hib*er*n*ie* . Dux Norm*annie* *et* Aquit*annie* . Come*s* And*egauie* . Dil*ecto* *et* fideli suo Hug*oni* de Neuill' [1]// Sal*utem* . Mandam*us* uob*is* q*uo*d cu*m* vice*comes* Eborac' uob*is* mandau*er*it q*uo*d securitate*m* cep*er*it de Roaldo fil*io* Alan*i* de [2]// fine que*m* nob*is*cum fecit p*ro* habendo castro de Richem*und*' unde dissaisit*us* est p*er* p*re*ceptu*m* n*ost*ru*m* p*ro* tredecimo suo ;' [3]// *tunc* eide*m* Roaldo saisina*m* h*abe*re faciatis de castro illo . Et in huius rei testim*onium* ;' has litt*er*as n*ost*ras patentes [4]// in*de* uob*is* mittim*us* . T*este* . me ip*s*o ap*ud* Wudest' . iiij . die Iun*ii* . [5]//

b. Duchy of Lancaster, Royal Charters (D.L. 10), no. 63

CHARTER of King John for Roesia of Dover, dated at Lincoln, 10 January, regnal year 14 (1213). Parchment. Sealed with the great seal in green wax, appended on dark-brown silk cords (*in filis sericis*); turn-up (*plica*).

Enrolled on Charter Roll 14 John (C. 53/10), m. 2: *Rot. Chart.* I. i. 190a.

. I . d*ei* g*ra*t*ia* Rex Angl*ie* . D*omi*n*us* Hib*er*nie . Dux Normann*ie* . *et* Aquit*annie* . Comes Andeg*auie* . Archiep*iscop*is . Ep*iscop*is . Abb*atibus* . Comit*ibus* . Baron*ibus* . [1]// Iustic*iis* . vicecom*itibus* . Preposit*is et* Omnib*us* Ball*iu*is *et* fidelib*us* suis Sal*utem*. Sciatis nos reddidisse Roesie de Douera totam [2]// parte*m* suam tam i*n* t*er*ris *et* redditib*us* q*uam* feodis *et* seruiciis . *et* om*n*ib*us* aliis que eam hereditarie co*n*tingu*n*t . de heredi[3]//tate Ricardi de Lucy aui sui . Tenenda*m* sibi *et* heredib*us* suis . p*er* seruicia q*ue* tenementa illa debent . Et in hui*us* rei [4]// testimoniu*m* hanc carta*m* n*ost*ram ei inde fecim*us* . Teste . W . Comit*e* Sarr' f*ra*tre n*ost*ro . Will*elm*o Briwerr' . Rob*er*to de Ros . Warin*o* fil*io* [5]// Geroldi . Will*elm*o de Albiniac' . Sim*one* de Kyma . Thom*a* de Muleton' . Hug*one* de Berneual' . Brian*o* de Insul' . Data p*er* ma[6]//nu*m* mag*ist*ri Ric*ardi* de Marisc' Archid*iaconi* Norhumb' *et* Richemund' . ap*ud* Lincoln' . x . die Ian*uarii* . anno Regni n*ost*ri . x°iiij° . [7]//

c. Ancient Correspondence (S.C. 1), vol. 47, no. 1

WRIT CLOSE of King John to W[illiam] Brewer, dated at Dover, 18 September [1215]. Parchment. A tear in the bottom left-hand corner represents a lost tongue. Filing hole.

The letters patent to Henry fitzCount mentioned in lines 3 and 9 are enrolled on Patent Roll 17 John (C. 66/14), m. 15: *Rot. Litt. Pat.* I. i. 155b, under date: Dover, 18 September, regnal year 17 (1215).

. I . d*ei* g*ra*t*ia* Rex Angl*ie* D*omi*n*us* Hyb*er*n*ie* Dux Norm*annie* . Aquit*annie et* Come*s* And*egauie* Dil*ecto et* fideli suo . W . Brigwerr' . Sal*utem* . Sci[1]//atis q*uo*d uolumus q*uo*d fidelis n*oste*r Rad*ulfus* Gernun Nepos n*oste*r custodiat castrum n*ost*ru*m* de Porcestr' . *et* mandamus [2]// p*er* litter*as* n*ost*ras patentes Henr*ico* fil*io* Comitis q*uo*d castrum illud eide*m* Rad*ulfo* s*ine* dil*at*ione liberet . Et ideo uob*is* manda[3]//mus q*uo*d ips*um* Rad*ulfum* ad castrum illud recipiend*um* mittatis . tradentes ei quotq*uo*t pot*er*itis milites *et* s*er*uientes bene [4]// p*ar*atos ad custodia*m* eiu*s*de*m* castri salua munitione castri n*ost*ri Winton'. Et o*mne*m warnistura*m* de victualibu*s* [5]// q*uam* pot*er*itis sep*ar*atim ex p*ar*te n*ost*ra ad denarios n*ost*ros faciatis h*abe*re eid*em* . p*ro*uidentes sicut nos diligitis ;' [6]// q*uo*d idem castrum sicut ad presens meli*us* possit . gente . armis *et* uictualib*us* muniatur . Faciatis etia*m* h*abe*re eid*em* [7]// Rad*ulfo* . *et* sociis suis vadia sua sic*ut* illa h*abe*re debent *et* uos expedire uid*er*itis . Et festinetis ip*sum* Rad*ulfum* q*uantu*m pot*er*itis [8]// q*uonia*m fidelis n*oste*r . Ioh*annes* Mariscallus ' cui*us* mora p*er*iculosa nob*is* ess*e*t ' expectat apud Porcestr' aduentum suu*m* cum litt*er*is n*ost*ris patentib*us* dir*ect*is d*ict*o [9]// Henrico de d*ict*o castro[a] lib*er*ando ip*s*i Rad*ulfo* . T*este* . me ip*s*o apud Douer' . xviij . die Sept*embris* . [10]//

[a] *Followed by a false start, partly erased.*

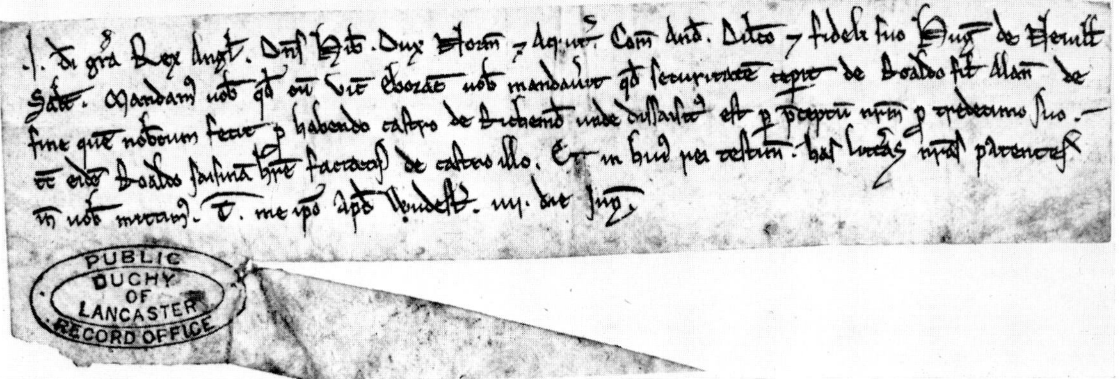

J. di gra Rex Angl. Dns Hib. Dux Norm. & Aquit. Com And. Dilco & fideli suo Hug de Nevill salt. Mandam vob qd cu vic Eboraci vob mandaver qd securitate cepit de Roaldo fil Alan de fine que nobcum fecit p habendo castro de Richemund unde dissaisit est p preceptu nrm p credentum suo. Et eide Roaldo saisina hre faciatis de castro illo. Et in huis rei testim has litt nras patentes vob mittim. T. me ipo apd [illegible] xiiij die Jun.

J. di gra Rex Angl. Dns Hibnie. Dux Normann. & Aquit. Comes Andeg. Archiepis. Epis. Abb. Comit. Baron. Justic. Vicecom. Prepositis & Omnib; Ballivis & fidelib; suis Salt. Sciatis nos reddidisse Roesie de Doura totam partem suam eam i tris & redditib; & feodis & servitiis & omnib; aliis que eam hereditarie contingunt de heredi tate Ricardi de Luci avi sui. Tenenda sibi & heredib; suis p servitia q tenementa illa debent. Et in huius rei testimonium hanc cartam nram ei inde fecim. Teste W. Comite Sar fre nro. Willo Briwer. Rob de Ros. Warin fil Geroldi. Willo de Albiniaco. Hug de Kyma. Thom de Muleton. Hug de Berneval. Brian de Insula. Data p manu magri Ric de Marisc Archid Northumb & Richemund. apd Lincoln. x. die Jan. anno Regni nri xiiij.

J. di gra Rex Angl. Dns Hibn. Dux Norm. Aquit. & Com And. Dilco & fideli suo [illegible]

[illegible]

... T. me ipo apud Dover. xiiij die Sept.

H. dei gratia Rex Angl. Dominus Hib. Dux Norm. et Aquit. et Com. And. Ballivis Widonis de la Pouconer
in Haffeld salutem. Precipimus vobis quod si dicto (?) plegium fecerit de recto tenendo Hugoni de Neuill de una carrucata
terre cum pertinentiis in Haffeld quam clamat tenere de predicto Widone per liberum tenementum ... per annum et diem sine (?)
... eidem Wido ... Et nisi feceritis vicecomes Essex faciat. Ne amplius inde clamorem audiamus pro defectu recti.
T. H. de Burgo justic. nostro apud Westm. xiii die Decembr. 3

¶ Prima propositio ¶ In primis proponatur quod omnes terre transmarine reddantur Regi Angl. preter Normanniam. et de
Normannia permittatur ad opus Regis unus episcopatus uel duo. ad transitum habendum
ad terras predictas. scilicet episcopatus Abricensis. et Constantiensis.

¶ Secunda propositio sic. ¶ Quod eadem forma seruetur de terris predictis et de Normannia. excluso predicto transitu.

¶ Tercia propositio. sic. ¶ Si forme predicte possint emendari per maritagium inter Reges et sorores suas. emendentur
sicut melius uiderint expedire. Vel per unum maritagium tantum. Vel per duo maritagia.

¶ Quarta propositio. ¶ Si nulla istarum formarum acceptetur. Remaneat Normannia imperium (?). et terre subscripte
dentur maritagium cum sorore Regis Angl. scilicet Andegauia citra Ligerim. et tota Ceno-
mannia. ita quod si habeat heredem. remaneat heredi. et si non habeat heredem. reuertatur
ad Regem Angl. et si non potest sic fieri. suppleatur per nuncios.

¶ ¶ Si aliqua istarum formarum possit emendari per denarios. emendetur per denarios.

H. dei gratia Rex Angl. Dominus Hibern. Dux Norm. et Aquit. Com. And. vic. Surr. salutem. Pone ad
petitionem petentis coram justic. nostris apud Westm. a die Sancti Trinitatis in tres septimanas Loquelam
que est in comitatu tuo per breue nostrum inter Andream ... et Rollandum de Hosted (?) de uirgata terre
cum pertinentiis in ... [*ab eodem Rollando*] ... et summone per bonos summonitores predictum R. quod tunc sit ibi
ibi eidem Andree inde responsurus. Et habeas ibi summonitores et hoc breue. T. me ipso apud Lamhid (?)
.iii. die Maii. Anno Regni nostri. xiiii. 8

H. dei gratia Rex Angl. Dominus Hibn. Dux Norm. et Aquit. Com. And. Omnibus ad quos presentes Littere
peruenerint. salutem. Sciatis quod concessimus dilecto et fideli nostro Joh. de Lasci Constabulario Cestr.
Maneria nostra de Colingeham et de Berdeseya cum pertinentiis. Unde Abbas de Kyrkestall
nobis reddidit per annum Quater uiginti et decem Libras de firma. tenenda. donec ei de
derimus racionabile escambium ad valentiam eorundem maneriorum in escaetis uel Wardis.
In cuius rei testimonium has litteras nostras patentes fieri fecimus. T. me ipso apud Nyrebel (?). xxviii.
die Jul. Anno regni nostri xiiii.

a. King's Bench Writs (K.B. 136), 1/2/3

WRIT OF RIGHT (? PATENT) of Henry III, attested by H[ubert] de Burgh, justiciar, and dated at Winchester, 13 December [1219]. Parchment. Filing slit.

. H . dei gra*tia* Rex angl*ie* . Do*minus* Hib*ernie* . Dux Norm*annie* . Aquit*annie* . *et* Comes Andeg*auie* Balli*uis* Widonis de La ponconer' 1// In Haffeld . Salu*tem* . Precipim*us* uob*is* q*uod* s*ine* dil*ati*one plen*um* rectu*m* teneatis Hug*oni* de Neuill' de vna carucata 2// t*er*re cu*m* p*er*tin*entiis* In Haffeld q*u*am clamat ten*er*e de p*re*d*ic*to Widone p*er* Lib*er*um s*er*uiciu*m* . xx . s' . p*er* ann*um* p*ro* om*n*i s*er*uicio . 3// Q*u*am Ide*m* Wido ei deforc*iat* . Et n*is*i fec*er*itis vic*ecomes* Essex' fac*iat* . Ne ampli*us* Inde clam*orem* audiam*us* p*ro* defec*t*u recti . 4// T*este* . H . de Burgo Iustic*iario* n*ost*ro ap*ud* Wint' . xiij . die . Decem*bris* . 5//

b. Chancery, Diplomatic Documents (C. 47), 27/1/5

INSTRUCTIONS to Henry III's ambassadors to France [? 1229, January–April]. Parchment, indented chirograph.

Printed in *Diplomatic Documents*, ed. Pierre Chaplais, i, no. 215.

¶ Prima p*ro*positio ¶ In p*r*imis p*ro*ponat*ur* q*uo*d om*n*es t*er*re t*r*ansmarine reddant*ur* Regi Angl*ie* . preter Norman*niam* . *et* de 1// Normannia retineatur ad opus Regis unus Ep*iscop*atus uel duo . ad transitum habend*um* 2// ad t*er*ras pred*ic*t*as* . scil*icet* . Ep*iscop*atus Abbricens*is* . *et* Constantiens*is* . 3//

¶ *secun*da p*ro*positio sic . ¶ Q*uo*d eadem[a] forma seruet*ur* de t*er*ris pred*ic*t*is* *et* de Norman*n*ia ∴ excluso[b] pred*ic*to transitu . 4//

¶ t*er*cia p*ro*positio . sic . ¶ Si forme pred*ic*te possint emendari p*er* Maritagiu*m* int*er* Reges *et* sorores suas ∴ emendant*ur*[c] 5// sicut melius uiderint expedire . vel p*er* unu*m* Maritagiu*m* tantu*m* . v*el* p*er* duo Maritagia . 6//

¶ q*u*arta p*ro*positio . ¶ Si nulla istar*um* formar*um* acceptetur ∴ Remaneat Normannia i*m*p*er*petuu*m* . *et* terre subsc*r*ipte 7// dentur maritagiu*m* cum sorore Reg*is* Angl*ie* . scil*icet* . Andegauia cit*r*a Ligerim . *et* tota Ceno8//-mannia . Ita q*uo*d si hab*e*at heredem ∴ remaneat heredi . *et* si no*n* hab*e*at heredem ∴ reuertat*ur* 9// ad Regem Angl*ie* . *et* si no*n* potest sic fieri ∴ suppleat*ur* p*er* nu*n*cios . 10//

¶ It*em* ¶ Si aliq*u*a istar*um* formar*um* pot*er*it emendari p*er* denarios ∴ emendet*ur* p*er* denarios . 11//

C I R O G R A P H V M

[a] Q*uo*d eadem *over an erasure.* [b] excluso *over an erasure.* [c] *Sic in MS.*

c. King's Bench Writs (K.B. 136), 1/2/8

'ORIGINAL' WRIT 'PONE' of Henry III, dated at Lambeth, 3 April, regnal year 14 (1230). Undoubtedly sent close. Parchment. Small step in the bottom left-hand corner. Filing hole.

Printed in *Curia Regis Rolls*, xiv, no. 2472.

. H . d*e*i gr*ati*a Rex Angl*ie* . Do*min*us Hib*er*nie . Dux Norm*annie* *et* Aquit*annie* Come*s* And*egauie* . vic*ecomiti* Surr' sal*utem* . Pone ad 1// petit*i*onem petentis coram iustic*iariis* n*ost*ris apud Westm' a die S*anc*te T*r*initatis in tres septimanas Loquela*m* 2// q*ue* est in Comitatu tuo p*er* br*eue* n*ost*rum int*er* Andr*eam* Bukerel *et* Rotlandum[d] de Acsted' de auerijs 3// ip*s*ius Andr*ee* captis *et*ˋ ab eodem Rollando ˊ iniuste detentis ut d*icit*ur . Et sum*m*one p*er* bonos sum*monitores* p*re*[dict]*um* Rotlaundum[d] q*uo*d 4// tunc sit ibi eidem Andr*ee* inde responsurus . Et h*abe*as ibi sum*monitores* *et* hoc br*eue* . T*este* me ip*s*o apud Lamhid' 5// . iij . die Ap*r*ilis anno Regni n*ost*ri . xiiij° . 6//

[d] e *erased after* Rot.

d. Duchy of Lancaster, Royal Charters (D.L. 10), no. 72

LETTERS PATENT of Henry III for John de Lacy, constable of Chester. Dated at Mirambeau, 27 July, regnal year 14 (1230). Parchment. Sealed with the great seal in natural wax, appended on a tongue.

Enrolled on Patent Roll 14 Henry III (C. 66/40), m. 4: *Patent Rolls, 1225–1232*, p. 388.

. H . d*e*i gr*ati*a Rex Angl*ie* . Do*min*us Hyb*er*nie . Dux Norm*annie* *et* Aquit*annie* . Come*s* And*egauie* . Om*n*ib*us* ad quos presentes Litt*er*e 1// p*er*uen*er*int . Sal*utem* . Sciatis q*uo*d concessimus Dil*ect*o *et* fideli n*ost*ro Ioh*anni* de Lascy Constabulario Cestr' 2// Maneria n*ost*ra de Colingeham *et* de Berdeseya cu*m* p*er*tinentiis . Vnde Abbas de Kyrkestall' 3// nobis reddidit p*er* annu*m* Quater uiginti *et* decem Libras de firma ∴ tenenda . donec ei de4//derim*us* *ra*tionabile escambium ad valentiam eoru*m*dem Manerior*um* in escaetis vel wardis . 5// In cui*us* rei testimoniu*m* has litt*er*as n*ost*ras patentes fieri fecim*us* . T*este* . Me ip*s*o apud Myrebel . xxvij . 6// die Iul*ii* . Anno regni n*ost*ri xiiij° . 7//

3

a. Patent Roll 22 Henry III (C. 66/48), m. 1 (schedule)

WARDROBE ENROLMENT of great-seal letters, 22 Henry III (1238). Parchment. Stitched to the Patent Roll.
Calendared in *C.P.R. 1232–1247*, p. 232.

Anno Regni Regis Henrici filii Regis Iohannis[a] facta fuerunt hec breuia apud Wudestok' in Guarderoba domini Regis Clericis de Cancella[1]//ria domini Regis ea ignorantibus eo quod fuerunt contra Cancellarium tunc postulatum Winton' . et postea redditus fuit rotulus[b] . [2]//

Anno Regni Regis Henrici filii Regis Iohannis . xxij . Circiter festum Natiuitatis beate Marie Missus est magister . S . de Steiland' ad [3]// Curiam Romanam cum literis procuracionis in hec uerba . Summo pontifici Rex etc' . Nouerit sanctitas vestra nos Dilectum [4]// et specialem clericum nostrum Magistrum . S . de Steiland clericum vestrum in negocio eleccionis seu postulacionis nuper de [5]// venerabili patre . R . dei gracia Cycestr' Episcopo in Ecclesia Winton' a Priore et quibusdam monachis facte procura[6]//torem nostrum constituisse . Ratum et gratum habituri quicquid idem magister . S . coram vobis in Curia Romana [7]// uel coram auditoribus a vobis deputatis :' impetrando . contradicendo . Agendo . defendendo . excipiendo . opponendo . [8]// tam contra personas eligencium seu postulancium quam contra personam Electi seu postulati . Tam contra eciam formam ipsius [9]// eleccionis seu postulacionis in dicto negocio nomine nostro duxerit faciendum . Damus eciam eidem magistro . S . potestatem [10]// specialem Iurandi in animam nostram si necesse fuerit . pro eo eciam Iudicatum solui promittimus . Hoc idem omnibus presen[11]//tes literas inspecturis significamus . In cuius rei etc'. Teste me ipso apud Wodestok' . iiij° . die septembris . anno . regni . nostri . xxij . [12]//

Item alie litere procuracionis Date eidem . [13]//

Summo Pon[ti]fici[c] Rex etc' . Nouerit paternitas vestra nos dilectum et specialem clericum nostrum magistrum . S . de Steyland' [14]// capellanum vestrum in omnibus agendis nostris in Curia Romana et in omnibus causis nostris motis et mouendis et spe[15]//cialiter in causis que uertuntur inter nos ex vna parte et priorem et Conuentum de Norwico Item priorem et Conuen[16]//tum Dunholm' ex altera :' procuratorem nostrum constituisse . Ratum et gratum habituri quicquid idem . S . Agendo . defenden[17]//do . Impetrando . contradicendo . in omnibus predictis nomine nostro duxerit faciendum . pro eo eciam si necesse fuerit Iudicatum solui [18]// promittimus . Idem eciam omnibus presentes literas inspecturis significamus . Et in huius rei testimonium eidem fieri fecimus [19]// literas nostras patentes . Teste me ipso apud Wodestok' . iiij . die septembris . anno . eodem . [20]//

Data sunt eciam eidem tria paria literarum de mutuo accipiendo singulas continentes[d] mutuum trecentarum marcarum[21]// in hec uerba . H . dei gracia Rex anglie etc' . Omnibus mercatoribus ad quos presentes litere peruenerint Salutem . Sciatis quod [22]// quicumque vestrum dederint Dilecto clerico nostro Magistro Simoni de Steiland' quem mittimus in nuncium nostrum ad Curiam [23]// Romanam pro negociis nostris mutuum trecentarum marcarum :' nos dictum mutuum soluemus has literas nostras [24]// deferenti simul cum literis predicti magistri Simonis mutuum illud testificantibus . locis et terminis ibidem ex[25]//pressis secundum formam in contractu contentam . In cujus rei testimonium has literas nostras fieri fecimus patentes . teste [26]// me ipso apud Wodestok' quarto die septembris . anno eodem . [*Crossed out for cancellation*] quia littere reddite fuerunt mutuo non facto[e] . [27]//

Data sunt eciam eidem tria paria literarum de mutuo accipiendo singulas continentes[d] mutuum ducentarum marcarum [28]// et vnum par literarum continentes[d] mutuum Centum marcarum sub forma prescrip[t]a[f] . [*Crossed out for cancellation*] quia similiter reddite fuerunt littere[e] [29]//

Idem magister . S .[g] vnum par literarum ad Bonaouillin'. Bonincontry . franketum . Bencheuennum . Bernardum Rustic' [30]// Ciues et mercatores florencie de mutuo mille librarum sub forma prescripta . [31]//

Idem habet Breue de liberate ad Thesaurarium et Camerarios de predictis mille libris liberandis predictis mercatoribus in Qu[i]ndena[h] [32]// sancti Michaelis anno . xxij . [33]//

[a] *Regnal year omitted.*
[b] *This heading was added later, in a different hand and ink, probably by a chancery scribe.*
[c] Ponfici *MS.*
[d] *Sic in MS.*
[e] quia . . . *written in a different hand and ink, probably by a chancery clerk.*
[f] prescripa *MS.*
[g] habet *omitted here.*
[h] Qundena *MS.*

b. Eyre, Writ Files (J.I. 4), 1/1/113

'JUDICIAL' WRIT OF ATTACHMENT BY GAGE AND PLEDGES, attested by R[oger] de Thurkelby, [justice in eyre], and dated at Gloucester, 1 June, regnal year 32 (1248). Sent close. Parchment. Filing hole.

Note the form of *F* in the name *Fuilyet*, line 3. There is one single mark of punctuation, a full point at the end of the writ.

H dei gracia Rex Anglie Dominus Hybernie Dux Normannie Aquitannie et Comes Andegauie vicecomiti Wilt' salutem Pone per vadium et saluos plegios Hugonem [1]// de Walton' quod sit Coram Iusticiariis nostris Itinerantibus apud Rading' die Iouis proxima post festum sancte Trinitatis ad respondendum Reginaldo [2]// Fuilyet et Mabilie vxori eius de placito quod ipse simul cum Ascelina Matre eius teneat eis conuencionem inter eos factam de quatuor [3]// acris Prati cum pertinenciis in Reuenham pro vt in Curia nostra Coram Iusticiariis nostris vltimo Itinerantibus apud Norh't' inter eos conuenit[i] [4]// Et habeas ibi nomina plegiorum et hoc Breue Teste R de Thurkelby apud Glouc' primo die Iunii anno regni nostri xxxij° . [5]//[j]

[i] *Followed by an erasure.*
[j] *The writ is endorsed:* Istud breue returnatum fuit libertati de Merleberg' In quam vicecomes non habet Ingressum set Ricardus clericus. Bailliuus eiusdem libertatis significauit vicecomiti quod Hugo de Waulton' nichil habet In comitatu vnde possit distringi nisi tantum bladum In campo

4

a. Exchequer Writs (E. 202), 1/2/13

EXCHEQUER WRIT OF 'VENIRE FACIAS', attested by H[enry] de Tracy, [baron of the exchequer], and dated at Westminster, 30 June, regnal year 44 (1260). Sent close. Parchment. Filing hole. A step in the bottom left-hand corner represents a lost tongue. The writ was originally sealed with the exchequer seal, probably the same as that of which two fragmentary impressions still survive among the Westminster Abbey Muniments (W.A.M. 6888 and 9003, both attested by J[ohn of Caux], abbot of Peterborough, treasurer, and dated 25 April 1262): the seal, apparently single-sided, represents the three leopards of England on a shield; the legend is missing.[a]

H . dei gr*aci*a Rex Angl*ie* D*omi*n*us* Hyb*er*n*ie* *et* Dux Aquit*annie*[b] vice*comiti* Norff' sal*ute*m . Quia Galfridus Pecche [1]// fecit nos securos p*er* Nichol*au*m de Wynton' . *et* Will*elmu*m de Stowe . de clam*ore* suo p*rosequendo* . t*ib*i p*re*cipim*us* q*uo*d venire fac*ias* [2]// cora*m* Baron*ibus* de scacc*ar*io n*ost*ro apud Westm'. In c*ra*stino s*anc*ti Mich*aelis* . Ric*ardu*m de Vall' . f*ra*trem *et* heredem . Rob*er*ti de Vall' [3]// *et* Ioha[n]nam Matre*m* p*re*d*ic*ti Rob*er*ti . qui tenent quanda*m* p*ar*te*m* t*er*rar*um* que fueru*n*t p*re*d*ic*ti Rob*er*ti vt d*icitu*r . [4]// ad respond*endum* p*re*d*ic*to Galfr*ido* de . I . marc*a* . q*u*am ab eo recepit p*ro* h*abe*ndo bre*ui* te*m*p*o*re quo Ide*m* Rob*er*tus fuit [5]// Ball*iuu*s in Hundr*edo* de Heyngeford' . *et* de qua . debuit ip*su*m acquietasse ad id*e*m scacc*ariu*m n*ostru*m *et* no*n* [6]// acquietauit vt dicit sicut r*aci*onabil*ite*r monstrare pot*er*it q*u*od inde respond*ere* debeant . Et h*abe*as [7]// ibi tunc hoc bre*u*e . T*este* . H . de Tracy apud Westm' . xxx . die Iun*ii* . a*nn*o . r*e*g*ni* . n*ost*r*i* . xliiij . [8]//[c]

[a] *I am indebted to Mr. N. H. MacMichael, Keeper of the Muniments of Westminster Abbey, for bringing the existence of these two fragments to my notice. At that date, the exchequer seal appears to have been similar to the privy seal at least in design, although it must have been larger. While Henry III was in France in 1242–3, exchequer writs were sealed* quodam privato sigillo nostro cum quodam scuto de armis nostris cum circumscriptione sigilli de scaccario (*Maxwell-Lyte, p. 41*).

[b] *The last three words are written over, and followed by, an erasure (apparently of* Dux Norm*annie* Aquit*annie et* Come*s* Andegau*ie*)*. See P. Chaplais, 'The Making of the Treaty of Paris (1259) and the Royal Style', English Hist. Rev. lxvii (1952), p. 251, n. 3.*

[c] *The writ is endorsed in two contemporary hands:* [1] Precept*um* s*it* sene*scallo* s*an*cti Eadm*undi*. [2] Precept*um* fuit sene*scallo* lib*er*t*atis* s*an*cti Eadm*undi* vbi h*abe*nt returna bre*ui*um *et* execuc*ione*m eorumdem *et* nich*il* inde respondit .

b. Duchy of Lancaster, Royal Charters (D.L. 10), no. 96

CHARTER of Henry III for his son Edmund, dated at Westminster, 6 December, regnal year 50 (1265). Parchment. Sealed with the great seal in natural wax, appended on a tag (*in duplici cauda*); turn-up.

Enrolled on Charter Roll 50 Henry III (C. 53/55), m. 1B (damaged): *C.Ch.R.* vi (1427–1516; Appendix), p. 287.

Henricus dei gr*aci*a Rex Angl*ie* Dominus Hib*er*n*ie* *et* Dux Aquitann*ie* Archiep*iscop*is Ep*iscop*is Abbatib*us* Priorib*us* Comitib*us* Baronib*us* Iusticiarijs [1]// vicecomitib*us* prepo*s*itis Ministris *et* omnib*us* Balliuis *et* fidelib*us* suis sal*ute*m . Sciatis nos dedisse concessisse *et* hac carta n*ost*ra confirmasse Edmu*n*[2]//do filio n*ost*ro dil*ec*to Castra de Keremerdyn *et* Kardigan cum om*n*ib*us* p*er*tinencijs suis que dudum dedimus k*arissi*mo filio Edwardo p*r*imogenito n*ost*ro [3]// *et* que idem Edwardus in manus n*ost*ras reddidit ad opus prefati Edmundi . Dedimus eciam *et* concessimus eidem Edmundo Manerium de [4]// Dunamenel cum p*er*tinencijs quod fuit escaeta n*ost*ra de terris Normannor*um* . habenda *et* tenenda de nobis *et* heredib*us* n*ost*ris eidem Edmundo *et* [5]// heredib*us* suis imp*er*petuu*m* . faciendo seruicia inde debita *et* consueta . Quare volumus *et* firmit*er* precipimus pro nobis *et* heredib*us* n*ost*ris [6]// q*uo*d pred*ic*tus Edmundus *et* heredes sui habeant *et* teneant pred*ic*ta castra *et* manerium cum omnib*us* p*er*tinencijs suis de nobis *et* heredi[7]//bus n*ost*ris imp*er*petuu*m* faciendo s*er*uicia inde debita *et* consueta sicut pred*ictu*m est . Hijs testib*us* venerabili p*at*re . W . Bathon*iensi* *et* Wellens*i* Ep*iscop*o [8]// Hugone le Bygod . Ph*ilipp*o Basset . Rog*er*o de Clyfford . Rog*er*o de Leyburn' . Rob*er*to Waleraund . Rob*er*to Aguyllon' . Will*elm*o de Aette . Will*elm*o Belet . Bar[9]//th*olome*o le Bygod . Gilb*er*to filio Hugonis *et* alijs . Dat*a* p*er* manu*m* n*ost*ram apud Westm' sexto die Decembr*is* anno regni n*ost*ri Quinq*u*agesi*m*o . [10]//

5

a. Duchy of Lancaster, Royal Charters (D.L. 10), no. 138

LETTERS PATENT OF SAFE-CONDUCT of Edward I for his brother Edmund, dated at Westminster, 29 April, regnal year 5 (1277). Parchment. Formerly sealed with the great seal, appended on a tongue. The great seal is lost, but the tongue remains.

Enrolled on Patent Roll 5 Edward I (C. 66/96), m. 20: *C.P.R. 1272–1281*, p. 199.

Edward*us* dei gr*aci*a Rex Angl*ie* . D*omi*nus Hib*er*n*ie* *et* Dux Aquit*annie* Om*n*ibus Balliuis *et* fidelib*us* suis ad quos p*re*sentes [1]// littere p*er*uen*er*int sal*ute*m . Sciatis q*uo*d suscepimus in saluu*m* *et* secur*um* conductum no*str*um carissimu*m* f*ra*trem *et* [2]// fidelem no*str*um Edmundu*m* . *et* homi*n*es suos in eundo p*ro* negociis no*str*is ad partes Marchie . ibidem [3]// morando *et* inde redeundo . Et ideo vob*is* mandam*us* q*uo*d eide*m* Edmundo uel homi*n*ib*us* suis in [4]// eundo ad partes illas pro negociis p*re*dict*is* . ibide*m*[a] morando . *et* inde redeundo no*n* inferatis [5]// aut inferri p*er*mittatis dampnu*m* impedimentu*m* aut grauamen / In cui*us* rei testimon*ium* / has [6]// l*itt*eras no*s*tras fieri fecim*us* patentes . duraturas usq*ue* ad festu*m* *sancti* Mich*ae*lis p*ro*xi*m*o futur*um* . T*este* [7]// me ip*s*o apud Westm' . xxix . die April*is* . a*nn*o . r*egni* . *nostri* . Quinto . [8]//

[a] *The last four words appear to be written over an erasure.*

b. Chancery Warrants (C. 81), 1/34

PRIVY-SEAL WRIT CLOSE of Edward I, ordering R[obert Burnell], bishop of Bath and Wells, [chancellor], to issue letters of presentation under the great seal. Dated at Lyndhurst, 20 January, regnal year 8 (1280). Parchment. Step in the bottom left-hand corner. Three vertical folds. Filing hole.

The great-seal letters are enrolled on Patent Roll 8 Edward I (C. 66/99), m. 24: *C.P.R. 1272–1281*, p. 360 (Lyndhurst, 20 January [1280]).

Edward*us* dei gr*aci*a Rex Angl*ie* . D*omi*nus Hybern*ie* . *et* Dux Aquitann*ie* . vene*r*abili p*at*ri in c*rist*o . *domi*no . R . eadem gr*aci*a [1]// Baton*iensi* *et* Wellen*si* ep*iscop*o :˙ salu*te*m . Cum Laur*encius* de Windlesor' quonda*m* canonic*us* lib*er*e cap*e*lle no*st*re de Hasting' [2]// p*re*benda*m* de Buleware-heth' q*ua*m h*ab*uit in manib*us* no*st*ris lib*ere* . plene *et* absolute tenore l*itter*a*rum* suar*um* [3]// resig*n*au*er*it . qua*m* quide*m* p*re*benda*m* Rob*er*to cle*r*ico no*st*ro d*ict*o Eylward caritatis *in*tuitu co*n*tulim*us* *et* co*n*cessim*us* :˙ [4]// uob*is* mandam*us* q*ua*tin*us* l*itt*eras no*s*tras p*re*sentat*io*nis s*u*p*er* eade*m* p*re*benda h*ab*enda in for*m*a debita *et* co*n*sueta *sibi* fieri [5]// faciatis . T*este* . me ip*s*o ap*u*d Lindhurst s*u*b sigillo no*st*ro priuato . xx° . die Ianuar*ii* . Ann*o* regni no*st*ri . viij° . [6]//

c. Chancery Warrants (C. 81), 1/40A

PRIVY-SEAL WRIT CLOSE of Edward I, ordering R[obert Burnell], bishop of Bath and Wells, chancellor, to issue letters of protection under the great seal. Dated at Devizes, 16 April, regnal year 10 (1282). Parchment. Step in the bottom left-hand corner. Filing slit. Traces of the privy seal in red wax in the centre of the dorse.

Edwardus dei gr*aci*a Rex Angl*ie* D*omi*n*us* Hib*er*n*ie* *et* Dux Aquit*annie* venerabili in c*rist*o patri / R . eadem gr*aci*a / Bathon*iensi* *et* Wellen*si* Ep*iscop*o Cancel[1]//lario suo sal*ute*m Quia ‵ dil*ec*tus *et* fidel*is* nost*er* . ′ Thom*as* de Multon' iunior in no*st*ro obsequio ad p*ar*tes Wallie p*ro*fecturus est / vob*is* mandam*us* / q*uo*d om*n*ia [2]// debita no*st*ri no*mi*n*e* / seu cuiuscu*m*q*ue* alterius / p*er* no*st*ros vicecomites / Lincoln' / Norff' ./ et Suff' ab eo exacta / poni faciatis [3]// in respectum . Et districc*io*nem / ei ea occasione f*ac*tam / relaxari / donec iidem vicecom*ites* / aliud a nob*is* sup*er* hoc habuerint [4]// in mandatis / . P*ro*tecc*io*nem no*st*ram similit*er* ei *et* om*n*ib*us* aliis / quos in no*st*ro s*er*uic*io* / p*ro*fecturos sciu*er*itis ad p*ar*tes supra-d*ic*tas / h*ab*ere faci*atis* . [5]// Dat' sub priuato sigillo no*st*ro apud Devis' . xvj . die April*is* . anno . r*egni* . no*stri* . Decimo .   p*er* Regem . [6]//

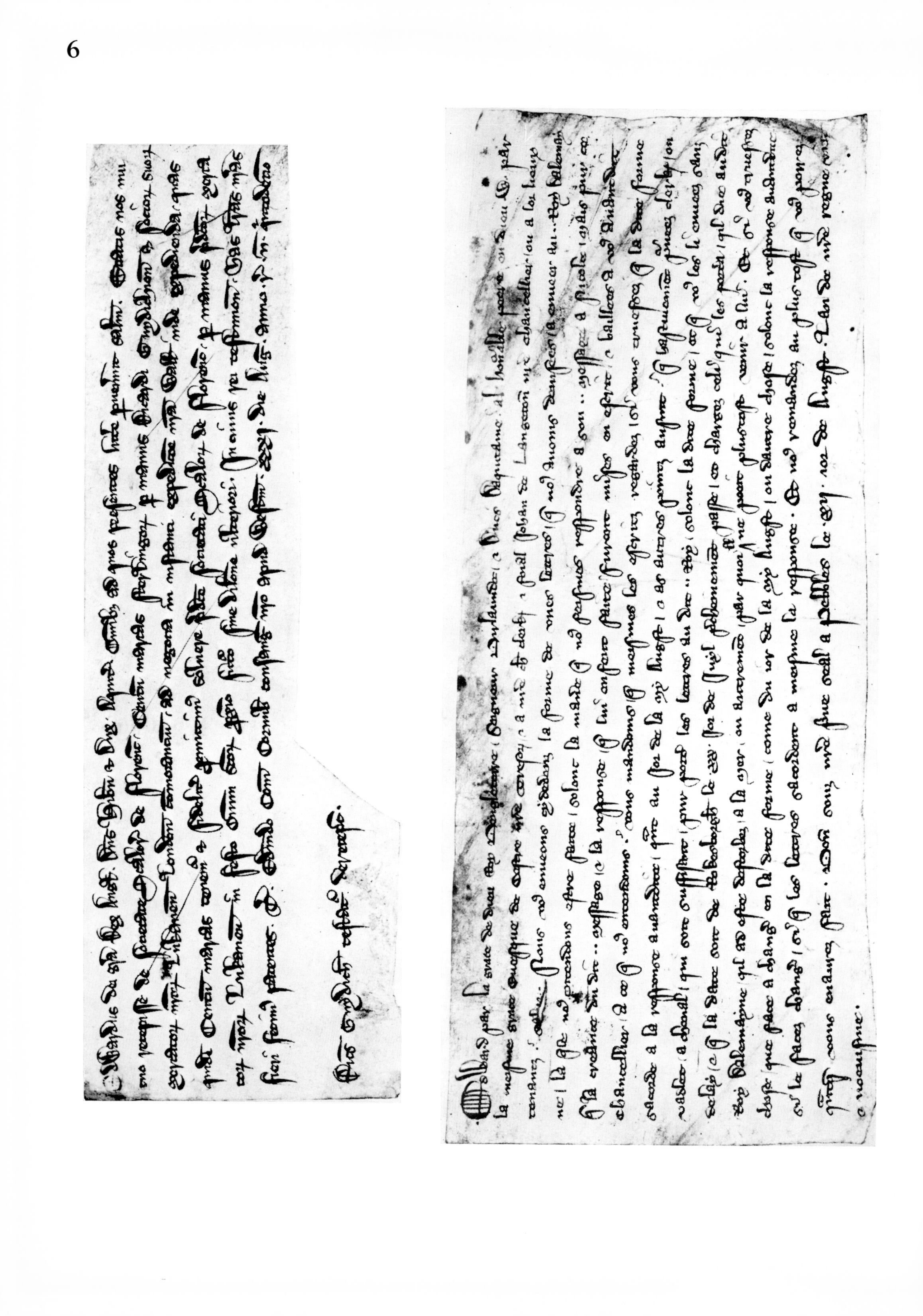

6

6

a. Chancery Files (C. 202), Cancelled Letters Patent, H. 3/31

CANCELLED LETTERS PATENT (RECEIPT) of Edward I, attested by Edmund, earl of Cornwall, [regent], during the king's absence in France. Dated at Westminster, 31 August, regnal year 15 (1287). Parchment. Formerly sealed with the seal of absence on a tongue, but the tongue has been torn off. Step in the bottom left-hand corner. Four oblique cuts for cancellation. Filing slit.

Enrolled on Welsh Roll 15 Edward I (C. 77/7), m. 9: *Cal. of Various Chancery Rolls*, p. 309.

Edwardus dei gr*aci*a Rex Angl*ie* . D*omi*n*us* Hib*ernie et* Dux Aquit*annie* . Om*nibus* ad quos presentes litt*er*e p*er*uen*er*int sal*ute*m . Sciatis nos mu[1]//tuo recepisse de societate Scalor*um* de Florenc*ia* / Centu*m* marcas sterlingor*um* p*er* manus Ricardi Guydichion*is et* socior*um* suor*um* [2]// Mercator*um* n*ostr*or*um* Lukanen*sium* London' co*m*moranciu*m* / ad negocia in instanti expedic*i*o*ne* n*ost*ra Wall*ie* inde expedienda / quas [3]// quide*m* Centu*m* marcas tene*mur et* fideli*ter* p*ro*mittim*us* soluere p*re*d*ic*te societati Scalor*um* de Florenc*ia* / p*er* manus p*re*d*ic*tor*um* Merca[4]//tor*um* n*ost*ror*um* Lukanen*sium* in festo O*mn*ium s*anc*tor*um* p*ro*x*im*o fut*ur*o sine dil*ac*io*ne* ulteriori . In cuius rei testimon*ium* / has l*itte*ras n*ost*ras [5]// fieri fecim*us* patentes . T*este* . Edm*und*o Com*ite* Cornub*ie* consang*uineo* n*ost*ro apud Westm' . xxxj . die Aug*usti* . anno . r*egni* . n*ostr*i . quintodeci*m*o [6]//

Ric*ardus* Guydichi*onis* testat*ur* de recepc*i*o*ne*[a]. [7]//

[a] *This sentence was written later, in a different hand.*

b. Chancery Warrants (C. 81), 23/2331

PRIVY-SEAL WRIT CLOSE of Edward I, ordering W[alter Langton], treasurer, John Langton, chancellor, or their lieutenants, to examine the enclosed draft (*forme*) of a letter to the king of the Romans and correct it, if necessary. Dated at Peebles, 12 August, regnal year 29 (1301). Parchment. Tear in the bottom left-hand corner. Filing slit. Two horizontal and two vertical folds. Traces of the privy seal in red wax in the centre of the dorse.

For the enclosure, see Plate 7*a*.

Calendared in *Cal. of Chancery Warrants*, i (1244–1326), p. 132.

. Edward par la grace de dieu Roy Dengleterre / Seigneur Dirlaunde / *et* Ducs Daquitaine ꝰ al hon*ur*able peere en dieu . W . par [1]// la meisme grace Euesque de Cestre n*ost*re Tresor*ier* / *et* a n*ost*re ch*ier* clerk' *et* foial Iohan de Langeton' n*ost*re Chancellier / ou a lor lieux [2]// tenantz ꝰ saluz . Nous vo*us* enueons cydedenz la forme de vnes lettres / q*ue* no*us* auoms deuisees / a enueer au . . Roy Dalemay[3]//ne / la q*ue*le no*us* entendons estre faite / solonc la man*er*e q*ue* no*us* feismes respondre a son . . Message a Nicole / Mais pur ce [4]// q*ue* la creance du dit . . Message / *et* la response / q*ue* lui en feut faite / furent mises en escrit / *et* baillees a vo*us* auantdit [5]// Chancellier / a ce q*ue* no*us* entendoms ꝰ vous mandoms / q*ue* meismes les escritz regardez / si vous truefsez q*ue* la dite forme [6]// sacorde a la response auantdite / q*u*ant au Ior de la My Augst / *et* as autres pointz ausint ꝰ q*ue* hastiueme*n*t p*ur*ueez clerk' / ou [7]// vadlet / a cheual / qui soit suffisant / pur port*er* les lettres au dit . . Roy / solonc la dite forme / et q*ue* vo*us* les li enueez sanz [8]// delay / *et* q*ue* la date soit de Rokesborgh' le . xx . Ior de Iuyl p*re*cheineme*n*t passe / et chargez celi / qui les port*er*a / qil die au dit [9]// Roy Dalemayne / qil ad este destorbez / a la Mer / ou autreme*n*t / par quoi ‵ il ′ ne poeit plus tost venir a lui . Et si vo*us* truefsez [10]// chose / que face a chang*er* en la dite forme / come du ior de la My Augst / ou dautre chose / solonc la response auantdite [11]// si le facez chang*er* / si q*ue* les lettres sacordent a meisme la response . Et no*us* remandez au plus tost q*ue* vo*us* porrez [12]// q*ua*ntq*ue* vous en aurez fait . Don' souz n*ost*re p*ri*ue seal a Pebbles le . xij . ior de Augst . Lan de n*ost*re regne vint [13]// *et* noeuisme . [14]//

7

a. Ancient Correspondence (S.C. 1), vol. 12, no. 28

DRAFT OF GREAT-SEAL LETTERS CLOSE, prepared in the wardrobe (enclosure to **6***b*, above). Back-dated at Roxburgh, 20 July, regnal year 29 (1301). Parchment. Filing slit.

R*oi* :' au Roi Dalem*ayne* :' saluz . Sire il nous souient bien / coment no*us* vous feismes piecea sauoir par nos lettres . *et* par mestre Iohan Burcard v*ostre* 1// notaire *et* Message / qui vous enuoiastes[a] a nous en Englet*erre* / q*ue* no*us* vous feriens response par nos p*ro*pres Messages / entour ceste my augst / 2// sur les busoignes / pur quoi vous enuoiastes a nous le dit Message . Et pur ce sire / q*ue* no*us* sumes a meintenant en n*ost*re guerre descoce / p*ur* la quele / et 3// p*ur* autres busoignes que no*us* touchent / no*us* auoms tant a faire de nos gentz / q*ue* ' no*us* ' ne porriens vncore enuoier v*er*s vous si suffisantz messages / come 4// no*us* voudriens :' vous prioms sire come n*ost*re chier amy / q*ue* vous no*us* en vueillez tenir pur excusez q*u*ant a ores . Et sachez sire / q*ue* au plustost q*ue* no*us* 5// porrons bonement / no*us* enuoierons nos messages vers vous / tielx come il afferra de enuoier p*ur* tielx busoignes / et qui aueront plen*er* poer 6// *et* mandement / de faire sur ce q*u*antquil verront / q*ue* a faire se face / pur honeur *et* pur p*ro*fit de vous *et* de nous ./ V*ost*re volunte sire / *et* v*ost*re 7// estat / le quel nous desirons touz iours estre bon / nous vueillez remander par vos lettres *et* par le porteur de cestes . Don' *etc*' a Roukes8//bourgh' . le xx . iour de Iuyl . Lan de n*ost*re regne vint *et* noeuisme . 9//

[a] *Followed by* nadgueres *partly erased and crossed out.*

b. Exchequer, K.R., Accounts Various (E. 101), 12/32/6

EXCHEQUER WRIT of Edward I, sent patent, attested by J[ohn] de Droxford, lieutenant of the treasurer, and dated at York, 29 November, regnal year 30 (1301). Parchment. Sealed with the exchequer seal (small fragment remaining) in green wax, appended on a narrow tongue.

Enrolled on K.R. Memoranda Roll 29–30 Edward I (E. 159/75), m. 74 (Brevia irretornabilia, Mich. 29 Edward I).

Edwardus dei g*ra*c*ia* Rex Angl*ie* D*omi*n*us* Hib*erni*e *et* Dux Aquit*annie* / dilecto *et* fideli suo Will*el*mo Russel Custodi sue Insule Vecte sal*utem* . Manda1//mus vob*is* firmit*er* iniungentes q*uo*d q*u*antumcu*m*q*ue* h*ab*eatis ad presens in custodia v*est*ra ' de bladis terr*arum* n*ost*rar*um* Insule p*re*d*ic*te / videlicet ' de ordeo / Auena / Fabis *et* pis*is* / excepto dumtaxat 2// quod inde n*ecessar*io noue*r*itis fore retinend*um* tam p*ro* semine / q*uam* aliis misis n*ecessar*ijs / hoc instanti anno / spectantib*us* ad terras p*re*d*ic*tas :' sine 3// dilac*i*one in Nauib*us* secure poni / *et* vsq*ue* Berewycum sup*er* Twedam t*ra*nsmicti / *et* ibidem Custodi stauri n*ost*ri lib*er*ari / faciatis . Recipientes 4// ab eod*em* lict*er*as suas patentes / de num*er*o q*u*art*er*ior*um* cuiuscumq*ue* gen*er*is bl*ador*um p*re*d*ic*tor*um* / plenar*iam* facientes menc*i*o*n*em . Et de custib*us* quos 5// apposueritis / tam in frectagio Nauium / q*uam* aliis misis n*ecessar*io / circa blada predicta apponendis / vt predictum est[b] 6// Necnon de eisdem bladis :' vobis in compoto v*est*ro ad scacc*ariu*m n*ost*r*u*m / debitam allocac*i*o*n*em h*ab*ere faciem*us* . T*este* . I . de Dro7//knesford' tenente locum Thes*aurar*ii n*ost*ri apud Ebor' . xxix . die Nouembr*is* anno . *regni* . *nostri* . xxx . p*er* ipsum Ioh*ann*em. 8//

[b] *Followed by an erasure.*

c. Ancient Correspondence (S.C. 1), vol. 12, no. 176

DRAFT PRIVY-SEAL WRIT (WARRANT FOR ISSUES) of Edward I, addressed to the treasurer and chamberlains of the exchequer and dated at St. Radegunds, 29 September [1302]. Parchment. Filing hole.

For other drafts coming from the same file (September 1302), see Pierre Chaplais, 'Privy Seal Drafts, Rolls and Registers (Edward I–Edward II)', *English Hist. Rev.* lxxiii (1958), p. 272, n. 2.

R*oy* au Tresor*ier* / *et* as Chamb*er*leins de n*ost*re Eschekier :' *saluz* . Pur ce q*e* mons' Richard Suiward demoert a Loghmaban *et* aillors celes p*ar*ties 1// gardein des pais ' de Gaweye *et* du val Danaund'[c] . ' tantq*e* no*us* eoms autrement ordene / *et* deust auoir receu deniers des executors mons' Iohan de seint 2// Iohan pur sa sustenance illueq*es* / dont il nad ' gueres[d] ' receu a ce q*e* nous auoms entendu :' vous m*a*nd*oms* q*e* a meisme celi Richard facez 3// auoir . xx . li*ures* dap*re*st sur ses gages ' taunt q*e* a la touz seinz p*re*chein auenir'[e] . ' issint q*e* les dites p*ar*ties ne soient desgarniz ne en p*er*il p*ar*[f] defaute ' de sa sustenaunce[g] ' en nule man*ere* . 4// Seinte Radegunde. xxix . iour de Septembre . 5//

[c] de . . . Danaund' *interlined, in a corrector's hand, above* depar nous *crossed out.*

[d] gueres *interlined, in the same corrector's hand, above* rien *crossed out.*

[e] taunt . . . auenir' *interlined, in the same corrector's hand.*

[f] *Followed by* vostre *crossed out.*

[g] de sa sustenaunce *interlined, in the same corrector's hand.*

8

8

a. Exchequer, K.R., Brevia Baronibus (E. 208), 1

GREAT-SEAL WRIT of Edward I to the treasurer and barons of the exchequer, dated at Westminster, 21 April, regnal year 33 (1305). Sent close. Parchment. Step in the bottom left-hand corner.

The petition from the hospitallers which is mentioned in the warranting note '*per* petic*ion*em de consilio' has survived in Ancient Petitions (S.C. 8), 100/4959. The petition has several endorsements, one of which reads 'Cumbr' Cora*m* Consilio', and another (in a different hand) 'h*ab*eant bre*ue* de Canc*ellaria* Thes*aurario et* Baron*ibus* de sc*accario* . *secun*d*um* forma*m* pet*icionis* / *et* q*uo*d inspecta inq*uisicione* / fac*iant* 'quod' fu*er*it faciend*um*.' The name *Tymparon*' is that of the chancery clerk responsible for the writing of the writ; his name is also found in the bottom right-hand corner of a pardon dated at Dunfermline, 10 November, regnal year 31 (Chancery Files (C. 202), Cancelled Letters Patent, H. 5/42).

The writ is enrolled on K.R. Memoranda Roll 34–35 Edward I (E. 159/80), m. 19 (Brevia directa baronibus, Trin. 35 Edward I).

Edwardus dei gr*ac*ia Rex Angl*ie* D*omi*n*us* Hib*er*n*ie et* Dux Aquit*annie* / Thes*aurario et* Baronib*us* suis de Scacc*ar*io .' sal*ute*m . Quia Magister *et* fratres hospitalis s*an*cti Nich*ola*i extra [1]// Karliolum / asserunt se quietos esse / de quat*er* viginti libris *et* septem denariis / qui p*er* sum*m*onic*ion*em eiusdem Scacc*ar*ij ab eis ad opus *nos-trum* exigunt*ur* p*ro* arrera[2]//giis cuiusdam firme n*ost*re / in suburbio Karlioli / de tempore d*omi*ni . H . quondam Regis Angl*ie* patris n*ost*ri / eidem patri n*ost*ro debitis vt dicit*ur* / p*er* quandam [3]// inquisic*ion*em / inde coram Thoma de Normanuill' / *et* Ranulpho de Dacre / anno regni n*ost*ri terciodecimo / p*er* bre*ue* n*ost*r*u*m apud Karliolu*m* captam / *et* [4]// que nu*n*c in eodem Scacc*ar*io residet / vt accepim*us* .' Nos eisdem Mag*ist*ro *et* fratrib*us* celeris iusticie complementum fieri volentes in hac parte .' [5]// vobis mandamus / q*uo*d inspecta inquisic*ion*e illa / si p*er* eandem vobis constare possit / q*uo*d ijdem Magister / *et* f*ra*tres de p*re*dic*t*is quater viginti libris [6]// *et* septem denariis / quieti esse debeant //*f* tu*n*c ips*o*s inde ad idem Scacc*ar*ium exon*er*ari / *et* quietos imp*er*petuu*m* esse faciatis . T*este* . me ip*s*o apud [7]// Westm' . xxj . die Aprilis / anno . *regni* . *nostri* . Tricesimo t*er*cio . p*er* petic*ion*em de consilio. Tymparon' . [8]//

b. Exchequer, T.R., Ancient Deeds, Series AA (E. 41), no. 460

CHARTER of Edward II, granting the earldom of Cornwall to Peter Gaveston. Dated at Dumfries, 6 August, regnal year 1 (1307). Parchment (26·8″ × 17·7″). Sealed with the great seal in green wax, appended on green and orange silk cords; turn-up. Decorated with ink drawings. Only the lower right-hand section is reproduced here.

The script is unlike that of the other contemporary documents sealed with the great seal. The scribe, whose name is given in the note 'T de Newehagh' scrips*it*', is Thomas de Newhay, not a chancery scribe, but a well-known clerk of Edward II's wardrobe, who in that capacity wrote royal letters sealed with the privy seal, not with the great seal (see Tout, *Chapters*, ii, p. 288, n. 3; v, p. 112; see also Brit. Mus., Cotton MS. Nero C. viii, fol. 59[v]). Thomas de Newhay also witnessed a charter of Peter Gaveston to Edward II, dated at London, 19 May 1308 (*C.C.R. 1307–1313*, p. 65). Note the text form of *r* with a foot-serif.

Enrolled on Charter Roll 1 Edward II (C. 53/94), m. 9: *C.Ch.R.* iii, p. 108: Rymer, *Foedera* (Rec. Comm.), II. i. 2.

. . . [ha]buit / *et* tenuit die obitus sui de p*er*quisito suo / *et* antecessor*um* suor*um* / tam de donis / *et* concessionib*us* p*ro*genitor*um* n*ost*ror*um* quon[1]//[dam] . . . nobis / *et* heredib*us* n*ost*ris s*er*uicium feodor*um* trium militum / pro omni s*er*uicio ad nos / *et* heredes n*ost*ros inde p*er*tinente Et eciam [2]// . . . [Ab]baciar*um* / Prioratuum / Hospitalium / Capellaniar*um* / s*er*uiciis libere tenenciu*m* / villenagiis / villanis / *et* eor*um* catallis *et* sequelis / simul [3]// . . . de hereditate n*ost*ra / et que post mortem eiu*s*dem Margarete ad nos / vel heredes n*ost*ros reu*er*ti deberent .' post deces[4]//[sum] . . . solidate redditus / quas Ph*ilipp*us de Kancia ad vitam suam / et decem marcate redditus / quas Henricus de Cicestr' [5]// . . . [Henr]ici ad nos / *et* heredes n*ost*ros similit*er* reuerti deberent .' post decessum *pre-dictorum* / Will*elm*i / Ph*ilipp*i / *et* Henrici remaneant eide*m* [6]// . . . [supra]dic*t*is quib*us*cumq*ue* p*er* s*er*uicium supradic*tu*m . Volumus insup*er et* firmit*er* p*re*cipimus p*ro* nobis *et* heredib*us* n*ost*ris / q*uo*d p*re*dictus [7]// . . . [qui]b*us*cumq*ue* p*re*nomin*a*tis omnes libertates / *et* liberas consuetudines / quas p*re*fatus Edmundus die obit*us* sui habuit *et* quib*us* [8]// . . . Comite Surr' / Humfrido de Bohun Comite Hereford' *et* Essex' *et* Constabulario Angl*ie* / Edmundo [9]// . . . [Aug]usti . Anno regni n*ost*ri Primo . . T de Newehagh' . scrips*it* . [10]//

9

a. Oxford University Archives, S.E.P. Y 6

GREAT-SEAL WRIT of Edward I to the mayor and bailiffs of Queen Margaret in Oxford, dated at Westminster, 16 March, regnal year 33 (1305). Presumably sent close. Parchment. Step in the bottom left-hand corner. Filing hole.

The name *Brom*, which is found in the bottom right-hand corner, is that of the scribe of the writ, Adam de Brome, later to become first provost of Oriel College, Oxford. A document of Edward II's reign informs us that in the last year of the previous reign (1307), during the chancellorship of Ralph Baldock, bishop of London, Adam de Brome as clerk of the chancery wrote letters of protection at the command of the chancellor (Selden Soc., vol. 57, p. cxxxii).

Printed in *Mediaeval Archives of the Univ. of Oxford*, ed. H. E. Salter, i (Oxford Hist. Soc. lxx), p. 82, no. 43.

Edwardus dei gr*aci*a Rex Angl*ie* D*omi*n*us* Hib*erni*e *et* Dux Aquit*annie* :ʾ Maiori *et* Ball*iu*is Margarete Regine Angl*ie* Consortis sue de Oxon' sal*utem* . Quia volumus q*uo*d Can[1]//cellarius Mag*ist*ri *et* scolares vniu*er*sitatis Oxon' vtant*ur* *et* gaudeant om*n*ib*us* lib*er*tatib*us* / priuilegiis / *et* inmunitatib*us* eis p*er* cartas p*ro*genitor*um* n*ost*ror*um* quondam Regum [2]// Angl*ie* concessis / quib*us* ip*s*i hucusq*ue* vsi su*n*t *et* gauisi :ʾ vobis p*ro*hibemus / ne Cancellariu*m* / Mag*ist*ros / seu scolares p*re*d*ic*tos contra lib*er*tates / priuilegia / aut inmuni[3]//tates p*re*d*ic*ta / seu eciam contra consuetudines hactenus vsitatas in villa p*re*d*ic*ta / vexetis / vel in aliquo vexari p*re*sumatis / ip*s*is / Cancellario / Mag*ist*ris / *et* scolarib*us* [4]// p*re*d*ic*ta lib*er*tates / priuilegia *et* inmunitates illesa conseruantes / *et* ab aliis quantu*m* in vobis est ˋ illesa ˊ conseruari facientes . T*este* me ip*s*o apud Westm' . xvj^o^ . [5]// die Marcij . anno *regni* . n*ost*ri . Tricesimo tercio . . Brom .

b. Duchy of Lancaster, Royal Charters (D.L. 10), no. 135

GREAT-SEAL WRIT OF 'CERTIORARI' of Edward II, dated at Westminster, 6 May, regnal year 2 (1309). Undoubtedly sent close. Parchment. Very small step in the bottom left-hand corner. Filing hole.

The name *Suwell'*, which is found in the bottom right-hand corner, is that of the scribe of the writ, probably John de Southwell, who in a petition addressed to Edward II in 1314 (Ancient Petitions (S.C. 8), 233/11632) styled himself *Johan de Suthewell' son clerk' de sa chauncellerie*, adding that he had served in the king's chancery from the time of Edward I's accession, 'making and writing the writs of the crown which concern the king's peace and dignity in his realm' ('desicome il ad servi son piere jadis roi Dengleterre qi Dieux assoille del temps qil estait roi coronez jusqes a sa mort e puis la mort son piere a lui come a son seignur en fesaunt e en escrivaunt les brefs de sa corone qe touchent sa pees e sa dignite en son roialme'). This passage suggests that Southwell was a clerk of the crown, not a chancery clerk of the higher rank, but one of those described as *clerici de secunda forma* in the chancery ordinance of 12 Richard II (B. Wilkinson, *The Chancery under Edward III*, p. 218).

The writ was issued without a royal warrant, at the direct command of the chancellor, as the dorsal warranting note '*per* Canc*ellarium*' shows.

Southwell also wrote the commission of gaol delivery reproduced below, *c*. For evidence that the clerks of the crown wrote such commissions, see Selden Soc., vol. 82, p. 148. When he wrote *b* and *c* Southwell was an old man: his handwriting, typical of the 1270s rather than of the first decade of the fourteenth century, contrasts sharply with that of the young Adam de Brome in *a*; see for example the form of *S* in *Suwell'*, *b* and *c*.

Edwardus dei gr*aci*a Rex Angl*ie* D*omi*n*us* Hib*erni*e *et* Dux Aquit*annie* dil*ect*o *et* fideli suo Hugoni de Neyuile sal*utem* . Quia quib*us*dam c*er*tis de causis [1]// c*er*ciorari volum*us* sup*er* indictame*n*tis feloniar*um* de quib*us* Ioh*an*-*nes* Rauel capt*us* *et* detent*us* in p*ri*sona n*ost*ra de Colecestr' coram vob*is* [2]// *et* sociis v*est*ris ad pac[e]m n*ost*ram in Com*itatu* Essex' co*n*seruandam assignatis indictatus est vt dicit*ur* :ʾ vob*is* mandam*us* q*uo*d indicta[3]//menta feloniar*um* p*re*d*ic*tar*um* nob*is* sub sigillo v*est*ro distincte *et* ap*er*te sine dil*aci*one mittatis *et* hoc br*eu*e T*este* . me ip*s*o apud Westm' . [4]// .vj^o^ . die Maij . anno . *regni* . n*ost*ri . sec*un*do . Suwell' [5]//

c. Duchy of Lancaster, Royal Charters (D.L. 10), no. 143

LETTERS PATENT (COMMISSION OF GAOL DELIVERY) of Edward II, dated at St. Albans, 1 April, regnal year 7 (1314). Parchment. Sealed with the great seal in natural wax, appended on a tongue: the seal, of which only the upper half is on the tongue, seems to be intact and should probably be regarded as an example of the use of the 'half-seal' (*pes sigilli*). See Maxwell-Lyte, pp. 306–9, 349.

The commission was written by John de Southwell, clerk of the crown in chancery, without a royal warrant, at the command of one of the higher chancery-clerks (a *preceptor*), as the dorsal note 'R*obertus* de Bard*elby* *precepit*' shows (see Wilkinson, *The Chancery under Edward III*, p. 77).

Note the use of two dots (one slightly higher than the other) as a punctuation mark (line 4 before *et ideo*; line 5 before *Facturi*).

Enrolled on Patent Roll 7 Edward II, Part II (C. 66/141), m. 15d. Non-enrolment of a commission of gaol delivery on the chancery rolls was an argument against its authenticity (Selden Soc., vol. 82, p. 148).

Edwardus dei gr*aci*a Rex Angl*ie* D*omi*n*us* Hib*erni*e *et* Dux Aquit*annie* dil*ect*is *et* fidelib*us* suis Hugoni de Neyuill' . Will*elm*o de Goldington' *et* Humfrido [1]// de Waledenne sal*utem* . Sciatis q*uo*d co*n*stituim*us* vos Iustic*iarios* n*ost*ros ad gaolam n*ost*ram de Releye tam de prisonib*us* qui cora*m* [2]// Custodib*us* pacis n*ost*re in Com*itatu* Essex' de feloniis aliquib*us* indictati sunt / q*uam* de aliis in ip*s*a gaola existentibus deli[3]//berandam . . Et ideo vob*is* mandam*us* q*uo*d ad c*er*tum diem que*m* ad hoc p*ro*uideritis co*n*ueniatis apud Releye ad p*re*d*ic*tam [4]// gaolam in forma p*re*d*ic*ta deliberandam . . F*ac*turi inde quod ad Iustic*iarios* p*er*tinet sec*un*du*m* lege*m* *et* consuetudine*m* regni n*ost*ri [5]//. Saluis nob*is* am*er*ciame*n*tis *et* aliis ad nos inde spectantib*us* . Mandauim*us* eni*m* vicecomiti n*ost*ro Essex' q*uo*d ad c*er*tum die*m* quem [6]// ei scire fac*ietis* / om*n*es p*ri*sones eiusdem gaole *et* eor*um* attach*iatores* coram vob*is* ibidem venire fac*iat* . In cuius rei testimoniu*m* [7]// has litt*er*as n*ost*ras fieri fecim*us* patentes T*este* . me ip*s*o apud s*anctu*m Albanu*m* . p*ri*mo die Aprilis . anno . r*egni* . n*ost*ri . septimo [8]// Suwell' [9]//

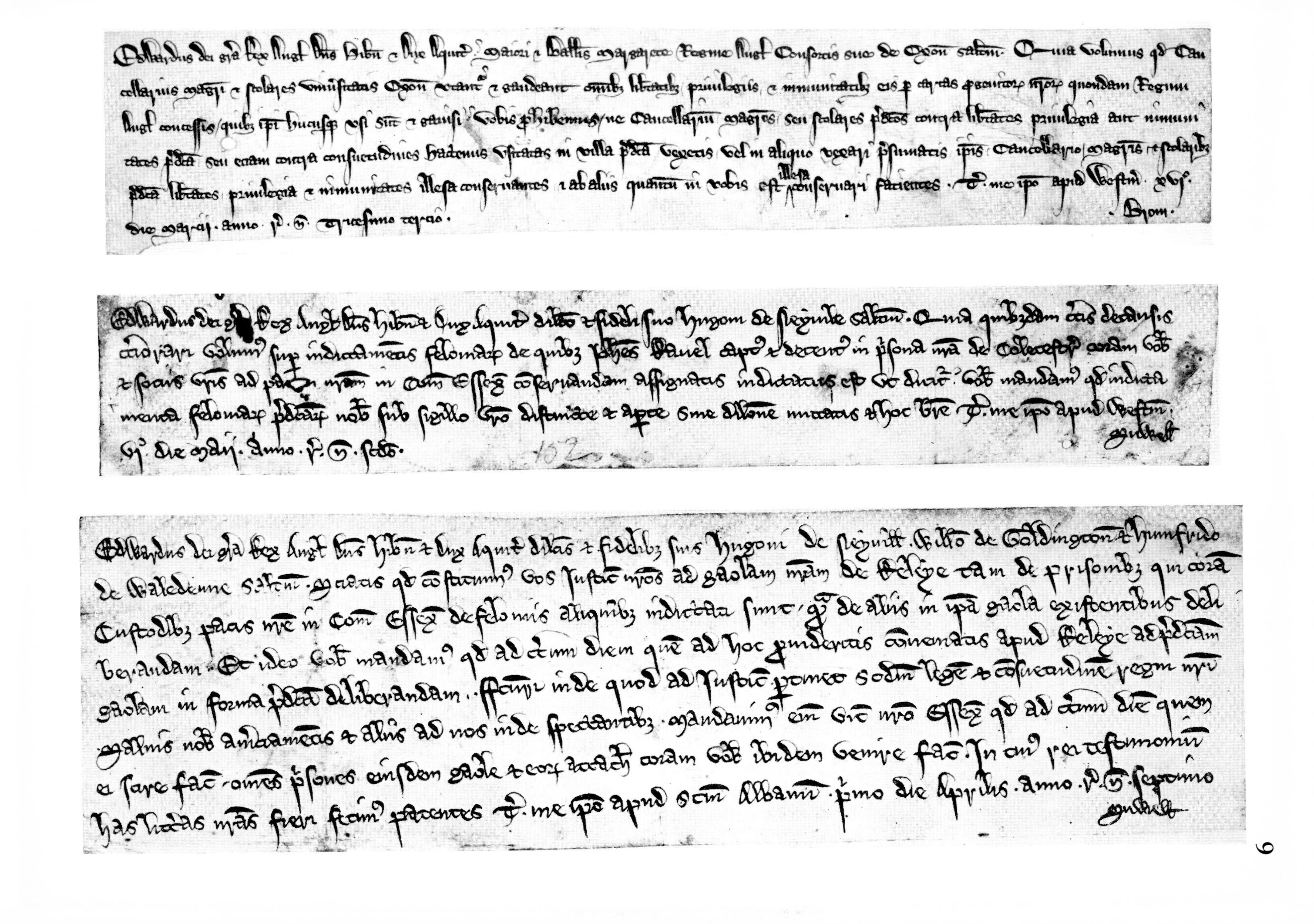

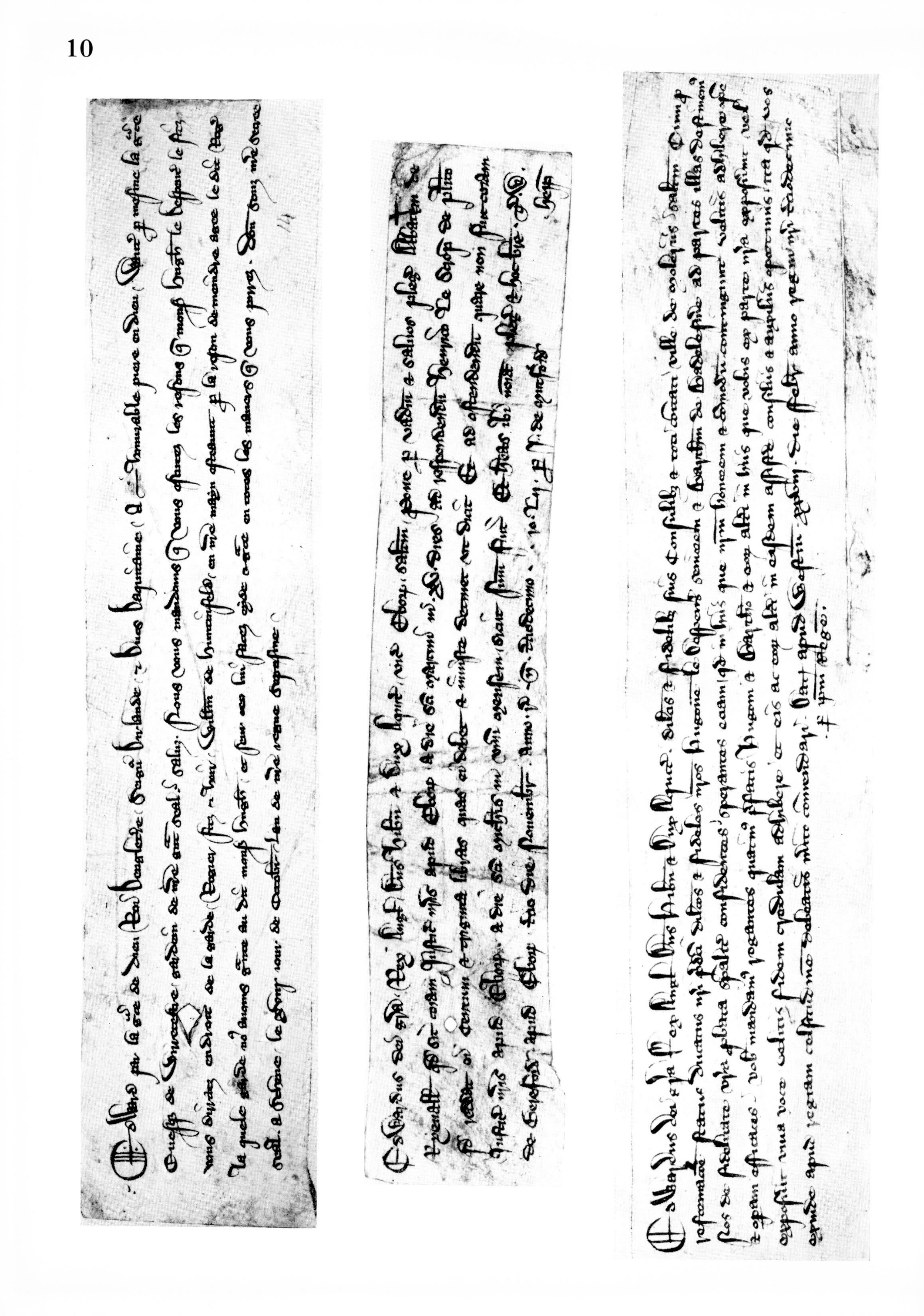

10

a. Chancery Warrants (C. 81), 1328/15

SECRET-SEAL WRIT CLOSE of Edward II to Walter [Reynolds], bishop of Worcester and keeper of the great seal, dated at Sheen, 18 October, regnal year 7 (1313). Parchment. Step in the bottom left-hand corner. Filing hole.

See *C.P.R. 1313–1317*, p. 20 (9 October 1313); *C.F.R.*, ii, p. 181 (18 October 1313).

∴ Edward par la g*r*ace de dieu Roi Dengleter*r*e / Seign*ur* Dirlande / *et* Ducs Daquitaine / a[a] honurable piere en dieu / Wauti*er* p*ar* mesme la g*r*ace [1]// Euesq*ue* de Wirrecestre / gardein de n*ost*re g*r*ant seal ∴ saluz . Nous vous mandoms q*ue* vous escutez les resons q*ue* mons' Hugh' le Despenc*er* le fitz [2]// vous dirratz endroit de la garde / Rogier fitz *et* heir / Will*iam* de Huntinfeld / en n*ost*re mayn esteaunt p*ar* la reson de meindre agee le dit Rogi*er* [3]// la quele garde no*us* auoms g*r*ante au dit mons' Hugh' / et seur ceo lui facez eyde *et* g*r*ace en totes les maners q*ue* vous porrez . Don' souz n*ost*re secree [4]// seal . a Schene / le xviij iour de Octobr*e* / Lan de n*ost*re regne septisme / [5]//

[a] *Followed by one letter erased.*

b. Chancery Files (C. 202), A. 18

'JUDICIAL' WRIT OF ATTACHMENT BY GAGE AND PLEDGES, attested by W[illiam] of Bereford, [chief justice of the common bench], and dated at York, 3 November, Edward II's regnal year 13 (1319). Sent close. Parchment. Step in the bottom left-hand corner. Two filing holes.

The note 'ro. Lij' is a reference to the membrane (*rotulus*) of the plea roll on which are recorded the proceedings in the common bench which led to the issue of the writ. See C.P. 40/231, rot. lij[d] (*De mense sancti Michaelis*): 'Ebor'. Henricus Le Scrop' per Galfridum de Fynghale attornatum suum optulit se iiij[to] die versus abbatem de Ryevall' de placito quod reddat ei centum et triginta libras quas ei debet et injuste detinet etc. Et ipse non venit. Et summonicio. Judicium: attachietur quod sit hic a die sancti Martini in xv dies, per J[ohannem] de Mutford etc.' John de Mutford, a colleague of William de Bereford (whose name in the form *Bereford'* is found at the head of both sides of the membrane) on the bench, ordered the issue of the writ. *Hepp'* is the name of the clerk of the common bench who wrote the writ and the membrane lij of the plea roll or supervised their writing: his name occurs at the foot of the recto of the membrane. The next stage in the proceedings is recorded on the recto of membrane ccxvj of the same roll (*De quindena sancti Martini*): 'Ebor'. Henricus Le Scrop' per Galfridum de Fyngal attornatum suum optulit se iiij die versus abbatem de Ryevall' de placito quod reddat ei centum et triginta libras quas ei debet et injuste detinet etc. Et ipse non venit. Et fuit attachiatus per Hugonem Le Coupere et Ricardum Le Fevre. Ideo ipsi in misericordia. Et preceptum est vicecomiti quod distringat eum per omnes terras etc. et quod de exitibus etc. et quod habeat corpus ejus hic in octabis sancti Hillarii, per justiciarios etc.'

Edwardus dei g*ra*c*ia* / Rex Angl*ie* / D*omi*n*us* Hib*er*n*ie* *et* Dux Aquit*annie* / vice*comiti* Ebor' / sal*utem* / Pone p*er* vadiu*m* *et* saluos pleg*ios* Abbatem de [1]// Ryeuall' q*uo*d sit coram Iustic*iariis* n*ost*ris apud Ebor' / a die s*anc*ti Martini in . xv . dies ad respondendu*m* Henrico Le Scrop' de pl*acit*o [2]// q*uo*d reddat ei Centum *et* triginta libras quas ei debet *et* iniuste detinet vt dicit Et ad ostendendu*m* quare non fuit coram [3]// Iustic*iariis* n*ost*ris apud Ebor' . a die s*anc*ti Mich*ae*lis in vnu*m* Mensem / sicut sum*monitus* fuit Et h*ab*eas ibi no*m*ina pleg*iorum* *et* hoc breu*e* . T*este* . W . [4]// de Bereford' . apud Ebor' . t*er*cio . die . Nouembr*is* . anno . r*egni* . n*ost*ri . t*er*ciodecimo .

. ro . Lij . p*er* I . de Mutford'

. Hepp' [5]//[b]

[b] *The writ is endorsed in three contemporary hands*: [*1*] Respons*io* Simonis Warde vice*comitis* Ebor' Pleg*ii* Abb*atis* de Ryeuall' Hugo le Coup*er* Ric*ardus* le Feure [*2*] *preceptum est* Ridale [*3*] *est*

c. Chancery Miscellanea (C. 47), 24/3/12 (1)

GREAT-SEAL LETTERS (PATENT) OF CREDENCE of Edward II, dated at Westminster, 28 February, regnal year 13 (1320). Formerly sealed on a tongue, but only the tongue remains. Brought back to the chancery and cancelled 'eo quod H[ugo] et B[artholomeus] non adiverunt partes Vasconie' (Gascon Roll 13–14 Edward II (C. 61/33), m. 11d).

Edwardus dei g*ra*c*ia* Rex Angl*ie* D*omi*n*us* Hib*er*n*ie* *et* Dux Aquit*annie* / dilect*is* *et* fidelib*us* suis Consulib*us* *et* toti co*mmun*itati ville de Moleriis / sal*utem* . Cum p*ro* [1]// reformac*io*n*e* status ducatus n*ost*ri p*re*dic*t*i dilec*t*os *et* fideles n*ost*ros Hugone*m* le Despens*er* seniorem *et* Barth*olome*u*m* de Badelesmer*e* ad partes illas destinem*us* [2]// Nos de fidelitate v*est*ra p*ro*bata spec*ia*lit*er* confidentes / sperantes eciam / q*uo*d in hiis que n*ostr*um honorem *et* com*m*odu*m* contingunt velitis adhibere op*us* [3]// *et* op*er*am efficaces / vob*is* mandam*us* rogantes quatin*us* p*re*fatis Hugoni *et* Barth*olome*o *et* eor*um* alt*er*i in hiis que vobis ex parte n*ost*ra exposu*er*int vel [4]// exposu*er*it viua voce / velitis fidem credulam adhibere / et eis ac eor*um* alt*er*i in eisdem assist*er*e consiliis *et* auxiliis oportunis / ita q*uo*d vos [5]// exinde apud regiam celsitudine*m* debeatis m*er*ito com*m*endari . Dat' apud Westm' . xxviij . die Feb*ruarii* anno regni n*ost*ri t*er*ciodecimo . [6]// . p*er* ips*um* Rege*m* . [7]//

11

a. Exchequer, K.R., Miscellanea of the Exchequer (E. 163), 4/11, no. 72

CORRECTED ENGROSSMENT (*LITTERE RESCRIBENDE*) OF A PRIVY-SEAL WRIT of Edward II to Stephen of Abingdon, his butler, dated at Fenham, 6 September, regnal year 16 (1322). Parchment. Filing hole.

Edward p*ar* la g*ra*ce de dieu Roi Dengleterre Seign*ur* Dirlande *et* Ducs Daquitaine :' A n*ost*re che*r* s*er*geant Estephne Dabyndon' n*ost*re Botiller / saluz . Nous vo*us* [1]// mandoms q*ue* a n*ost*re che*r* en dieu P*ri*our de Halieland' ou a son attornez en cele p*ar*tie facez liue*r*er vn tonel de vyn :' *et* a n*ost*re che*r* *et* foial Richard [2]// Tuyt vn tonel de vyn / *et* a Rees ap Griffith' vn tonel de vyn ˋ p*ur* les galeys qil mesne[a] ˊ *et* a Griffith' ap Rees vn tonel de vyn / ˋ p*ur* les gal*eys* qil mesne[a] ˊ *et* a Morgan ap Cruky vn [3]// tonel de vyn ˋ p*ur* les galeys qil mesne[a] ˊ de n*ost*re doun . Et nous vous en feroms aue*r* due alloance s*ur* v*ost*re aconte . Don' souz n*ost*re p*ri*ue seal a Fenham le . vj . iour [4]// de Septembr*e* Lan de n*ost*re regne . xvj[me] . [5]//

[a] *This interlineation is in a different hand.*

b. Exchequer, K.R., Miscellanea of the Exchequer (E. 163), 4/11, no. 11

DRAFT PRIVY-SEAL WRITS of Edward II, ordering the keeper of the great seal to issue letters under the great seal. Dated at Durham, 25 September [1322]. Parchment. Filing hole.

The original engrossments of the writs have survived in Chancery Warrants (C. 81), 120/6221 and 6220 (Durham, 26 September 1322): the latter is reproduced below, *c*. For the enrolments of the great-seal letters issued in pursuance of the writs, see *C.C.R. 1318–1323*, p. 598 (Durham, 26 September 1322), and *C.P.R. 1321–1324*, p. 206 (same place and date of issue).

:'. R*oy* au gardein de n*ost*re g*ra*nt seal salutz :' Come[b] de n*ost*re grace especiale eoms g*ra*nte a ˋ Alianore[c] ˊ la compaigne Rich*ard* de Waleys Cheualer les terres [1]// *et* ten*ementz*[d] que le dit Rich*ard* *et* li tiendrent en dower mesme cele ˋ Alianore del assignement Rob*er*t de Bruys iadis son barom[e] ˊ *et* les queux ensemblement od touz les autres terres *et* ten*ementz* [2]// le dit Rich*ard* sont pris en n*ost*re mein . p*ar* la reson qil fuist[e] aerdant a noz enemis *et* rebealx / auoir en eide de la sustinance mesme cele [3]// ˋ Alianore[c] ˊ vo*us* mandoms q*ue* s*ur* ce la facez auer l*ett*res[f] souz n*ost*re dit seal tantz *et* teles come y apendent . Don' souz n*ost*re[g] p*ri*ue [4]// seal a Duresme le . xxv . iour de sept*embre*[h] p*er* ips*um* R*egem* Nunc*iante* dom*ino* Rob*er*to de Kendale . [5]//

R*oy* as gardeins de n*ost*re g*ra*nt seal salutz / Come a la requeste noz chiers *et* fealx Hugh' le despens*er* Counte de Wincestr*e* *et* Hughe son fuitz [6]// eoms p*ar*done / a Ad*am* de Swinynton' cheualer cink' Centz marcz des Mil marcz . par queux y fist nadgaires fin ouesq*ue* no*us* p*ur* sa vie [7]// terres *et* ten*ementz* p*ar* lencheson qil fust[e] aerdant a noz enemis *et* rebealx . *et* li ˋ eoms[i] ˊ g*ra*nte de n*ost*re g*ra*ce especiale estallement des autr*es* [8]// cink' Centz marcz a paier L li*ures* . p*ar* an ˋ a n*ost*re Escheqer ˊ as t*er*mes de la Pasch*e* *et* ˋ de ˊ seint Mich*el* ˋ tanq*ue* no*us* soioms p*ar*paiez de meismes les cink' centz marcs[j] ˊ le p*ri*m*er* t*er*me comenceant a la Pasq*ue* p*re*cheine auenir [9]// vo*us* mandoms q*ue* s*ur* ce li facez auoir l*ett*res souz[k] n*ost*re dit seal tantz *et* teles come mest*er* y serront . Don' vt sup*ra* / p*er* ips*um* R*egem*

[b] *Written over* Pur *partly erased.*
[c] *Interlined above* Isode *struck out.*
[d] *Followed by* que ele tient en *struck out.*
[e] *Followed by* en *struck out.*
[f] *Followed by* sur *struck out.*
[g] *Followed by* secre sea *struck out.*
[h] *Followed by* la (*false start of* lan) *struck out.*
[i] *Interlined above* auoms *struck out.*
[j] *This interlineation is in a different hand.*
[k] *Written over an erasure.*

c. Chancery Warrants (C. 81), 120/6220

PRIVY-SEAL WRIT CLOSE of Edward II, ordering the keepers of the great seal to issue letters under the great seal. Dated at Durham, 26 September, regnal year 16 (1322). Parchment. Tear in the bottom left-hand corner. Filing hole. Traces of the privy seal in red wax in the centre of the dorse.

This is the original engrossment of the second part of the draft reproduced above, *b*. Note the change of date and the corrections in lines 2 and 3.

The same scribe wrote *b* and *c*.

:'. Edward par la g*ra*ce de dieu Roi Dengleterre Siegn*ur*[l] Dirlaunde *et* Ducs Daquitaine / As gardeins de n*ost*re g*ra*nt seal salutz :' Come a [1]// la requeste noz chiers *et* fealx Hugh'[m] le Despens*er* Counte de Wyncestre / *et* Hugh' son fuitz / eoms p*ar*donez a Adam de Swinlinton'[n] [2]// Cheualer cink' Centz marcs des Mill*e* marcs / par queux y fist nadgaires fin ouesq*ue* no*us* p*ur* sa vie ˋ *et* p*ur* ses ˊ terres *et* tenementz par lencheson [3]// qil fust aerdant a noz enemys *et* rebealx . *et* li eoms g*ra*ntez de n*ost*re g*ra*ce especiale estallement des autres cink' Centz marcs a paier [4]// Cinquante liures p*ar* an a n*ost*re escheqer as termes de la Pasq*ue* *et* de seint Michiel tantq*ue* no*us* soioms p*ar*paiez de mesmes les cink' [5]// Centz marcs le p*ri*mer terme comenceant a la Pasq*ue* p*re*scheine auenir :' vous mandoms q*ue* s*ur* ceo li facez auer l*ett*res souz n*ost*re dit [6]// seal tantz *et* teles come mest*er* ly[o] serront Don' souz n*ost*re p*ri*ue seal a Duresme le . xxvj . iour de septembre lan de n*ost*re [7]// regne . xvj[me] . [8]//

[l] *Sic in MS.*
[m] *Corrected from* Hughe.
[n] *The letters* li *are written over an erasure.*
[o] *The letter* l *was added by another hand.*

n° 280. — Westminster, 17 mars 1324 n.

Treschier et tresames frere, por ce qe nous savoms bien qe vous orriez volunters bones noueles de nous, voillez savoir treschier et tresames frere qe
nous estoioms en bone sante de corps, mercy dieux, au partir de cestes, ce qil vous voille touz iours ottroier par sa puissance selonc nostre desir;
et vous pryoms treschier et tresamez frere, qe de vostre estat, quel tordis voille dieux qe bon soit, la certeinete nous voillez mander, si sovent come vous
plerra. Car nous simes molt reconfortez totes les foiz qe nous en oioms plesantes noueles. Treschier et tresamez frere, come nous vous prissions autrefoiz
par noz messages et par lettres souz nostre grant seal, qe pres si nul fait comencez par nous du fait qest dit estre fait a Seint Sardos en nostre terre Dagenes
et totes autres choses pendantes en vostre plement a Pariys, touchantes nous par reson de nostre dite Duchee et nostre Seneschal, conseillers, procurours
et noz autres ministres celes parties, voilliez bonement respiter, tanqz a un autre plement ou tanqz a nostre entreveue, pur meillour et plus
gracious esploit aid des dites busoignes a honur de vous et de nous, des queux messages nous navoms uncore receu nulle certification. Vous pryoms
derechief treschier et tresamez frere et requeroms si adcertes et de quer come nous poems qe toutes noz dites busoignes voillez bonement respiter
selonc ce qe nous vous en avoms avant requis par noz ditz messages et lettres. Car treschier et tresamez frere, nous nous asseuroms tant de vostre grant
bonte qe vous ne vorriez qe nous ne les noz feussoms surpris ne grevez es busoignes qe nous pount toucher vers vous. Dautre part treschier et tresamez
frere, pur ce qe nous envoioms presentement vers vous nostre cher frere et foial Esmon conte de Kent, pur grosses busoignes qe nous touchent, et pur aler outre
en nostre dite Duchee, a viseer lestat dycele, vous pryoms affectuosement tresamez frere qe vous voillez comander voz lettres de conduyt bones
et suffisantes pur li et pur ses gentz, et mesmes les lettres faire liverer a nostre cher et foial Robert de Echingham ou mestre Bertin Ferrant port de cestes, qil les puisse amener
a nous si come nous li avoms chargez. Treschier et tresamez frere le seint espirit vous eit et garde. Don souz nostre prive seal a Westmostre
le xvij jour de marz lan de nostre regne xvij^me

12

Brussels, Archives Générales du Royaume, Chartes de Brabant, no. 280

PRIVY-SEAL LETTERS CLOSE of Edward II to Charles IV, king of France, dated at Westminster, 7 March, regnal year 17 (1324). Parchment.

Printed in *The War of Saint-Sardos*, ed. Pierre Chaplais (Camden Third Series, lxxxvii, 1954), no. 24.

Tresch*er et* tresamez frere / por ce q*ue* nous sauoms bien q*ue* vous orriez volunt*er*s bones nouelles de no*us* ſ voillez sauoir tresch*er et* tresamez frere q*ue* [1]// nous estoioms en bone sancte de corps m*er*cy dieux au partir de cestes ſ ce quil vous voille touz iours ottroier p*ar* sa puissance selonc n*ost*re desir / [2]// et vous p*r*ioms tresch*er et* tresamez frere / q*ue* de v*ost*re estat / quel totdis voille dieux q*ue* bon soit ⁏ la c*er*teinete no*us* voillez mander / si souent come vo*us* [3]// plerra . Car no*us* sumes molt reconfortez / totes les foitz / q*ue* no*us* en ooms pleissantes nouelles . Tresch*er et* tresamez frere / come no*us* vo*us* p*r*iissiens autr*e* foitz [4]// p*ar* noz messages / *et* p*ar* l*ett*res souz n*ost*re grant seal / q*ue* p*r*oces / si nul feut comencez / p*ar* vo*us* du fait / qest dit estr*e* fait / a seint Sacerdot' en n*ost*re t*er*re Dagent [5]// *et* totes autr*e*s choses pendantes en v*ost*re p*ar*lement a Parys / touchantes no*us* / p*ar* reson de n*ost*re dite Duchee / *et* n*ost*re seneschal / conseillers / procurous [6]// *et* noz autr*e*s Ministres celes p*ar*ties / vousissiez bonement respit*er* / tantq*ue* a vn autre p*ar*lement / ou soueaux tantq*ue* a n*ost*re entr*e*ueue / p*ur* meillour / *et* plus [7]// gracious exploit au*er* / des dites bosoignes / a hon*ur* de vous / *et* de nous / des queux messages / no*us* nauoms vncore receu / nulle c*er*tificacion / Vo*us* p*r*ioms [8]// derechief' tresch*er et* tresamez frere / *et* requerroms / si adec*er*tes *et* de cuer / come no*us* pooms / q*ue* toutes noz dites bosoignes / voillez bonement respiter / [9]// selonc ce q*ue* nous vous en auoms auant requis / p*ar* noz ditz messages *et* l*ett*res . Car tresch*er et* tresamez frere / no*us* no*us* asseuroms tant de v*ost*re grant [10]// bountie / q*ue* vous ne vorriez q*ue* no*us* / ne les noz feussoms suppris / ne sedutz / es bosoignes q*ue* no*us* p*ur*ront toucher v*er*s vous . Dautr*e* p*ar*t tresch*er et* tresamez [11]// frere / p*ur* ce q*ue* no*us* enueoms p*r*echeinement v*er*s vous / n*ost*re ch*er et* foial Esmon Conte de Kent / p*ur* grosses bosoignes q*ue* no*us* touchent / *et* p*ur* aler outre [12]// en n*ost*re dite Duchee / a s*ur*ueer lestat dycele ſ vous p*r*ioms affectuosement tresamez frere q*ue* vous voillez co*m*mander voz l*ett*res de conduyt s*ur* [13]// ce suffisantes p*ur* li / *et* p*ur* ses gentz / *et* meismes les l*ett*res faire liu*er*er a n*ost*re ch*er et* foial Robert de Echingham ' ou maistr*e* Bert*r*am Ferrant ' port*ur* de cestes / qil les puisse enueer [14]// a no*us* / sicome no*us* li auoms chargez . Tresch*er et* tresamez frere le seint espirit' vous sauue *et* garde . Don' souz n*ost*re p*r*iue seal a Westmost*er* . // le . vij . iour de Marz Lan de n*ost*re regne . xvij^{me} . [16]//

13

a. Exchequer of Receipt, Writs and Warrants for Issues (E. 404), 4/22

PRIVY-SEAL WRIT CLOSE (WARRANT FOR ISSUES) of Edward III to the treasurer and chamberlains of the exchequer, dated at Westminster, 27 September, regnal year 11 (1337). Parchment. Two filing holes. Three vertical and possibly one horizontal folds. Traces of the privy seal in red wax on the dorse, on the right of the central vertical fold.

Edward p*ar* la g*ra*ce de dieu Roi Dengleterre Seign*ur* Dirlande *et* Ducs Daquit*aine* :' As Tresorer *et* Chamb*er*leins de n*ost*re Escheqier / [1]// salutz . Nous vous mandoms q*ue* a les executours Mons' Guy Lumbard qest a dieu comandez facez paier dys Marcs [2]// de n*ost*re Tresor p*ur* son ent*er*rement de n*ost*re doun . Don' souz n*ost*re p*r*iue seal a Westmost*er* le xxvij . iour de septembre [3]// lan de n*ost*re regne vnzisme . [4]//[a]

[a] *One endorsement reads*: ∫ Persoluit*ur* vt p*ate*t in pelle . xxxj°. die Ian*uarii* anno . xij°.

b. Chancery Files (C. 202), Cancelled Letters Patent, H. 9/53

CANCELLED LETTERS PATENT (MORTMAIN LICENCE) of Edward III for the prior and convent of Merton, dated at the Tower of London, 6 October, regnal year 11 (1337). Parchment. Originally sealed with the great seal, appended on a tag, but the tag has been torn off. Herring-bone cuts for cancellation.

Line 1, note the unfinished initials 'H' of *Hibernie* and 'D' of *Dux*, which were obviously meant to be decorated.

The privy-seal writ mentioned in the warranting note 'p*er* bre*ue* de priuato sig*illo*' has survived in Chancery Warrants (C. 81), 239/10322, dated at the Tower of London, 6 October, regnal year 11 (Latin).

The letters patent are enrolled on Patent Roll 11 Edward III, Part III (C. 66/191), m. 30: *C.P.R. 1334–1338*, p. 533.

Edwardus dei g*ra*cia Rex Angl*ie* Dominus Hib*er*nie *et* Dux Aquit*annie* Omnib*us* ad quos p*re*sentes litt*ere* p*er*uene[1]//rint :' sal*ute*m . Sciatis q*uo*d de g*ra*cia n*ost*ra spe*ci*ali concessimus *et* licenciam dedimus p*ro* nobis *et* heredib*us* n*ost*ris q*u*antu*m* [2]// in nobis est dil*ect*is nob*is* in c*ris*to . . Priori *et* Conuentui de Merton' q*uo*d ipsi decem libratas t*er*re *et* redditus cu*m* [3]// p*er*tinenciis p*er* annu*m* tam de feodo suo p*ro*prio q*u*am alieno exceptis t*er*ris *et* redditib*us* que de nobis tenent*ur* in capite adqui[4]//rere possint h*abe*ndo*s* *et* tenendo*s* sibi *et* successorib*us* suis imp*er*petuu*m* . Statuto de t*er*ris *et* ten*ementis* ad manu*m* mortuam non ponend*is* [5]// edito non obstante . Dumtamen p*er* inquisici*o*nes inde in forma debita faciend*as* *et* in Cancellar*ia* n*ost*ra vel heredu*m* n*ost*roru*m* rite [6]// retornand*as* comp*er*tum sit ∫ q*uo*d id fieri pot*er*it absq*ue* dampno *et* p*re*iudicio n*ost*ri *et* heredum n*ost*roru*m* ac alt*er*ius cuiuscumq*ue* . In [7]// cuius rei testimoniu*m* has l*itt*eras n*ost*ras fieri fecimus patentes . Teste me ip*s*o apud Turrim London' sexto die [8]// Octobr*is* anno regni n*ost*ri vndecimo . :' p*er* bre*ue* de priuato sig*illo*[b] . [9]//

[b] *This note is in lighter ink. The document is endorsed:* [*1*] Prior *et* Conuentus infrascripti virtute istius licencie adquisi*uerunt* terras *et* tene*menta* ad valorem decem solidoru*m* p*er* annu*m* sub dat*a* . xv[mi] . diei Decembr*is* anno regni R*egis* E . terc*ij* . vide*licet* angl*ie* xxxiij . *et* Franc*ie* vicesimo / in p*ar*tem satisfacc*ionis* *etc*' . [*2*] vaca*nt* *et* restitute fuerunt eo q*uo*d Prior *et* Conuentus infrascr*ipti* xx die Iulij anno regni Regis Ric*ardi* sec*un*di post conquestu*m* sextodecimo adquisiuer*unt* c*er*ta terras *et* tene*menta* in plenam satisfacc*io*nem Et ideo iste l*itt*ere cancellant*ur* *et* dampnant*ur* ∫ *These are references to two licences for alienation in mortmain, one for alienation by Thomas Cook* (*C.P.R. 1358–1361, p. 319: 15 Dec. 1359*)*, the other by Adam Tychesey* (*C.P.R. 1391–1396, p. 127: 20 July 1392*)*. The writs and inquisitions ad quod dampnum for both alienations have survived: Inquis. ad quod dampnum* (*C. 143*)*, file 333, no. 12* (*writ dated 6 Nov. 1359*)*, and file 422, no. 13* (*writ dated 18 June 1392*)*. The note* dampn*atur* in rotulo (*not reproduced*)*, on the face of the document, in the top left-hand corner, refers to the cancellation on the Patent Roll; it is in a different hand*

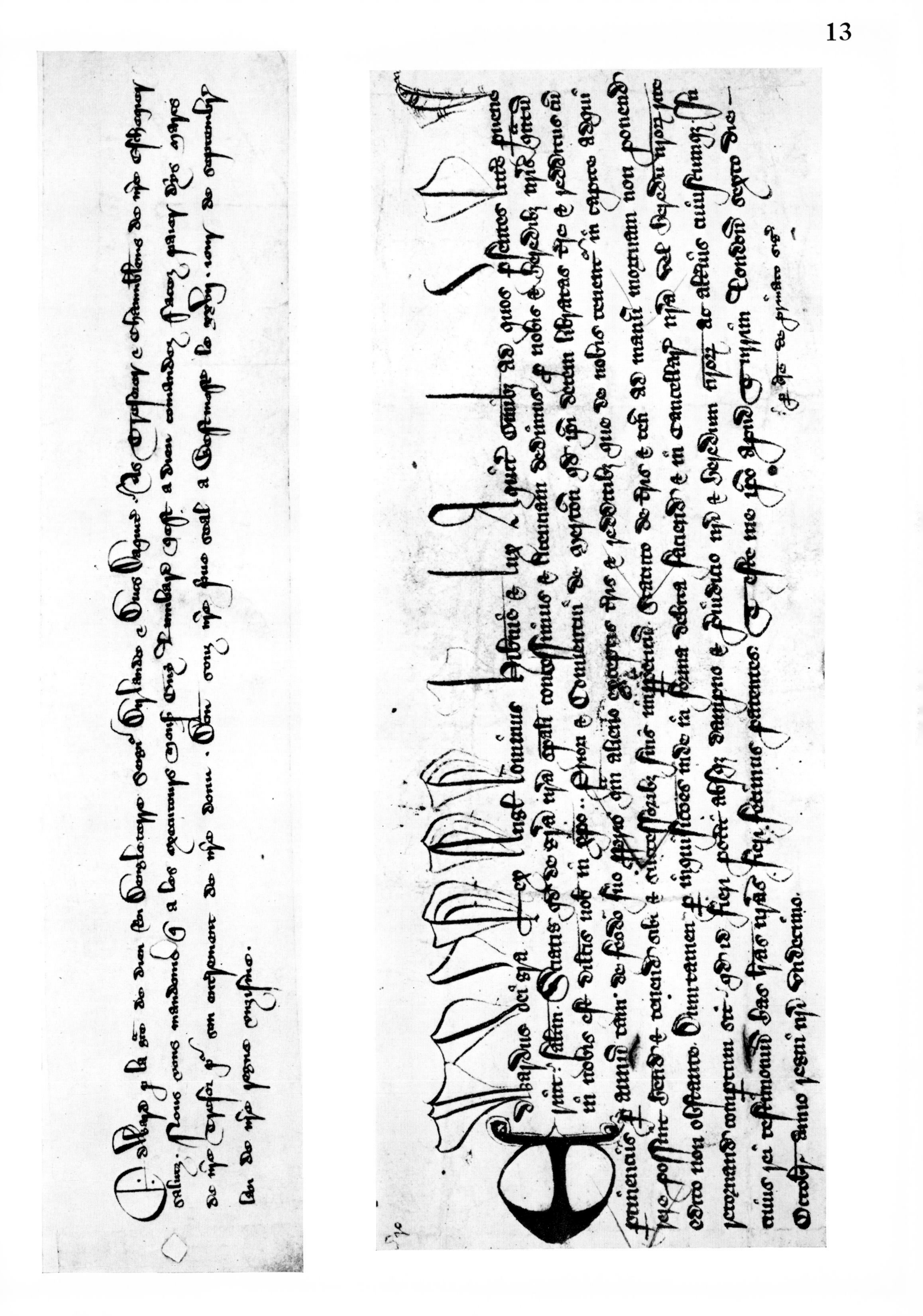

14

a. Chancery Warrants (C. 81), 909/6A

COUNCIL BILL (PATENT) forwarded close under the privy seal to Master John de Offord, dean of Lincoln, Edward III's chancellor, and ordering him to issue a commission under the great seal. Delivered to the chancellor on 27 October [1347]. Parchment. Nine slits for insertion of a thong. Filing hole. Traces of the privy seal in red wax on the dorse, close to the right margin, over two slits.

The commission under the great seal is enrolled on Patent Roll 21 Edward III, Part I (C. 66/220), m. 3d: *C.P.R. 1345–1348*, p. 321 (Westminster, 20 [*sic*] October [1347]; warranted *per billam de privato sigillo*).

Pur ceo qe n*ostr*e seign*ur* le Roi ad entendu qe diu*er*ses deceites concelementz faus allowances *et* autres errours sount en[a] la Count / rendu [1]// en leschequer' p*ar* ceux qe furent iadis coillours ` vend*ours* *et* asse*ours* ′ des neouismes iadis a n*ost*re dit seign*ur* le Roi grauntez en le Northrythyng' en le Counte [2]// Deu*er*wyk' de mesme la subside / *et* les Barouns del eschequer' sount taunt ocupez p*ar* autres bosoignes qe cels errours ne poount ils [3]// en hast redrescer / Si voet n*ost*re dit seign*ur* le Roi qe co*m*mission soit fait a mons' William de Thorp William cusance Iohan [4]// de Howton' ` Nichol. de Bokeland' clerc[b] ′ *et* Richard de la Pole ` s*er*geant[b] ′ a quatre / ou trois[c] ` deux[b] ′ de eaux desquels il voet qe mons' William de Thorp vn soit pur oier *et* [5]// t*er*miner touz les deceites concelementz faus allowances *et* touz les autres ` errours[b] ′ en la susdit acompt trouez resceiuaunt deu*er*s eaux [6]// touz les euidences qe demorent en leschequer' t[o]uchaunt cele acompt *et* la recitacion / oiauntz les plaintz de chescuny qe ` sure[d] ′ [7]// mesmes les coill*ours* vodraient pleindre [8]//

Soit assignez ` iour ′ a les p*ar*ties lundy qi vendra p*re*schein[e] / [9]// ¶ Me*morandum* q*uo*d ista billa lib*er*ata fuit Cancellar*io* vicesimo septimo die Octobr*is* ad faciend*um* inde co*m*missione*m* iuxta tenorem [10]// eiusde*m* bill*e* . quo p*re*textu co*m*missio illa f*act*a fuit *et* co*n*signata ∴ vno[f] cu*m* quoda*m* br*eui* clauso *et* lib*er*at*a* Walt*er*o de Iernemuth' . [11]//[g]

[a] en *written over a false start* l.

[b] *This interlineation is in a different hand and ink.*

[c] quatre ou trois *written over an erasure, in the same hand as the interlineation mentioned in note b.*

[d] *Interlined above* deuers *struck out.*

[e] *This sentence may be written in the same hand and ink as the interlineations.*

[f] *Sic in MS. for* vna.

[g] *This paragraph is in a third hand, that of a chancery scribe. The document is endorsed in a contemporary hand:* A n*ost*re ch*er* Clerc maistre Iohan de Offord' Dean de Nicole / n*ost*re Chanc*ellier* .

b. Chancery Warrants (C. 81), 1334/8

SIGNET LETTERS CLOSE of Edward III, ordering the issue of letters under the great seal. Dated at Clipstone, 1 September [1354]. Parchment. Three vertical folds. Traces of two seals in red wax on the dorse. Four slits for insertion of a tongue.

The commission under the great seal is enrolled on Fine Roll 28 Edward III (C. 60/155), m. 11: *C.F.R. 1347–1356*, p. 401 (Clipstone, 1 September [1354]).

depa*r* le Roi . [1]//

Nous auons grantez a n*ost*re ch*er* *et* foial Geffrey Sire de Say la Conestablerie de n*ost*re Chastel de Roucestr' [2]// a auoir a t*er*me de sa vie / Rendant ent a n*ost*re Escheqier attant come . . le Conte de Huntynd[a] [3]// qi mort est / *et* q*e* dieux assoille / fist / tancome il vesquit / Si vous mandons q*e* s*ur* ce facez auoir [4]// au dit Geffrey noz l*ett*res desouz le grant seal tielles qapp*ar*tienent . Don' souz n*ost*re signet a Clipston' [5]// le prim*er* io*ur* de sept*embre* .

[a] *The right-hand margin may have been trimmed and the two letters* on *lost at the end of this name.*

15

Wolfenbüttel, Herzog-August-Bibliothek, MS. 31 Aug. 2° (extracts)

ROYAL BOOK written by royal scribes. This manuscript (parchment, 32×22 cm.), known as 'Recognitiones feodorum in Aquitania', was copied in 1354 from an earlier exemplar. See J.-P. Trabut-Cussac, 'Les cartulaires gascons . . .', *Biblioth. de l'École des Chartes*, cxi (1953), pp. 69–71, 76–85. Printed in *Recueil d'actes relatifs à l'admin. des rois d'Angleterre en Guyenne au XIIIe siècle*, ed. C. Bémont (*Doc. inédits*, Paris, 1914).

In the majority of cases the names of the scribe and examiner of each quire are given either at the foot of the verso of the last folio or, more often, at the foot of the recto of the first folio, normally in the form *scribitur per* . . . (or *scribitur per manus* . . .) and *examinatur per* . . . The examiners include such well-known chancery clerks as Thomas Brayton, William Burstall, Thomas and William Newenham (see Wilkinson, *The Chancery under Edward III*, pp. 205–8). The scribes are less easily identified, but at least some of them—among whom John de Colyngbourn—were also chancery clerks.

a. Extract from folio 16^{v}: hand of William de Burgh the younger

Bertrandus de mota fil*ius* suus cu*m* eius concensu Iur*atus* dix*it* q*uo*d tenebat de d*omi*no [1]// Rege Miliciam Daudinon cu*m* suis p*er*tin*enciis* r*aci*one successionis mat*er*ne cu*m* homagio *et* [2]// fidelitate[a] *et* ius ac legem in Curi*a* s*anct*i Seu*er*ij *et* exercitu*m* de suo corpore cu*m* armis [3]// vel si non possit cu*m* trib*us* s*er*uientib*us* De allod*iis* nich*il* de sporla nich*il* [4]//

b. Extract from folio 23^{r}: hand of Edmund le Blount

Arn*aldus* de Renum Domicellus de Renum tenet de d*omi*no Rege *et* Duce . viij . casa[1]//lia in p*a*roch*ia* de sent seuini / a la lanuce p*ro* quibus debet homag*ium et* fidelit*atem et* ius ac [2]// legem vt alij de vig*er*ia *et* ex*er*c*itum* vni*us* s*er*uientis de allod*iis* nichil De alienatis nichil [3]//

c. Extract from folio 41^{v}: hand of Hawclerk

¶ Petrus Hugos *et* frat*er* eius debe*n*t ij . s' . iij . d' . *et* tene*n*t quicquid h*a*bent[b] a d*ic*to d*omi*no [1]// Rege excepto vsq*ue* ad sex quartaladas terre vel plus quas h*a*bent[b] in loco vocato [2]// ahugos . et teneba*n*t a Bert*r*ando de la Dils cu*m* xxx . s' burd' de feodo . [3]//

d. Extract from folio 53^{r}: hand of John de Colyngbourn

¶ Item eode*m* die Grimoardus de Moncl*er*ico iur*atus* dix*it* q*uo*d nichil tenebat[c] nec [1]// debebat tenere in feod*o* inmed*iato* a d*omi*no Rege Angl*ie* seu in allod*io* de hiis que [2]// h*ab*ebat sub eius dominio nec in aliquo deu*er*io tenebat*ur* T*estes* p*re*d*ic*ti . [3]//

e. Extract from folio 97^{v}: hand of John de Ditton

Edwardus illust*r*is Reg*is* Angl*ie* p*r*imoge*nitus* dil*ectis et* fid*elibus* suis sen*escallo* vascon*ie et* Castel[1]//lano Burd' ∴ sal*utem* . Cum nup*er* dederim*us et* co*n*cesserim*us* dil*ect*o *et* fideli n*ost*ro Bern*ardo* May[2]//conis Ciui Burd' B*ene*d*ictu*m Iudeum n*ost*ru*m* de Sparra p*r*out in l*itt*era ˋ n*ost*ra ˊ qua*m* inde h*abe*t plen*ius* [3]//

f. Extract from folio 104^{v}: hand of John de Digby

E es assab*er* que lo dits sen*escals* anres[d] *e* pauzat lo saget de la cort de Gasconha *e* lo [1]// dits˙ Naug*er*s apausat[e] lo geen[f] p*r*opri saget en acesta p*re*sent carta p*er* maiu flue[2]//tat[g] *e* c*er*tenetat de cesta causa E en testimonage de v*er*itat la quals carta a eu[h] [3]// deu auer entegra *e* plena *e* ferma valor *e* f*er*metat *e* auctoritad ab las aua*nt* [4]// dits sages o senes les auantdits sagetz Actum vt supra [5]//

g. Extract from folio 156^{r}: hand of Henry de Coventre

T*estes* huius rei sunt Gualhard*us* darieto domicell*us* Bern*ardus* de montib*us* Arn*aldus* de [1]// sauciras Gaucelm*us* damieyssan Amaneu*us* Artaudi ad hoc sp*eci*alit*er* vocati [2]// *et* rogati Et ego p*re*d*ic*tus notar*ius* burd' vocat*us et* rogat*us* ad h*e*c p*re*sens fui eaq*ue* [3]// conscripsi *et* in publica*m* forma*m* redegi *et* signu*m* meu*m* apposui in test*imon*ium p*re*missoru*m* [4]//

h. Extract from folio 159^{v}: hand of Kymberleye

Et ego p*re*d*ic*tus . P . Rob*er*ti public*us* notar*ius* Ciuit*atis* Burd' vocat*us et* rogatus ad hoc p*re*sens [1]// fui ea*que* conscripsi *et* in publica*m* fo*r*mam redegi *et* signu*m* meu*m* apposui in testim*onium* p*re*missoru*m* [2]//

[a] *Apparently corrected from* fidelius, *the latter being a misreading of* ? fidelit'. [b] *Corrected from* habet. [c] *Corrected from* tenebatur . [d] *Scribal error for* a mes . [e] *Scribal error for* a pausat . [f] *Scribal error for* seen . [g] *Scribal error for* fermetat . [h] *Scribal error for* e .

[illegible]

[illegible]

[illegible]

[illegible]

[illegible]

[illegible]

[illegible]

[illegible]

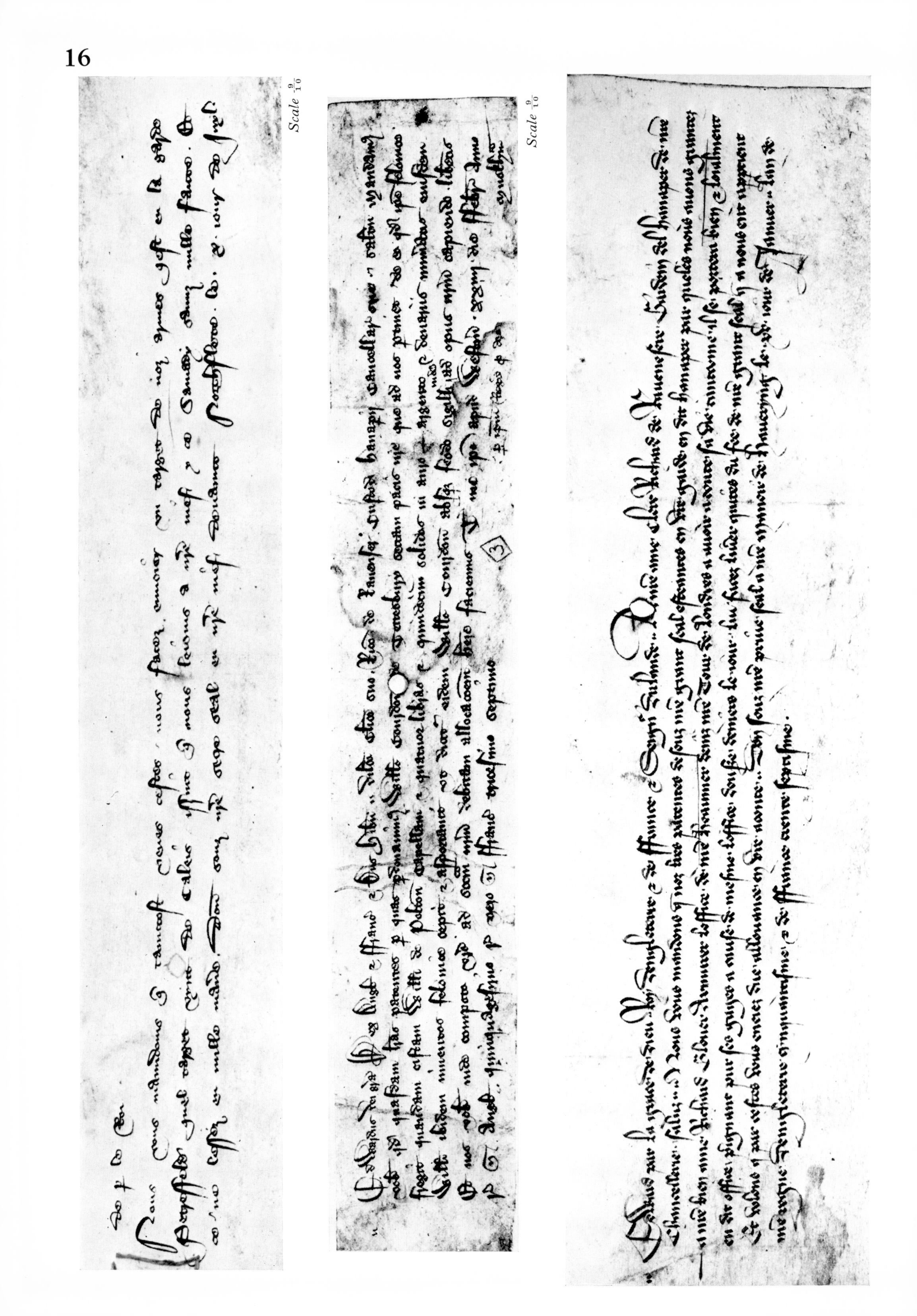

Scale $\frac{9}{10}$

Scale $\frac{9}{10}$

16

a. Exchequer, K.R., Accounts Various (E. 101), 392/15/65

SECRET-SEAL LETTERS CLOSE of Edward III [to the keeper of the privy wardrobe], dated on the royal ship, before Northfleet, 10 July [1355]. Parchment. Small step in the bottom left-hand corner. One horizontal and three vertical folds. Three slits for insertion of a tongue. Filing hole. Traces of the secret seal in red wax on the dorse, close to the right margin, over a slit. [*Reduction scale*: 9/10]

de p*ar* le Roi . [1]//
Nous vous maundoms q*e* tauntost veues cestes / nous facez enuoier vn target de noz armes qest en la garde [2]// Petresfeld' quel target vynt de Caleis / issint q*e* nous leioms a n*ost*re nief' y ce Samady saunz nulle faute . Et [3]// ce / ne lessez en nulle man*er*e . Don' souz n*ost*re secre seal en n*ost*re nief' deuaunt Northflete . le . x . iour de Iuyl . [4]//

b. Exchequer, K.R., Accounts Various (E. 101), 212/15/3

GREAT-SEAL WRIT of Edward III to Richard de Ravenser, keeper of the hanaper of the chancery, dated at Westminster, 24 February, regnal year of England 50 and of France 37 (1376). Parchment. Presumably sent close. Filing hole.

The *extra sigillum* note 'pro deo' signifies that no fee or fine was charged for this writ (see Maxwell-Lyte, p. 338). The name *Muskham* is that of the chancery clerk Robert Muskham, who —or a clerk under him—wrote the document. The same name occurs in the bottom right-hand corner of various great-seal documents (not all in the same hand) in Chancery Files (C. 202), Cancelled Letters Patent, H.20–H.24; Johnson and Jenkinson, plate xxx (*a*). In October 1360 he also wrote documents connected with the treaty of Brétigny (Exch. of Receipt, Warrants for Issues (E. 404), 41/21). The following comment by a chancery clerk about a forged 'original' writ of covenant dated 12 February 1372 explains the meaning of the clerk's name in the bottom right-hand corner of chancery documents: 'Thomas Duffeld, clericus de cancellaria domini regis, cujus nomen in fine brevis predicti inseritur, juratus et inde examinatus, dicit quod nec ipse nec aliquis alius subtus illum in dicta cancellaria nomine suo scribens breve predictum scripsit, nec quod ipse breve predictum unquam ante hoc tempus vidit' (Selden Soc., vol. 82, p. 165). [*Reduction scale*: 9/10]

~ Edwardus dei gr*aci*a Rex Angl*ie et* Franc*ie et* D*omi*n*us* Hib*er*n*ie* ~ dil*ect*o Cl*er*ico suo . Ric*ard*o de Rauenser Custodi hanap*er*ij Cancellar*ie* sue[a] / salut*em* Mandam*us*[1]// vob*is* q*uo*d quasdam l*itt*eras patentes p*er* quas p*er*donauim*us* Will*elm*o Gourdon' de Tettesbury sectam pacis n*ost*re que ad nos p*er*tinet / de eo q*uo*d ip*s*e felonice [2]// fregit quandam cistam Will*elm*i de Polton' Capellani *et* quatuor libras *et* quindecim solidos in auro[b] argento *et* denariis num*er*atis eiusdem [3]// Will*elm*i ibidem inuentos felonice cepit *et* asportauit vt dicit*ur* eidem Will*elm*o Gourdon' absq*ue* feodo sigilli ' inde ' ad opus n*ost*r*u*m capiendo . lib*er*etis [4]// Et nos vob*is* inde compoto v*est*ro ad scaccar*iu*m n*ost*r*u*m debitam allocac*ion*em h*ab*ere faciemus T*este* me ip*s*o apud Westm' . xxiiij . die Febr*uarii* anno [5]// *regni* n*ost*r*i* Angl*ie* quinquagesimo *regni* vero n*ost*r*i* Franc*ie* tricesimo septimo :' p*er* ip*su*m Rege*m*
p*r*o deo[c] Muskham [6]//

[a] sue *partly over an erasure.*
[b] *Followed by an erasure.*
[c] *This note is in a different hand and ink.*

c. Exchequer, K.R., Accounts Various (E. 101), 212/15/107

PRIVY-SEAL WRIT CLOSE of Edward III to Richard de Ravenser, keeper of the hanaper of the chancery, dated at Havering[-atte-Bower], 15 January, regnal year of England 50 and of France 37 (1377). Parchment. Tear in the bottom left-hand corner. One horizontal and two vertical folds. Six slits for insertion of a tongue. Traces of the privy seal in red wax on the dorse, close to the right margin, over a slit. Two filing holes.

~ Edward par la grace de dieu Roy Dengleterre *et* de France *et* Seign*ur* Dirlande ~ A n*ost*re ame Clerc Richard de Rauenesere Gardein del hanaper de n*ost*re [1]// Chancellerie / saluz ~ Nous vous mandons q*ue* noz l*ett*res patentes desouz n*ost*re grant seal esteantes en v*ost*re garde en dit hanaper par queles nous auons grantez [2]// a n*ost*re bien ame Richard Glouer Armurer loffice de n*ost*re Heaumer deinz n*ost*re Tour de Londres a auoir a toute sa vie tantcome il se portera bien *et* loialment [3]// en dit office p*r*eignant pur ses gages a cause de mesme loffice dousze deniers le iour / lui facez liu*er*er quites du fee de n*ost*re grant seal q*ue* a nous ent app*ar*tient [4]// Et volons q*ue* par cestes vous en eiez due allouance en v*ost*re aconte ~ Don' souz n*ost*re priue seal a n*ost*re Manoir de Haueryng' le . xv . iour de Ianuer ~ Lan de [5]// n*ost*re regne Dengleterre cynquantisme *et* de France trente septisme . [6]//

17

a. Exchequer, T.R., Council and Privy Seal Files (E. 28), 1

DRAFT PRIVY-SEAL WRIT of Richard II, ordering the chancellor to issue letters under the great seal [24 June 1389]. Parchment.

The original engrossment under the privy seal has survived in Chancery Warrants (C. 81), 505/5261, dated at Westminster, 24 June, regnal year 13 (1389): it differs from the draft on a number of points and particularly in the order of its various clauses.

The great-seal letters issued in pursuance of the writ are enrolled on Patent Roll 13 Richard II, Part I (C. 66/328), m. 37: *C.P.R. 1388–1392*, p. 73 (Westminster, 24 June [1389]).

⁓ R*oy* Au Chanceller ⁓ Come nous le quatorzisme iour de Feu*er*er darein [1]// passe pur le bon s*er*uice q*ue* n*ost*re b*ie*n ame Henri Ferrour nous auoit fait [2]// *et* ferroit ‵ lui ′ eussiens grantez ‵ par noz l*ett*res pat*entes* desouz n*ost*re grand seal ′ loffice de Feure ‵ en[a] ′ n*ost*re Chastel de [3]// Wyndesore le quel office Nichol Smyth' auoit quant il viuoit [4]// ʃ a auoir a toute la vie du dit Henri preignant eu dit office [5]// tieux gages fees *et* profitz *et* en mesme la man*er*e come feurent [6]// appartenantz[b] dancien[c] temps a loffice auantdit Et nous [7]// de n*ost*re grace espec*i*ale a la supplicacion du dit Henri *et* p*ar* cause qil [8]// nous ad offert noz d*ic*tes l*ett*res a restituer ‵ lui ′ eons grantez . loffice de [9]// Feure[d] en n*ost*re d[i]t Chastel de Wyndesore ʃ a auoir a toute [10]// sa vie preignant eu dit office sys deniers le io*ur* p*ur* ses gages [11]// des[e] issues de n*ost*re dit Chastel p*ar* les mains [12]// ‵ du[f] ′ Conestable dycel / qi p*ur* le temps serra Issint q*ue* le dit [13]// Nichol[g] face continuel demoere en mesme le Chastel sur son [14]// dit office ʃ *et* nous face le s*er*uice q*ue* affiert en loffice auantd[it] [15]// ⁓ vous mandons q*ue* receues deue*rs* vous noz d*ic*tes l*ett*res *et* ycelles [16]// cancellees en n*ost*re Chancellerie si facez faire sur ceste n*ost*re [17]// grace autres noz l*ett*res ⁓ [18]//

[a] *Interlined above* deinz *crossed out.*
[b] *Followed by* de *crossed out.*
[c] *Letter* d *written over* l.
[d] *Followed by* de *crossed out.*
[e] *Preceded by* par les mains de *crossed out.*
[f] *Interlined above* de nostre *crossed out.*
[g] *Recte* Henri.

b. Exchequer, K.R., Accounts Various (E. 101), 402/5, fol. 35[v]

EXTRACT FROM THE ACCOUNT-BOOK OF BALDWIN DE RADYNGTON, controller of Richard II's household (1 October 1389–26 July 1390). Parchment book. The book was written before 26 April, regnal year 16 (1393), on which day Radyngton delivered the book in person to the exchequer (note on fol. 43[v]).

⁓ Vadia Falconar*iorum et* put*ur*a Falconu*m* [1]//
¶ Petro Courtenay Custodi de les Mewes pro vadijs suis consuet*is*[h] [2]// pro eadem Custodia a primo die Octobr*is* vsq*ue* vj . diem Febr*uarii* p*ro*x*imo* [3]// sequent*em* computat*um* p*er* Cxxix dies vj li' ix s' Eidem Petro [4]// pro vadijs Gerardi Crawell' extra Curiam ad xij d' iiij[or] vall*ettorum* [5]// quoli*bet* ad iiij d' iiij portou*rs* quoli*bet* ad ij d' *et* put*ur*a xvj Falconu*m* [6]// quoli*bet* ad j d' p*er* diem . a primo die Octobr*is* vsq*ue* vltimum diem [7]// eiusdem mensis computat*um* p*er* xxxj . dies . vj li' . xiiij s' iiij d' [8]// Baldewino Berford' Militi Custod*i* de les Mewes p*ro* vad*iis* su*is* [9]// consuet*is* p*ro* eadem Custodia ad xij d' p*er* diem a . vij die Febr*uarii* [10]// vsq*ue* xxvj diem Iulij p*ro*x*imo* sequent*em* pro[i] . Clxx . dies viij li' x s'. [11]// Eidem Baldewino pro vadijs Grerardi[i] Crawell' ex*tra* Cur*iam* [12]// ad xij d' iiij[or] vall*ettorum* quoli*bet* ad iiij d' iiij[or] portitor*um* . quoli*bet* ad ij d' [13]// *et* put*ur*a xxj Falconu*m* . quoli*bet* ad j d' p*er* diem a xxvj . die Marcij [14]// vsq*ue* xxvj diem Iulij . p*ro*x*imo* sequent*em* vtroq*ue* die comput*ato* [15]// p*er* Cxxiij dies xxix li'. iiij s' . iij d' [16]//

[h] xij d' per diem *in the margin.*
[i] *Sic in MS.*

c. Exchequer, T.R., Council and Privy Seal Files (E. 28), 1

CORRECTED ENGROSSMENT (*LITTERE RESCRIBENDE*) OF A PRIVY-SEAL BILL ordering the issue of a protection (letters patent under the great seal). Dated at Westminster, 5 July, regnal year 13 (1389). Parchment. Filing hole.

The sealed engrossment has survived in Chancery Warrants (C. 81), 1051/3, dated at Westminster, 10 July, regnal year 13.

The great-seal letters are enrolled on Treaty Roll 13 Richard II (C. 76/74), m. 26 (Westminster, 10 July [1389]).

Fiat proteccio cum clausula volumus pro Ric*ardo* Mercer de Somersham qui in obsequium n*ostru*m ad partes Picardie p*ro*fectur*us* est / ibidem [1]// in comitiua dil*ecti et* fidelis n*ost*ri Thome [T]albot Militis Capitanei Castri n*ost*ri de Guynes in municione eiusdem Castri moratur*us* p*er* unu*m* [2]// annu*m* duratur*a* Dat' sub priuato sigillo n*ost*ro apud Westm' quinto die Iulij . Anno regni n*ost*ri[j] terciodecimo [3]//

[j] *Followed by* terciod *crossed out.*

a

b

c

18

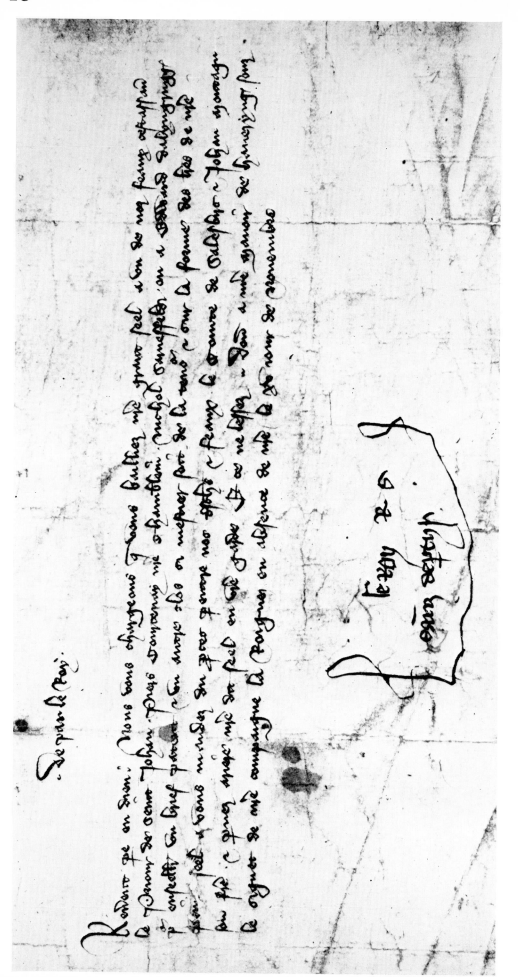

18

a. Chancery Warrants (C. 81), 1354/15

LETTERS CLOSE UNDER THE QUEEN'S SIGNET in the absence of Richard II's own signet, ordering [William of Wykeham], bishop of Winchester, chancellor, to deliver the great seal to one of several persons named in the letters. Dated in the royal manor of Havering[-atte-Bower], 15 November [1389]. Paper. Two vertical and one horizontal folds. Two sets of three slits for insertion of a thong.

At the foot of the letters, the words 'le Roy R*ichard* S*econd* sau*n*z dep*ar*tyr' are in Richard's own hand. Richard's signature proper (sign-manual), 'le Roy R S', occurs in other documents, e.g. Exchequer, T.R., Diplomatic Documents (E. 30), 317; Exchequer, T.R., Scottish Documents (E. 39), 95/12; Brit. Mus., Cotton MS. Vespasian F. iii, fol. 4; Paris, Arch. Nat., J. 644, no. 35/5 (reproduced in *The Dipl. Corr. of Richard II*, ed. E. Perroy (Camden Third Series, xlviii, 1933), frontispiece). The additional words 'saunz departyr' should probably be given the same meaning as the autograph annotation made by Charles V of France on royal letters patent, 'par dey que il ny ait defautey' (G. Tessier, *Diplomatique royale française* (Paris, 1962), plate xiv (1); compare also the autograph note of the Black Prince, 'depar homout Ich dene', reproduced in *Facs. of Nat. MSS.* I. xxix, and see Tout, *Chapters*, v, pp. 371, 380). In *Facs. of Nat. MSS.* I. xxx, Richard's sign-manual appears as 'Richard'. The first English king known to have written his sign-manual on a document is Edward III, who, in June 1362, added the words '*Edwardus* Rex' to letters patent empowering two proctors to negotiate and conclude various agreements with the king of Castile; the document ended with a notarial attestation, which stated that Edward III had written the two words with his own hand: 'Ego Johannes de Branketre . . . scripturam / . E . Rex / manu domini regis propria factam . . . sic fieri vidi . . .' (Treaty Roll 36 Edward III (C. 76/45), m. 6; see also E. 30/191–2: Rymer, *Foedera*, III. ii. 657; Tout, *Chapters*, iii, p. 28, n. 1). Here Edward was imitating Castilian practice (compare the sign-manual 'Yo el Rey' in Rymer, *Foedera*, III. ii, 753, 804). For the words 'Pater sancte' added in Edward III's own hand to a letter sent to the pope in about 1330 and still extant in the Vatican Archives, see Johnson and Jenkinson, plate xxii (*b*); see also V. H. Galbraith, 'The Literacy of the Medieval English Kings', *Proceedings of the British Academy*, xxi (1935), p. 223.

Printed in Maxwell-Lyte, p. 321.

ʃ De par le Roy . [1]//

⁓ Reuerent p*er*e en dieu ʃ Nous vous chargeons q*ue* vous bailliez n*ost*re grant seel a vn de noz feaux cestassau*er* [2]// le Priour de seint Iohan . Piers Courtenay n*ost*re Chamb*er*lein . Nichol Sarnesfeld' ou a Edward dalyngrugg' [3]// *pur* enseell*er* vn brief patent *et* vn autre clos si mestier soit de la tenou*r* *et* sur la forme des l*ett*res de n*ost*re [4]// priu[e] seel a vous mandez du p*ro*ces p*ar*entre nos t*re*schers *et* feaux le Counte de Salesbirs *et* Iohan Montagu [5]// son fr*ere*[a] ʃ *et* p*er*nez ariere n*ost*re dit seel en v*ost*re garde Et ce ne lessez ⁓ Don' a n*ost*re Manoir de Haueryng' souz [6]// le signet de n*ost*re compaigne la Roigne en absence de n*ost*re / le xv iour de Nouembre [7]//

le Roy R S [8]// sau*n*z dep*ar*tyr [9]//[b]

[a] *See Chancery Warrants (C. 81), 509/5693.*

[b] *The document is endorsed*: ⁓ A Reuerent pere en dieu leuesque de ⁓ Wyncestre n*ost*re Chaunceller ⁓

b. Chancery Miscellanea (C. 47), 18/4/13 (1)

GREAT-SEAL WRIT CLOSE OF PROHIBITION (debts and chattels) of Richard II to the abbot of Notley, dated at Westminster, 27 November, regnal year 14 (1390). Step in the bottom left-hand corner. Filing slit.

This is a writ 'of course', issued without any warrant. The name *Billyngford'* is that of a clerk of the crown in the chancery, James Billingford (Tout, *Chapters*, iii, p. 488, n. 3, and p. 492, n. 2). Since Billingford's name is written in a different hand and over an erasure, it is likely that the scribe of the writ was not Billingford himself, but one of the two clerks whom the chancery ordinance of 12 Richard II allowed each of the two clerks of the crown to have (Wilkinson, *The Chancery under Edward III*, p. 218). Billingford's name also occurs in the bottom right-hand corner of various documents in Chancery Files (C. 202), Cancelled Letters Patent, H. 25, H. 30–5, H. 41–4, etc.

ʃ Ricardus dei gr*aci*a Rex Angl*ie* *et* Franc*ie* *et* Do*minus* Hib*er*n*ie* Abb*at*i de Nottele ∴ sal*utem* . Prohibem*us* vob*is* ne sequamini pl*ac*itum in Cur*ia* cr*ist*ianitatis de catallis vel debitis [1]// vnde Ioh*ann*es Bolour Iunior Ioh*ann*es Wynter senior Ioh*ann*es Payn senior Will*elmus* atte Hull' Ioh*ann*es fil*ius* Will*elmi* atte Hull' *et* Rob*er*tus Euote querunt*ur* q*uo*d vos t*ra*hitis [2]// eos in pl*ac*itum in Cur*ia* cr*ist*ianitatis Nisi catalla illa vel debita sint de testamento vel matrimonio Quia pl*ac*ita de catallis *et* debitis que non sunt de [3]// testamento vel matrimonio spectant ad coronam *et* dignitatem n*ost*ram T*este* . me ip*s*o apud Westm' xxvij . die Nouembr*is* anno r*egni* n*ostri* . quartodecimo / [4]//

Billyngford'[c] [5]//

[c] *This name is in a different hand and seems to be written over an erasure.*

a. Paris, Archives Nationales, J. 644, no. 19

PRIVY-SEAL LETTERS PATENT of Richard II, promising to assist Charles VI of France against everyone. Dated in the royal tents near the mill of Ardres, 28 October, regnal year 20 (1396). Parchment. Sealed with the privy seal in red wax, appended on a tag; turn-up.

The wording of the *extra sigillum* notes 'Par le roi en soun consail . . . Frie' and their place on the parchment show a departure from normal English practice and a deliberate attempt at imitating the usage of the French chancery. To quote only one example, letters patent of Charles VI dated at Paris, 29 January 1399 (old style), bear the following note on the left-hand side of the turn-up: '⁓ Par le Roy en son conseil ou messires les ducs de Berry, de Bourgogne, Dorleans et de Bourbon, le Conte de Tancarville et plusieurs autres estoient. J. de Sanctis' (Arch. Nat., J. 644, no. 25; see also Tessier, *Diplomatique royale française*, plate viii). Perhaps Robert Fry, clerk of the privy seal, who signs the document and also seems to have written it, was responsible for this imitation. At any rate, two other documents, sealed with Richard II's privy seal, written and signed by Fry, and delivered to Charles VI, have similar *extra sigillum* notes (Arch. Nat., J. 655, nos. 23 and 23 *bis*). In these two documents Fry does not sign his full name (*Frie*) as here, but only uses the initial *F* as in the letter to his mother partially reproduced in *b*. On Fry's career see Tout, *Chapters*, v, pp. 79, 83, 111, 225, etc.

The document is printed in Froissart, *Œuvres*, ed. Kervyn de Lettenhove, xviii, pp. 582–3.

[*Reduction scale*: *approx.* 9/10]

⁓ Richard par la grace de dieu ⁓ Roy dangleterre *et* de Fraunce *et* Seignur Dirlande ⁓ A touz ceux qui ces l*ett*res verront salut ⁓ Sauoir faisons que a lonneur *et* reu*er*ence [1]// de dieu *et* de sa benoite miere *et* de sainte eglise *et* pour le b*ie*n vniu*er*sel de toute la cr*isti*aintee *et* pour lalliance amour *et* affeccion quele nous auons *et* portons au treshaut *et* tres[2]//puissaunt Prince n*ost*re treschier *et* tresame piere de Fraunce *et* que sembl*able*ment tenons de certain quil nous porte *et* auxi au fin que noz subgiz empuissent le mieux *et* [3]// le plus paisiblement *et* seurement viure a seruir dieu desouz n*ost*re obeissaunce :' Nous pour les causes s*us*dites *et* autres innume*r*ables / iurons *et* promettons par la foi de n*ost*re [4]// corps *et* en parole du Roi *et* par la vraie crois *et* sains euangiles par nous corporelment touches que nous serrons en aide a n*ost*re dit piere countre tous autres gens du mounde [5]// *et* que nous ne serrons durans les trieues prinses parentre lui et nous nulment armes countre lui / et auons comaunde *et* voulons que durant le dit terme nul de noz vncles [6]// cestassauoir les ducs de Guyene *et* de lencastre . York ne Gloucestre ne nul des autres de n*ost*re sanc portans noz armes ne soient nulment ne en nul lieu armez countre n*ost*re [7]// dit piere ne countre le dauphin n*ost*re treschier frere ne ses autres enfauntz p*re*sens *et* auenir ne countre ses Oncles *et* les n*ost*res ne soun frere n*ost*re vncle ne countre les autres de son sanc [8]// *et* de ses armes ⁓ Et voulons outre *et* promettons que se aucun attemptat ou autre chose auenist durans les dites trieues par quoi guerre debat courous ou haine pourroit [9]// aucunement sourdre que dieu deffende :' nous ferrons par les n*ost*res de n*ost*re dit sanc duement les amender *et* redresser par auis *et* counsail des susdiz du sanc de n*ost*re dit piere [10]// au fin que tous soient dun counsail *et* dun auis ⁓ Toutefoiz nous iurons *et* promettons comme dess*us et* sambl*abl*ement voulons *et* comandons que les desusdiz de noz sanc *et* [11]// armes le facent que nous ferrons n*ost*re loial deuoir *et* entier pouoir nonobstans les liens *et* seurementz susdiz au fin que bonne paix finale ce puisse faire parentre lui *et* no*us* [12]// *et* ce le plustost que faire le pouons bonnement / tous cauelacions fraudes *et* excusacions faites cessans ⁓ les trieues prinses parentre nous *et* les alliances f*aic*tes auecques [13]// les alliez dun coste *et* dautre demourans en leur force *et* vertu en la fourme *et* maniere que les trieues le portent ⁓ Toutes lesqueles choses susdites *et* chescune par soi de tenir [14]// *et* guarder *et* faire tenir *et* guarder nous iurons *et* promettons comme desus ⁓ En tesmoigne de ce nous auons fait mettre n*ost*re priue seal a ces presentes ⁓ Donne en noz tentes [15]// esteauntz en champ' pres du molin Dandre[a] le . xxviij . iour Doctobre lan de n*ost*re regne vintisme :'. [16]//

[*On the turn-up*] ⁓ Par le Roi en soun consail ou quel les ducs de Guyene *et* de lencastre [17]// *et* de Gloucestre . *et* les Comtes de derby . de Rutland' . de Huntyndon' . [18]// Mareschall' *et* de Northumbr' . feurent p*re*sens . Frie[b]

[a] *This is a scribal error: a French contemporary copy* (*Arch. Nat., J. 644, no. 19 bis*) *restores the correct reading* Dardre.

[b] rie *written below* F.

b. Exchequer, T.R., Council and Privy Seal Files (E. 28), 29

PRIVATE LETTER (*LITTERE DE STATU*) of Robert Fry to Agnes Fry, his mother, dated at London, 14 January (year unknown). Parchment. Filing hole. For some unknown reason the letter was not sent: it has no slit or traces of seal.

The letter is only reproduced in part, but the full text is given below. Compare the script and signature with those of *a*.

[⁓ Carissima ac dulcissima mater :' Humilima filiali recommendacione premissa :' Ingenti] desiderio affectans de statu v*est*ro vtinam semp*er* prospero *et* felici ʃ audire noua salubria *et* iocunda ∴ [1]// [dulcedinem v*est*ram deprecor affeccione filiali . quatinus de status v*est*ri continencia michi q*u*]amtocius certificare dignemini ʃ pro certo h*ab*itura q*uo*d naturali instinctu dilator gaudiis quociens [2]// [de v*estrorum* felicitate successuum noua michi prospera nunciant*ur* :' Et vtinam vobis ad] vota succedant dies prosperi *et* longeui ⁓ Script' London'. xiiij . die Ianuarij ʃ [3]//

⁓ P*er*humilis filius v*es*ter . F [4]//[c]

[c] *The letter is endorsed*: ⁓ Carissime ac dulcissime Matri sue ⁓ Agneti Frye ʃ

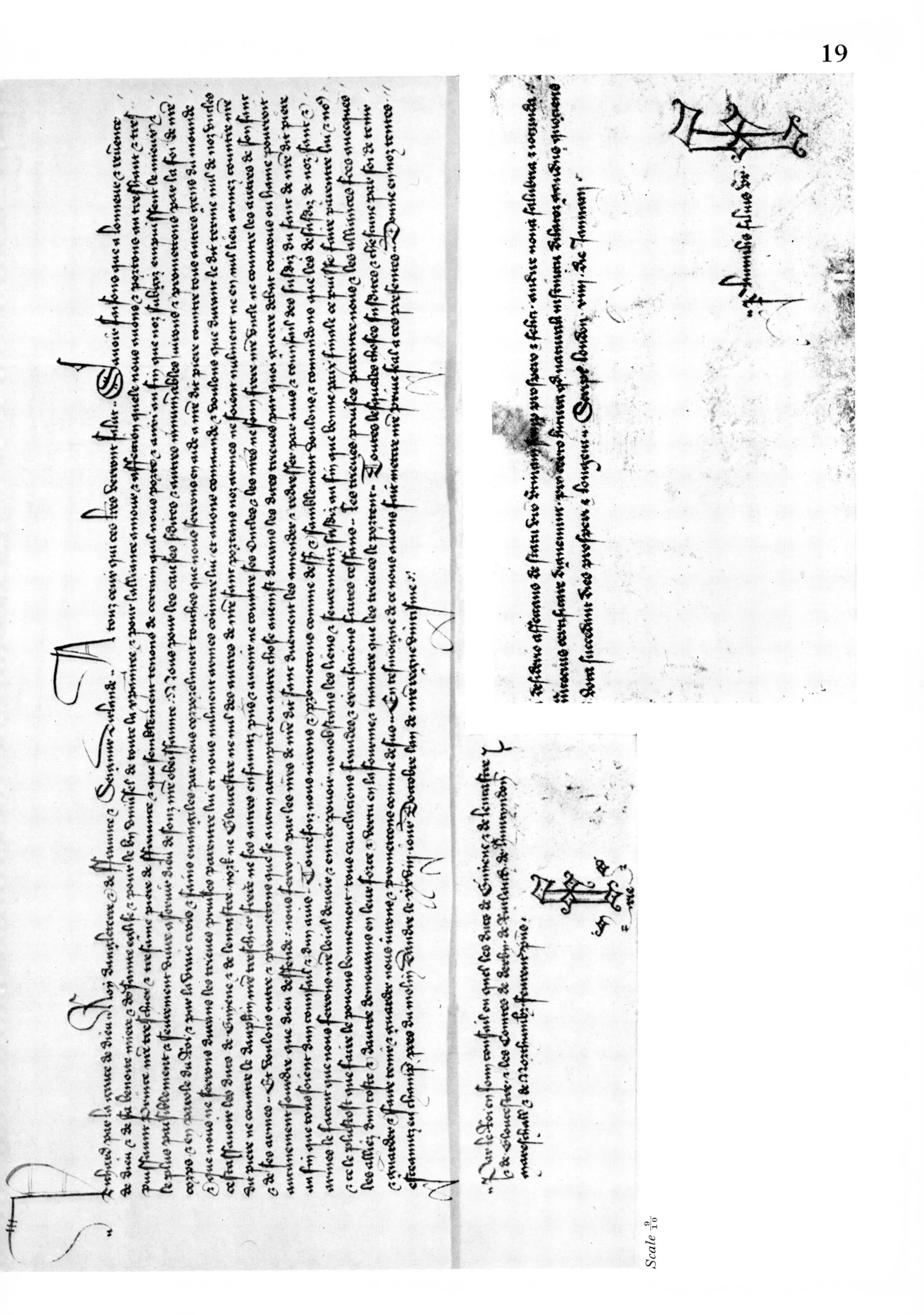

Scale $\frac{9}{10}$

De par le Roi

Tres cher et foial Nous vous chargeons de faire une Saufconduit desouz nostre grand seal de le tenour dune cedule enclose en cestes et le baillier al Currour nostre tres cher et foial cousin le Counte de Northumbr' portour dicestes pur apporter a nostre Adversaire Descoce issint qil poet estre al Abbeie de Kelcowe en Escoce lundy oeptasme iour de Novembr' proschein venant sanz defaute. Don souz nostre prive Signet de Seint Edward a nostre manoir de Wodestok le xxvij iour doctobr'

Ricardus dei gracia Rex Angl' et Franc' et Dominus Hibn' vic' Ebor' et Comit' salutem. Precipimus tibi quod Willelmum Setore idiotam ut dicitur coram nobis in Cancellaria nostra die sabbati proximo ante festum sancti Jacobi Apostoli proximo futurum ubicumque tunc fuerit salvo et secure ac modo honesto venire fac' ad faciendum et recipiendum quod Curia nostra consideravit in hac parte. Et hoc sub periculo quod incumbit nullatenus omittas. Et habeas ibi hoc breve. Teste me ipso apud Westm' xj die Julii anno r. n. vicesimo primo.

Hertilpole

Ricardus dei gracia Rex Anglie et Francie et Dominus Hibernie Omnibus ad quos presentes littere pervenerint salutem. Sciatis quod de gracia nostra speciali concessimus dilecto nobis Ricardo Covyngton officium parcarii parci de Eytoun in Wallia quod quidem officium ad nos pertinet occasione forisfacture Ricardi Comitis Arundell' defuncti. Habendum et tenendum officium illud eidem Ricardo Covyngton pro termino vite sue cum vadiis feodis et proficuis ad idem officium pertinentibus. In cuius rei testimonium has litteras nostras fieri fecimus patentes. Teste me ipso apud Westmonasterium tricesimo die Septembris anno regni nostri vicesimo primo

per breve de privato sigillo

Ffaryngton

Scale $\frac{9}{10}$

20

a. Chancery Warrants (C. 81), 1354/18

LETTERS CLOSE UNDER RICHARD II'S SIGNET OF ST. EDWARD, ordering John Scarle to issue a safe-conduct (letters patent) under the great seal as drafted in the enclosed schedule. Dated in the royal manor of Woodstock, 27 October [1395]. Paper. Fragment of the signet in red wax, applied in the centre of a red-wax cross, on the dorse. Possibly two vertical and one horizontal folds. Slits for insertion of a thong. Filing hole. The schedule (C. 81/1354/17) is stitched to the letters.

The great-seal safe-conduct is enrolled on Scotch Roll 19–20 Richard II (C. 71/74), m. 6: *Rotuli Scotiae*, ii, p. 130*a* (Woodstock, 27 October [1395]; *per litteram ipsius regis de signeto*).

Dep*ar* le Roi [1]//
Ch*er* *et* foial Nous vous chargeons de faire vne Saufconduit / desouz n*ost*re grand seal de le tenour dune cedule enclose [2]// [en] ycestes *et* le baillier al Currour n*ost*re ch*er* *et* foial Cousin le Count / de Northumbr' / portour dicestes pur [3]// apportier a n*ost*re Aduersaire Descoce :' issint qil poist / estre al Abbeie de Kelcowe en Escoce lundy oeptisme [4]// iour de Nouembr*e* proschein venant sanz defaute . Don' souz n*ost*re p*ro*pre Signet de Seint Edward' a n*ost*re [5]// Manoir de Wodestok / le xxvij[e] . iour Doctobre / [6]//[a]

[a] *The document is endorsed*: A n*ost*re ch*er* *et* foial s*ire* Iohan Scarle Gard (*the rest of the endorsement is cut off*). *John Scarle was at the time keeper of the rolls of the chancery, but he also acted as keeper of the great seal on several occasions before he became chancellor in 1399.*

b. Chancery Files (C. 202), C. 102/30

GREAT-SEAL WRIT CLOSE of Richard II to the sheriff of Dorset and Somerset, dated at Westminster, 6 July, regnal year 21 (1397). Parchment. Filing hole.

This writ was issued without a royal warrant, at the command of the chancellor, as its endorsement 'p*er* Cance*llarium*' shows. The name *Hertilpole* is that of the chancery clerk of the first bench (*de prima forma*) named John Hartipole in the chancery ordinance of 12 Richard II (Wilkinson, *The Chancery under Edward III*, pp. 218, 220). He took the responsibility for the writing of the document, but probably did not write it himself. His name is also found in the bottom right-hand corner of various documents in Chancery Files (C. 202), Cancelled Letters Patent, H. 30–43, etc.

Ricardus dei gr*aci*a Rex Angli*e* *et* Franci*e* *et* D*omi*n*us* Hib*er*ni*e* . vic*ecomiti* Dors' :' *et* Som*ers*' :' salutem . Precipim*us* tibi q*uo*d Will*elmu*m Brecore idiotam vt dicit*ur* . coram nob*is* in Cancellar*ia* n*ost*ra [1]// die sabb*at*i p*ro*xi*ma* ante festum s*anct*i Iacobi Ap*osto*li p*ro*xi*mo* futur*um* vbicumq*ue* tunc fu*er*it saluo *et* secure ac modo honesto venire fac*ias* . ad faciend*um* *et* recipiend*um* quod Cur*ia* n*ost*ra [2]// considerau*er*it in hac parte . Et hoc sub p*er*iculo quod incumbit . nullatenus omittas . Et h*ab*eas ibi hoc bre*ue* . T*este* me ip*so* apud . Westm' . vj . die Iulij . anno r*egni* . n*ostri* . [3]// vicesimo primo. . Hertilpole [4]//[b]

[b] *The name* Hertilpole *is in a lighter ink. The writ is endorsed in two contemporary hands:* [*1*] p*er* Cance*llarium* [*2*] Ego Ioh*ann*es Rodeneye vic*ecomes* vob*is* mitto Will*elmu*m Brecore infrascriptu*m* p*er* latorem p*re*senciu*m* ad faciend*um* *et* recipiend*um* p*ro*ut istud bre*ue* requirit

c. Chancery Files (C. 202), Cancelled Letters Patent, H. 34/24

CANCELLED LETTERS PATENT (GRANT OF OFFICE) of Richard II for Richard Donyngton, dated at Westminster, 30 September, regnal year 21 (1397). Parchment. Originally sealed with the great seal, appended on a tag, but the tag has been torn off. Three herring-bone cuts for cancellation. Filing hole.

The privy-seal writ mentioned in the warranting note 'p*er* bre*ue* de priuato sigillo' has survived in Chancery Warrants (C. 81), 567/11454, dated at Westminster, 30 September, regnal year 21 (French). The name *Faryngton*' stands for Robert Faryngton, a chancery clerk (see Maxwell-Lyte, pp. 12, 85). He either wrote the letters patent or at least took the responsibility for the writing. His name also occurs in the bottom right-hand corner of various documents in Chancery Files (C. 202), Cancelled Letters Patent, H. 20–4, H. 30–5, etc.

The letters patent are enrolled on Patent Roll 21 Richard II, Part I (C. 66/347), m. 13: *C.P.R. 1396–1399*, p. 205.

[*Reduction scale*: 9/10]

Ricardus dei gracia Rex Anglie *et* Francie *et* Dominus Hib*er*nie Omnib*us* ad quos p*re*sentes l*itt*ere p*er*uen*er*int :' sal*ute*m Sciatis q*uo*d de gr*aci*a [1]// n*ost*ra spe*ci*ali . concessimus dil*ec*to nobis Ric*ard*o Donyngton' officium parcarij parci de Eyton' in Wallia :' quod quidem officium [2]// ad nos p*er*tinet occ*asi*one forisfacture Ric*ard*i Comitis Arundell' defuncti :' habend*um* d*ictu*m officium eidem Ric*ard*o Donyngton' pro [3]// t*er*mino vite sue cum vadiis feodis *et* p*ro*ficuis ad idem officium p*er*tinentib*us* . In cuius rei testimonium has l*itt*eras n*ost*ras [4]// fieri fecimus patentes. Teste me ip*so* apud Westmonast*er*ium tricesimo die Septembris anno regni n*ost*ri vicesimo primo [5]// / p*er* bre*ue* de priuato sigillo / Faryngton' [6]//[c]

[c] *The document is endorsed:* vacant q*uia* restitute fueru*nt* eo q*uo*d d*omi*n*us* Re*x* infrascr*iptus* xij die Nou*embris* anno infrascr*ipto* concessit infrascr*ipto* Ric*ard*o officiu*m* infrascr*iptum* h*abendum* durante vita sua vna cum vadiis trium denarior*um* p*er* die*m* *et* aliis feodis *et* p*ro*ficuis eide*m* officio p*er*tinentib*us* . Et i*deo* iste l*itt*ere cance*llantur* *et* dampnant*ur* .

21

a. Warrants for the Privy Seal, Series I (P.S.O. 1), 1/52A

SIGNET LETTERS CLOSE of Henry IV to Thomas Langley, keeper of the privy seal, ordering him to issue a warrant to the sheriff of Gloucester under the privy seal. Dated at Abingdon, 5 January, [regnal year 5 (1404)]. Parchment. Two vertical and one horizontal folds. On the dorse, a red-wax cross where the signet was applied. Nine slits for insertion of a thong. [*Reduction scale*: 9/10]

~ Depar le Roy . [1]//

~ Trescher *et* bi*en* ame Nous vous mandons que par noz l*ett*res de garant a faire soubz n*ost*re priue seal en due forme . vous donez en mandement depar nous a n*ost*re [2]// visconte de Gloucestre . que a William Smyth de Gloucestre Nailer *et* a Thomas Malmesbury *et* cynk de ses compaignons Carpentiers . il face paier en [3]// la p*re*sence *et* par tesmoignance du Constable de n*ost*re Chastel de Gloucestre sessante *et* dys *et* oyt souldz *et* neuf deniers par nous a eux duz sicome ils dient [4]// po*ur* certeins ou*er*eignes par eux faitz a diu*er*ses foiz sur la reparacion *et* amendement des defaultes de n*ost*re dit Chastel . par lordenance *et* auis du dit Constable [5]// *et* dautres noz officers illoeques po*ur* la greindre seurete *et* defense de mesme n*ost*re Chastel ~ Donne souz n*ost*re signet a n*ost*re ville de Abyndon le . quint Iour [6]// de Ianuer .[7]//

¶[a] le xxviij . iour de Ianuer lan *etc*' quint p*re*sens en le Consail messeign*urs* lerceuesq*ue* de Cantirbirs . le Chan*cellier* . *et* le Gardein du [8]// priue seal . accordez estoit . q*ue* garant soit fait as Tresorer *et* Chamb*er*leins de leschequier . pur faire le susdit paiement . [9]//[b]

[a] *This council memorandum, which changes the royal order for a warrant to the sheriff of Gloucester into an order for a warrant to the treasurer and chamberlains of the exchequer, is written in a different hand, presumably that of a privy-seal or council clerk.*

[b] *The document is endorsed:* (*1*) ~ A n*ost*re tresch*er* clerc Thomas Longley Gardein de n*ost*re priue seal . . (*2*) . Pur William Smyth *et* autres .   . Soit fait . *These endorsements are in two different hands; the first was written by a signet clerk and the second presumably by a council or privy-seal clerk.*

b. Eyre, Writ Files (J.I. 4), 6/1/121

'JUDICIAL' WRIT CLOSE OF 'HABEAS CORPUS' (*non omittas*) of Henry IV to the sheriff of Worcester, attested by H[ugh] Huls, [justice of the king's bench and justice of assize *pro hac vice*]. Dated at Worcester, 3 March, regnal year 8 (1407). Parchment. Filing hole. The name *Heuster* is that of the clerk who wrote the document, possibly Thomas Heuster. There is no punctuation mark.

Henricus dei gr*aci*a Rex Angl*ie et* Franci*e et* Dom*in*us Hib*er*n*ie* vic*ecomiti* Wygorn' sal*utem* Precipim*us* tibi q*uo*d non omittas p*ro*pt*er* aliquam lib*er*tatem Com*itatus* tui quin capias Ioh*ann*em [1]// Rauenesby Thomam Rauenesby *et* Ioh*ann*em Draper de Kydermynster si inuenti fu*er*int in balliua tua Et eos saluo custod*ias* Ita q*uo*d h*ab*eas corpora eor*um* coram [2]// Iustic*iariis* nost*ri*s ad assis*as* in Com*itatu* tuo capiend*as* assign*atis* apud Wygorn' die ven*er*is p*ro*x*ima* post festum s*anc*ti Cedde Ep*iscop*i ad satisfaciend*um* nobis de redempc*ione* [3]// sua de eo q*uo*d ad nos p*er*tinet p*ro* quadam disseis*in*a Ric*ard*o Russeby vi *et* armis *et* cont*ra* pacem nost*ra*m de ten*emen*to in Kydermynstre f*ac*ta Et h*ab*eas ibi hoc breue [4]// T*est*e H Huls apud Wygorn' t*er*cio die Marcij anno r*egni* n*ost*ri octauo   Heuster [5]//[c]

[c] *The writ is endorsed:* Ricard*us* de bello Campo vic*ecomes* Ioh*ann*es Rauenesby *et* om*n*es alij in bre*ui* isto no*minati* no*n* sunt inuent*i* in balliua mea postq*ua*m breue istud m*ichi* liberatu*m* fuit . [*There is one extra minim at the beginning of* inuent*i*].

c. Exchequer of Receipt, Writs and Warrants for Issues (E. 404), 29/55

GREAT-SEAL WRIT CLOSE OF LIBERATE of Henry V to the treasurer and chamberlains of the exchequer, dated at Westminster, 7 November, regnal year 1 (1413). Parchment. Small step in the bottom left-hand corner. Filing hole.

Simon Gaunstede, whose name is found in the bottom right-hand corner, was a chancery clerk of the first bench (Tout, *Chapters*, iii, p. 488, n. 3, and p. 492, n. 2; iv, p. 63). His name also occurs in the bottom right-hand corner of various documents in Chancery Files (C. 202), Cancelled Letters Patent, H. 30–5, H. 47–55, etc.

The writ is enrolled on Liberate Roll 1 Henry V (C. 62/147), m. 6 (Westminster, 7 November [1413]).

Henricus dei gr*aci*a Rex Angl*ie et* Franci*e et* Dom*in*us Hib*er*n*ie* Thes*aurario et* Cam*er*ar*iis* suis . sal*utem* ſ lib*er*ate de th*esaur*o n*ost*ro dil*ect*o *et* fideli n*ost*ro Ioh*ann*i Colpeper vni [1]// Iustic*iariorum* n*ost*ror*um* ad assisas in diu*er*sis Com*itatibus* regni n*ost*ri Angl*ie* capiend*as et* ad gaolas deliб*er*and*as* assign*atorum* decem libras p*ro* termino s*an*c*t*i Mich*ae*lis vltimo [2]// p*re*t*er*ito de annuo feodo suo viginti librar*um* quod ei concessim*us* p*er*cipien*dum* in officio sup*ra*d*ic*to T*este* me ipso apud Westm' vij die Nouembr*is* [3]// anno r*egni* n*ost*ri primo.   Gaunstede [4]//

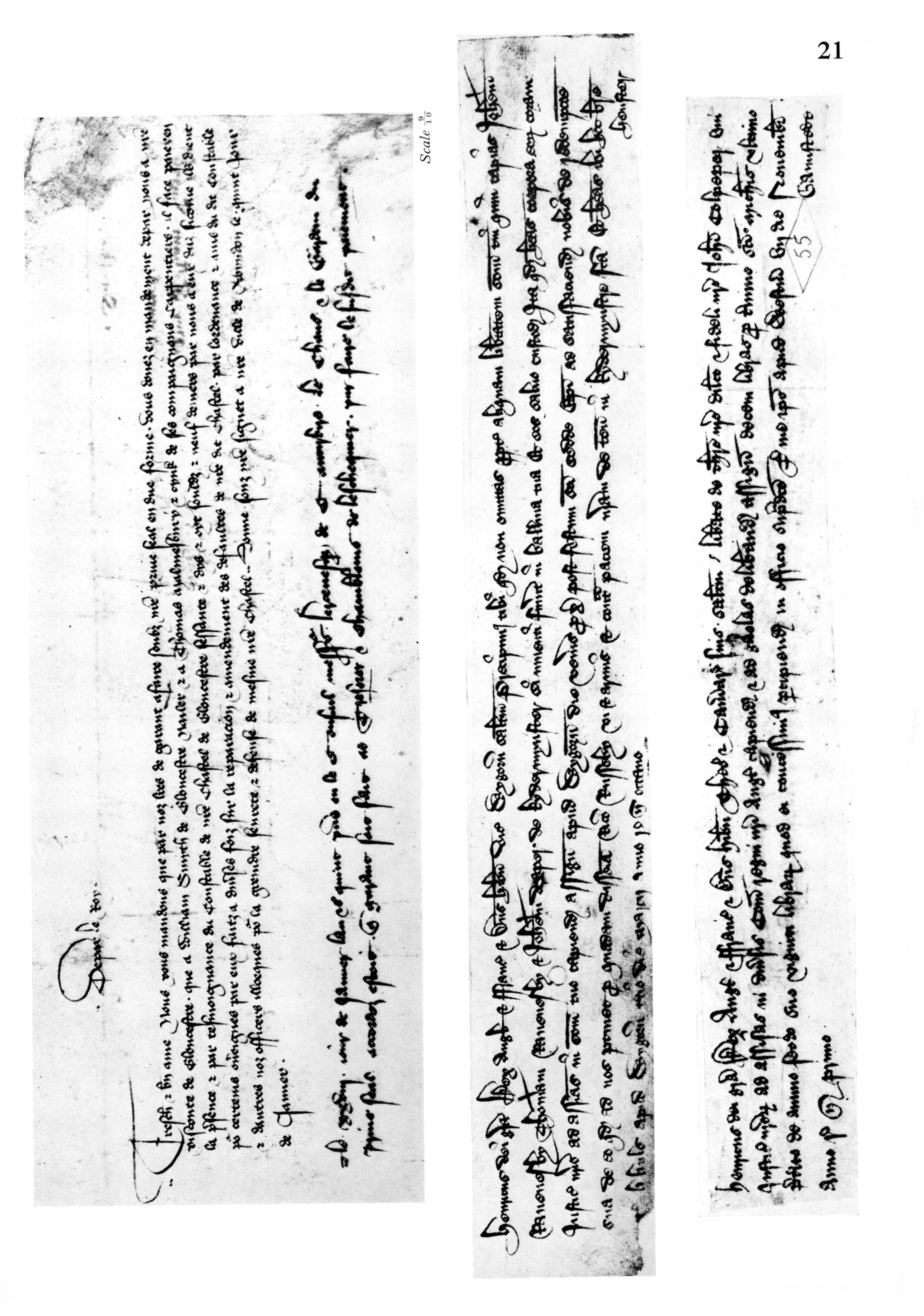

Scale $\frac{9}{10}$

Scale $\frac{9}{10}$

22

a. Exchequer of Receipt, Writs and Warrants for Issues (E. 404), 31/322

PRIVY-SEAL WRIT CLOSE (WARRANT FOR ISSUES) of Henry V to the treasurer and chamberlains of the exchequer, dated at Westminster, 27 May, regnal year 3 (1415). Parchment. Step in the bottom left-hand corner. One horizontal and two vertical folds. Traces of the privy seal in red wax on the dorse, close to the right margin, over a slit. Six slits for insertion of a tongue. Filing hole. [*Reduction scale*: 9/10]

Henri par la grace de dieu Roy Dengleterre *et* de France *et* Seignur Dirlande ⁓ As Tresorer *et* Chamb*er*leins de n*ost*re Eschequer ſ saluz ⁓ [1]// Nous vous mandons q*ue* veue lendenture f*aicte* parentre nous et Thomas Tunbrigge / William Bangore / Hugh' Bigge / Roger Chieff / [2]// Henri Shipley / Thomas Hampton' / Richard Burton' / Iohan Botiller / Iohan North'folk' / Iohan Hille / Roger Seinper / Iohan [3]// Birkyn / Thomas Swetenham / Iohan Spaldy[ng] / Iohan Walssh' / Richard Filongley / Iohan Bannebury / William Alcok' / Iohan [4]// Mikelfeld / Henri Scalder / Gregoire Scaldyr / William Shorn / Richard Breustere *et* Rauf Passenham vadletz de n*ost*re houstel [5]// de ce quils sont demorez deuers nous pur nous faire s*er*uice de guerre en le voiage q*ue* nous ferons se dieu plest deinz br*ef* ſ facez [6]// paier a ch*asc*un de eux tielx gages *et* par manere come preignent de nous les arch*er*s qui pass*er*ont ouesq*ue* les Esquiers qui ont [7]// endentez ouesq*ue* nous a cause du viage susdit *et* selonc leffect de lendenture auantd*icte* ⁓ Don' souz n*ost*re priue seal a Westm' le . [8]// xxvij . iour de May / lan de n*ost*re regne tierz ⁓[9]//[a]

[a] *Below the text of the writ the following note (not reproduced) is written in a second hand*: super vad*iis* s*uis* ad xx mar*cas* p*ro* die [*or* p*er* die*m*] quarto a*nno* cuil*ibe*t xxiiij p*er*sonar*um* pred*ic*tar*um* xxxiij s' iiij d' Sum*ma* tot*alis* xl li' *and in a third hand:* h*ab*et bill*am*

b. Chancery Warrants (C. 81), 1537/4

SIGNET LETTERS CLOSE of [Humphrey], duke of Gloucester, keeper of England, ordering [Thomas Langley], bishop of Durham, chancellor, to issue a writ of passage under the great seal. Dated at York, 8 August [1420]. Paper. Possibly two vertical and two horizontal folds. Slits for insertion of a thong.

⁓ Le duc de Gloucestre [1]// Gardein Dengle-t*erre* [2]//

⁓ Reu*er*end p*er*e en dieu n*ost*re tresch*er* *et* tresentierem*en*t b*ie*n ame Nous volons a linstance *et* priere du t*re*sreu*er*end p*er*e en dieu lercheuesq*ue* [3]// Deu*er*wike / que a son Cousin Henri Bowet Archediakne de Richemond' qui desire grandem*en*t dexercer son estudie a luniu*er*sitee [4]// de Boloigne pour son greindre honour *et* meilleur apris . veullez faire auoir vn brief de passage soubz le grant [5]// seal en due forme / par force du quel brief / il purra seurem*en*t passer ouec sept hom*me*s a cheual en sa co*m*paignie [6]// hors du Roialme / p*ar*deue*r*s la d*ic*te vniu*er*sitee / sans destourbance ou empeschement ⁓ Donne soubz n*ost*re signet a Eu*er*wik [7]// le viij[me] . iour daoust ⁓ [8]//[b]

[b] *The document is endorsed*: ⁓ Au Reu*er*end p*er*e en dieu n*ost*re tresch*er* *et* t*re*sent*er*ement b*ie*n ame leuesq*ue* de Duresme Chanc*ellier* Dengleterre .

23

a. Chancery Files (C. 202), Cancelled Letters Patent, H. 58/13

CANCELLED LETTERS PATENT (GRANT OF PENSION) of Henry VI for Robert Dauson, dated at Westminster, 12 January, regnal year 15 (1437). Parchment. Formerly sealed with the great seal, appended on a tongue, but the tongue has been torn off. Three herring-bone cuts for cancellation. Two filing holes. The name *Selby*, i.e. Richard Selby, a chancery clerk, also occurs in the bottom right-hand corner of various documents in Chancery Files (C. 202), Cancelled Letters Patent, H. 56–8; see also *Merton Muniments*, ed. P. S. Allen and H. W. Garrod (Oxford Hist. Soc., 1928), plate xviii.

Enrolled on Patent Roll 15 Henry VI (C. 66/440), m. 43: *C.P.R. 1436–1441*, p. 18.

Henricus dei gr*aci*a Rex Angl*ie et* Franc*ie et* Dominus Hib*ernie* Om*n*ib*us* ad quos p*re*sentes l*itt*ere p*er*uen*er*int ʃ sal*ute*m . Sciatis q*uo*d nos considerantes bona *et* gratuita 1// s*er*uicia que dil*ect*us s*er*uitor nost*er* Rob*er*tus Dauson' vnus valettor*um* de Corona nob*is* impendit *et* impendet infutur*um* de gr*aci*a n*ost*ra spe*ci*ali concessim*us* ei sex 2// denarios p*er* diem p*er*cipiend*os* annuatim q*ua*mdiu nob*is* placu*er*it de exitib*us et* p*ro*ficuis de Com*itatu* Deuon' p*ro*uenientib*us* p*er* manus vic*ecomitis* eiusdem Com*itatus* p*ro* 3// tempore existent*is* ad t*er*minos Pasche *et* s*an*c*t*i Mich*ael*is p*er* equales porc*ion*es ʃ eo q*uo*d p*re*dic*t*us Rob*er*tus h*ab*et ex concessione carissimi d*omi*ni *et* p*at*ris n*ost*ri 4// Regis defuncti ad t*er*minu*m* vite sue nouem libras vndecim solidos *et* quatuor denarios de vlnagio Com*itatus* Oxon' *et* Berk' aceciam ex concessione 5// n*ost*ra officiu*m* Parcarij parci n*ost*ri de Eltham non obstant*e* . In cuius rei testimoniu*m* has l*itt*eras n*ost*ras fieri fecim*us* patentes T*este* me ip*s*o apud 6// Westm' xij die Ianuarij Anno r*egni* n*ostri* quintodecimo

Selby 7//[a]

[a] *The document is endorsed:* ¶ vac*ant* q*uia* restitut*e* fuer*unt* eo q*uo*d d*omi*n*us* Rex infrascr*iptus* xxix die Septembr*is* anno r*egni* sui xvj°. conc*essit* infrascr*ipto* Rob*er*to infrascr*iptos* sex denarios p*ro* t*er*mi*no* vite sue Et i*deo* iste l*itt*ere cance*llantur et* dampn*antur*

b. Exchequer, T.R., Council and Privy Seal Files (E. 28), 65

WARRANT (BILL) UNDER THE SIGN MANUAL of Henry VI. Parchment. Two slits for insertion of a thong, which apparently attached the present document to the next one in the file; the date of both seems to be 16 November, regnal 19 (1440). Filing hole. At the top of the warrant, the letters 'R H' are in Henry VI's own hand.

R H 1//

The Kyng will' that the Chaunceller of England and the Keper of the priue seale do make warrantes fro tyme to tyme as many 2// and suche as semeth necessarie and expedient ∴ and for the causes and maters aforsaide by the avise and assent of the 3// Tresourer of England . any acte Statute ordinance or maundement made in contrarie noght withstondyng' . 4//

c. Exchequer, T.R., Council and Privy Seal Files (E. 28), 78

DRAFT PRIVY-SEAL LETTER of Henry VI to Charles [? count of Eu], dated at Westminster, 4 April, regnal year 27 (1449). Parchment.

De par le Roy 1//

Charles Nous auons entendu le contenu de voz l*ett*res q*ue* nagaires escriptes nous auez pour cause dune Barge a vous appartenant q*ue* on dit 2// nagaires auoir este prinse sur la mer par aucuns noz subgietz de pardeca en n*ost*re Roy*au*me Dangleterre contre la teneur des treues estans 3// entre nous *et* n*ost*re tresche*r* Oncle de france laquele prinse a este faicte a n*ost*re desplaisance Et pour ce bien effectuelme*nt* auons enchargie 4// *et* coma*n*de a gens notables *et* de grant auctorite que par prinse de corps *et* de biens delinquans la chose soit tantost Reparee Si 5// faichiez[b] que prochaineme*nt* vous en aurez tele deliurance ou Restituc*io*n que par raisou*n* en durez estre content Car de n*ost*re part 6// souueraineme*nt* nous desirons que les d*ict*es treuez soient gardees *et* entretenues Inuiolableme*nt* . sans enfraindre Donne *etc'* 7// a Westm' le iiij^me^ Iour dauril Lan de n*ost*re Regne xxvij^me^. / 8//

[b] *Scribal error for* saichiez.

Henricus dei gratia Rex Anglie & Francie & Dominus Hibernie Omnibus ad quos presentes littere pervenerint salutem. Sciatis quod nos considerantes bona & grata servicia que dilectus serviens noster Robertus Danson unus valettorum de corona nostra nobis impendit & impendet in futurum de gratia nostra speciali concessimus ei sex denarios per diem percipiendos annuatim quamdiu nobis placuerit de exitibus & proficuis de com Devon provenientibus per manus vicecomitis eiusdem com pro tempore existentis ad terminos Pasche & sancti Michaelis per equales porciones eo quod predictus Robertus habet ex concessione carissimi domini & patris nostri Regis defuncti ad terminum vite sue novem libras undecim solidos & quatuor denarios de ulnagio com Oxon & Berk ac etiam ex concessione nostra officium parcarii parce nostre de Eltham non obstante. In cuius rei testimonium has litteras nostras fieri fecimus patentes. Teste me ipso apud Westm xii die Januarii Anno r. n. quintodecimo.

Selby

R H

The kyng wol that the Chaunceller of England and the keper of the prive seale do make warrantes fro tyme to tyme as many and suche as semith necessarie and expedient &c and for the causes and materes aforsaide by the avise and assent of the Tresorer of England any acte Statute ordinance or mandement made in contrarie noght withstondyng.

De par le Roy

Charles Nous avons entendu le contenu de voz lettres nagaires escriptes a nous pour cause dune barge a vous appartenant quon dit nagaires avoir este prinse sur la mer par aucuns noz subgetz de pardeca en nostre Royaume dangleterre contre la teneur des treves estans entre nous & nostre treschier oncle de france laquele prinse a este faicte a nostre desplaisance Et pour ce bien effectuelment avons enchargie & comande a gens notables & de grant auctorite que par prinse de corps & de biens delinquans la chose soit tantost reparee Si sachiez que prochainement vous en aurez tele delivrance ou restitucion que par raison en devrez estre content Car de nostre part souverainement nous desirons que lesdites treves soient gardees & entretenues inviolablement sans enfraindre Donne &c a Westm le iiiime jour davril lan de nostre regne xxviime.

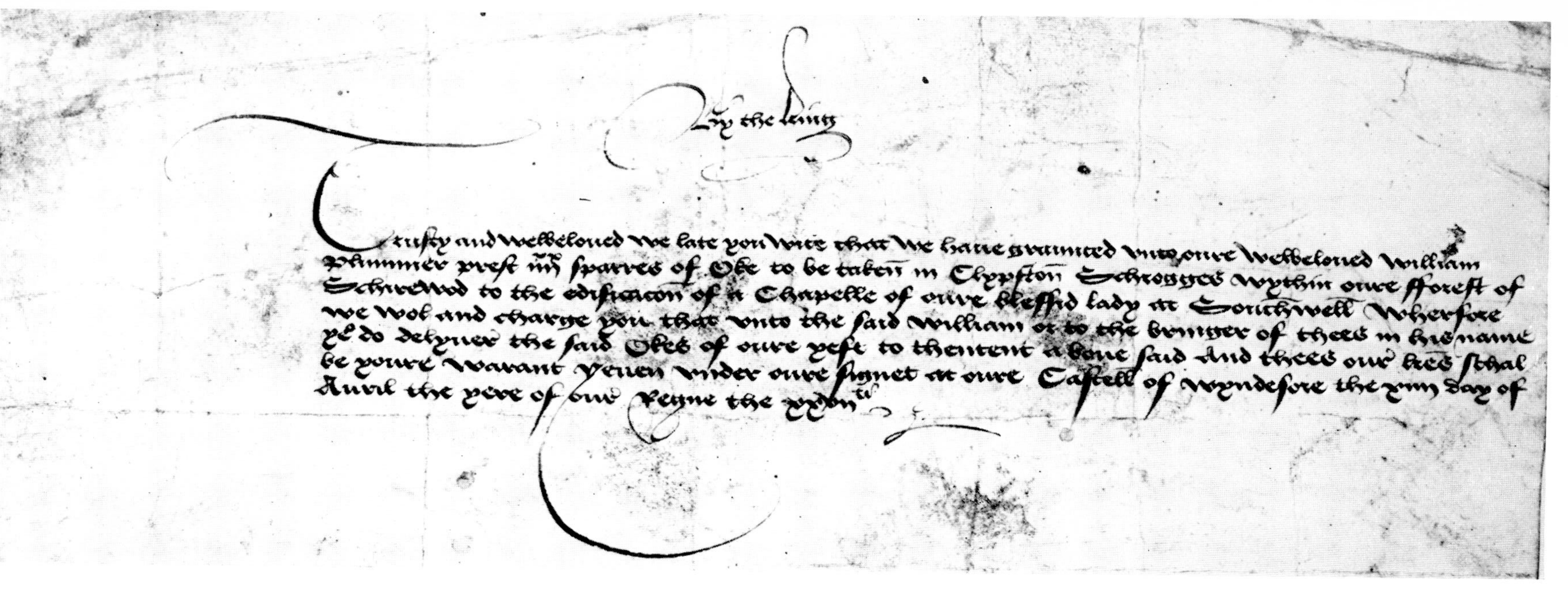

By the King

Trusty and welbeloved we late you wite that we have graunted unto oure welbeloved William Plummer prest iiij sparres of Oke to be taken in Clypston Schrogges within oure fforest of Schirewod to the edificacon of a Chapelle of oure blessed lady at Southwell Wherfore we wol and charge you that unto the said William or to the berrer of thees in his name ye do delyver the said Okes of oure yefte to thentent abovesaid And thees oure lettres shal be youre warant Yeven under oure signet at oure Castell of Wyndesore the xiiij day of Auril the yere of oure Reigne the xxxiiijti

Scale 9

24

a. Exchequer, T.R., Council and Privy Seal Files (E. 28), 78

SIGNET LETTERS CLOSE of Henry VI to the master forester of Sherwood Forest, dated at Windsor Castle, 14 April, regnal year 27 (1449). Parchment. On the dorse, a red-wax cross, where the signet was applied. Two vertical and one horizontal folds. Six sets of double slits for insertion of a thong.

By the King [1]//

Trusty and welbeloued we late you wite that we haue graunted vnto oure welbeloued William [2]// Plummer prest iiij[xx] sparres of Oke to be taken' in Clypston' Schrogges wythin oure Forest of [3]// Schirewod to the edificac*i*on of a Chapelle of oure blessid lady at South'well' Wherfore [4]// we wol and charge you that vnto the said William or to the bringer of thees in his name [5]// ye[o] do delyuer' the said Okes of oure yeft to thentent aboue said and thees our*e* l*ett*res schal [6]// be youre warant Yeuen vnder oure signet at oure Castell' of Wyndesore the xiiij day of [7]// Auril the yere of our*e* Regne the xxvij[ti] [8]//[a]

[a] *Endorsed:* To oure trusty and welbeloued the Maist*er* forster of oure Forest of Schirwode or to his lieuten*ant* or depute there .

b. Chancery, Parliament and Council Proceedings (C. 49), file 31/1

COUNCIL WARRANT for the issue of letters [patent] of safeguard under the great seal for the merchants of Genoa. Dated at Westminster, 26 June, Henry VI's regnal year 34 (1456). Parchment. Filing slit. Signed by T[homas] Kent, clerk of the council; compare the signature with that in Johnson and Jenkinson, plate xxxviii (*b*); *Facs. of Nat. MSS.* I. xlii–xliii. Not only is Kent's signature autograph, but the whole of the document appears to be in his hand; he also wrote the notes *Anno . . . consueta* in Johnson and Jenkinson, loc. cit., *Dictis anno . . . ut patet* in *Facs. of Nat. MSS.* I. xlii, and *xxx[mo] die . . . ut patet*, ibid. I. xliii.

The great-seal letters patent are enrolled on Treaty Roll 34 Henry VI (C. 76/138), m. 4, warranted *per ipsum Regem.* The enrolled safeguard was to last for only two years, whereas the council had apparently agreed to a period of seven years. [*Reduction scale*: 9/10]

Vicesimo sexto die Iunij . Anno *etc*[a] . xxxiiij[to] . apud Westm' / Rex de auisamento consilij sui suscepit in saluam et secura*m* gardiam / [1]// protect*ion*em / tuicionem / et defensionem suas spe*c*iales m*er*catores de Ianua ac factores / attornatos et s*er*uientes suos / in regnu*m* suum [2]// Anglie / ac do*m*inia *et* iurisdict*io*nes sua / quecu*m*q*ue* / cu*m* carracis / galeis / nauib*us* et alijs vasis suis / tam p*er* terra*m* q*u*am p*er* aqua*m* coniu*n*ctim vel diuisim [3]// veniendo ibidem morando ‵ et ′ *per*hendinando / bona et m*er*candisas sua ibidem vendendo / ac lanas pannos laneos stannu*m* *et* alias m*er*candisas [4]// emendo / et de eisdem Regno / do*m*inijs / et iurisdict*io*ne cu*m* carrac*is* / Galeis / nauib*us* / vasis / bonis / m*er*candisis / et hernesijs suis / quociens sibi placu*er*it [5]// t*r*anseundo et redeundo / Ac Carracas / galeas / naues / et vasa h*uius*mod*i* / necnon p*at*ronos / marinarios / et seruientes eor*um* / Ac bona / m*er*candisas [6]// et hernes*ia* sua quecu*m*q*ue* . [b] [7]// Prouiso [8]// semp*er* q*uo*d Carrace / galee / naues / et vasa p*redicta* de amicicia . R*egis* . existant / ac m*er*catores factores et attornati eorudem[c] legales exc*er*ceant [9]// m*er*candisas / ac Custumas subsidia et alia deu*er*ia / R*egi* in hac p*ar*te debita de tempore in tempus fidel*ite*r soluant ʃ q*uo*dq*ue* ijdem m*er*catores [10]// Attornati / p*at*roni / marinarij / et eor*um* s*er*uientes ligeis . R*egis* . pro victualib*us* ab eis empt*is* / et emend*is* satisfac*iant* / Ita tamen / et cu*m* declarac*io*ne [11]// q*uo*d p*er* hanc salua*m* gardia*m* aut eius concession*em* nullu*m* fiat p*re*iudiciu*m* aut derogac*io* amicicie / vnitati / confederac*ioni* / et lige / initis / fact*is* / *et* pen[12]//dentib*us* inter Regem ac vasallos ligeos subditos *et* districtuales eiusd*em* eccl*es*iasticos et seculares Regnu*m*q*ue* suu*m* Anglie /Ac terras p*at*rias Ciui[13]//tates atq*ue* villas *et* do*m*inia sua / et ducem Ianuen*sem* ac co*mmun*itatem Ianue / suosq*ue* subditos / districtuales / ligeos eccl*es*iasticos et sec*u*lares / territoriu*m*q*ue* [14]// eor*um* / terras p*at*rias / ciuitates atq*ue* villas / et do*m*inia sua / p*er* vij Annos duratur*as* . /

T Kent :7 [15]//

[b] *Followed by an erasure of almost two lines.*
[c] *Sic in MS.*

25

a. Oxford University Archives, W.P. β, E 6 (a)

GREAT-SEAL LETTERS PATENT of Henry III, granting to the University of Oxford that in future (*decetero*) the rent of all houses occupied by scholars should be reviewed every five years. Dated at Woodstock, 10 February, regnal year 40 (1256).

Sealed *in modum carte perpetue*. The great seal in green wax is appended on cords of red silk inserted through two sets of two eyelets in the folded lower margin.

Full text in *Mediaeval Archives of the Univ. of Oxford*, ed. H. E. Salter, i (Oxford Hist. Soc. lxx), p. 21, no. 12.

[*Much reduced*]

Henricus Dei gracia rex Anglie, dominus Hybernie, dux Normannie, Aquitannie et comes Andegavie, omnibus ad quos presentes littere pervenerint, salutem. Sciatis quod . . . In cujus rei testimonium has litteras nostras eidem universitati fieri fecimus patentes. Teste me ipso apud Wodestok' decimo die februarii, anno regni nostri quadragesimo.

b. Oxford University Archives, W.P. β, M 3

GREAT-SEAL LETTERS PATENT of Edward I, granting that the chancellor of the University of Oxford may hear personal suits and contracts between the masters and scholars of the University and the king's Jews. Granted during the king's pleasure. Dated at Westminster, 28 April, regnal year 14 (1286).

Sealed with the great seal in natural wax appended on a tongue. Note the presence of a wrapping-tie below the tongue.

Full text ibid., p. 40, no. 29. [*Much reduced*]

Edwardus Dei gracia rex Anglie, dominus Hibernie et dux Aquitannie, omnibus ad quos littere presentes pervenerint, salutem. Sciatis quod . . . In testimonium cujus rei litteras nostras fieri fecimus has patentes, quamdiu nobis placuerit duraturas. Teste me ipso apud Westm' xxviij° die aprilis, anno regni nostri quartodecimo.

c. Oxford University Archives, W.P. β, G 2

GREAT-SEAL LETTERS PATENT (*INSPEXIMUS*) of Henry IV, confirming a grant of Richard II to William Cousin made by letters patent. Dated at Westminster, 2 November, regnal year 1 (1399).

Sealed with the great seal in natural wax appended on a tag, which is inserted through a double slit in the folded lower margin.

Full text ibid., pp. 224–5, no. 139. [*Much reduced*]

Henricus Dei gracia rex Anglie et Francie et dominus Hibernie, omnibus ad quos presentes littere pervenerint, salutem. Inspeximus litteras patentes domini Ricardi nuper regis Anglie secundi post conquestum factas in hec verba: Ricardus Dei gracia rex Anglie et Francie et dominus Hibernie, omnibus ad quos presentes littere pervenerint, salutem. Sciatis quod . . . In cujus rei testimonium has litteras nostras fieri fecimus patentes. Teste me ipso apud Wodestoke decimo die octobris, anno regni nostri undecimo. Nos autem, concessionem predictam ratam habentes et gratam, eam pro nobis et heredibus nostris quantum in nobis est acceptamus, approbamus et tenore presencium de gracia nostra speciali confirmamus, prout littere predicte racionabiliter testantur. In cujus rei testimonium has litteras nostras fieri fecimus patentes. Teste me ipso apud Westm' secundo die novembris, anno regni nostri primo.

Per breve de privato sigillo et pro dimidia marca soluta in hanaperio. Cliderhowe

[*On the turn-up*]: Examinatur per Jacobum Bilyngford' et Johannem Cliderhowe, clericos.

d. Exchequer, K.R., Accounts Various (E. 101), 672/1

WRIT CLOSE OF THE REIGN OF HENRY VIII, plyed for the great seal, but never sealed or sent. A portion of the great seal was supposed to be appended on the tongue, close to the loop. The address on the tongue reads: Custodibus pacis sue in comitatu Hertf' ac vicecomiti ejusdem comitatus et eorum cuilibet de supers*edendo* tam pacis quam boni gestus et fame pro Roberto Frauncys. S. Asshton' [*Much reduced*]

e. Oxford University Archives, W.P. β, N 40

GREAT-SEAL WRIT CLOSE of Edward III to the chancellor and scholars of the University of Oxford. Dated at Westminster, 8 July, regnal year of England 29 and of France 16 (1355).

When it was received, the writ was apparently folded seven times vertically, and the tongue wrapped round the package once and looped through itself near its root. Only one-half of the great seal was used for closing the writ. Two-thirds of the half-seal are preserved on the tongue. In this instance the writ was opened by cutting the tongue a little beyond its original root (without detaching it completely from the main parchment) and sliding the packet out of the looped tongue to the right of the right-hand margin. The seal is in natural wax.

Full text in Salter, op. cit., p. 157, no. 101. [*Much reduced*]

Edwardus Dei gracia rex Anglie et Francie et dominus Hibernie, dilectis sibi cancellario et scolaribus universitatis Oxon', salutem. Cum . . ., nos inde ac de eo quod super hoc faciendum decreveritis reddatis in cancellariam nostram ad cicius quo poteritis cerciores, hoc breve nobis remittentes. Teste me ipso apud Westm' viij die julii, anno regni nostri Anglie vicecimo nono, regni vero nostri Francie sextodecimo.

Per consilium. Wynt'

[*On the tongue*]: Cancellario et scolaribus universitatis Oxon' pro [*sic*].

a

d

b

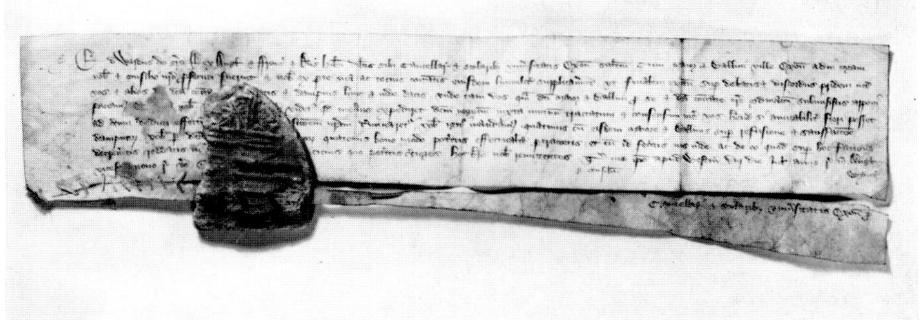

e

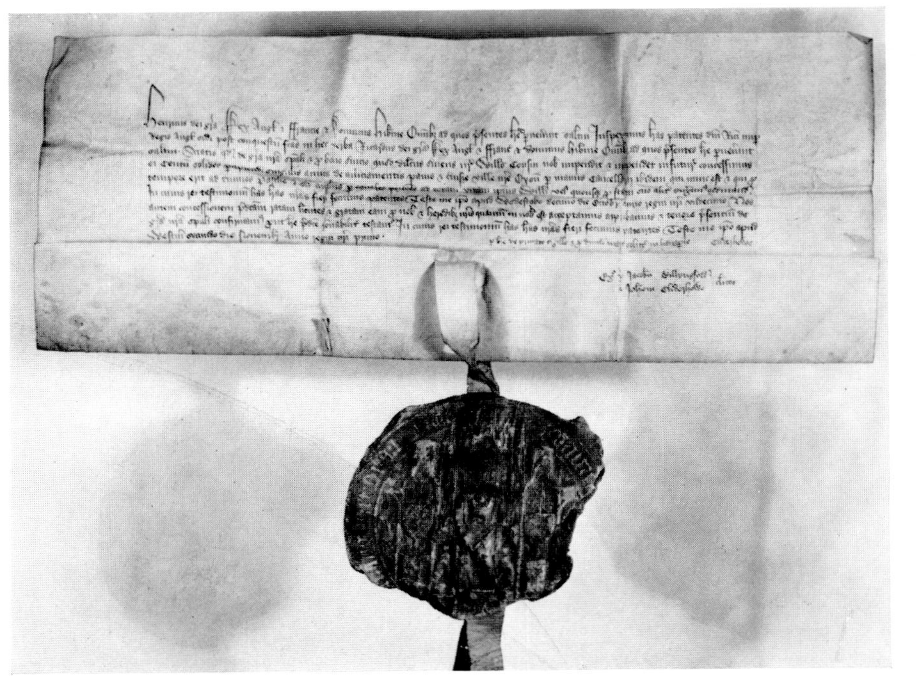

c

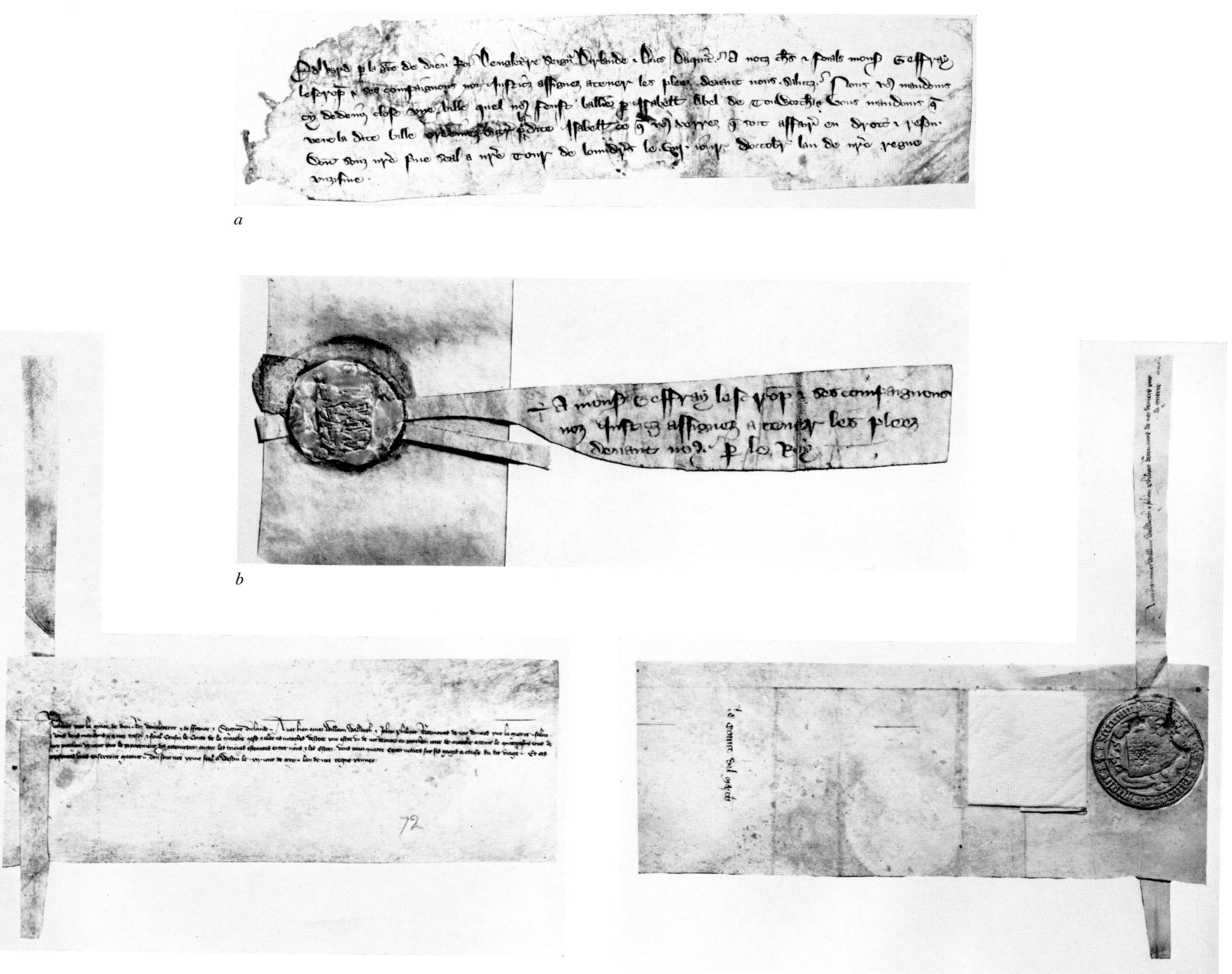

a

b

c

d

a–b. Ancient Correspondence (S.C. 1), vol. 63, no. 211

PRIVY-SEAL WRIT CLOSE of Edward III to Geoffrey Lescrope and his fellow justices of the king's bench, ordering them to examine the enclosed petition (*bille*) and provide remedy. Dated at the Tower of London, 8 October, regnal year 11 (1337).

Sealed with the privy seal in red wax applied over a tongue, approximately half-way between the vertical margins of the writ, fairly close to the lower margin. There are no slits. For the method of sealing, see above, p. 31, drawings 1–4. [(*a*) *more reduced than* (*b*)]

Edward par la grace de Dieu roi Dengleterre, seignur Dirlande et ducs Daquitaine, a notz chers et foials mons' Geffray Lescrop' et ses compaignons noz justicz assignez a tener les pleez devant nous, salutz. Nous vous mandoms cy . . . en droit et reson. Don*e* souz nostre prive seal a nostre Tour de Loundres le viij jour doctobre, lan de nostre regne unzisme.

[*On the tongue*]: A mons' Geffray Lescrop' et ses compaignons noz justicz assignez a tener les pleez devant nous. Par le roy.

c–d. Exchequer, K.R., Accounts Various (E. 101), 37/27/72

PRIVY-SEAL WRIT CLOSE of Richard II to William Walworth and John Philipot, receivers for war, ordering them to pay 400 marks to the earl of March. Dated at Westminster, 12 May, regnal year 1 (1378).

Sealed with the privy seal in red wax applied over a tongue and slit, in the upper right-hand corner of the dorse. One horizontal and two vertical folds. Three horizontal slits along the same horizontal line for insertion of the tongue (one slit covered by the seal). The extreme left-hand part of face and dorse is not shown on the photographs. For the method of sealing, see above, p. 31, drawings 5–8. [*Much reduced*]

Richard par la grace de Dieu roy Dengleterre et de France et seignur Dirlande, a noz bien amez William Walworth' et Johan Philipot, receivours de noz deniers pur la guerre, saluz. Nous vous mandons que . . Et ces presentes vous en serront garant. Don*e* souz nostre prive seal a Westm' le xij jour de may, lan de nostre regne primer.

[*On the tongue*]: A noz bien amez William Walworth et Johan Philipot, receivours de noz deniers pur la guerre. Marche.

27

a. Exchequer, T.R., Ancient Deeds, Series A (E. 40), no. 15105

PRIVY-SEAL LETTERS PATENT of Edward III, appointing his clerk William de Mulsho as his attorney to receive seisin of various lands granted to him by Walter Forester, citizen of London, and Agnes, his wife. Dated at Westminster, 22 February, regnal year of England 44 and of France 31 (1370).

Sealed with the privy seal in red wax appended on a tongue. A small step in the bottom left-hand corner (not shown on the photograph) is all that remains of the wrapping-tie, below the tongue. [*Much reduced*]

Edward par la grace de Dieu roi Dengleterre et de France et seignur Dirlande, a touz ceux qi cestes lettres verront, saluz. Savoir vous fesons que . . . En tesmoignance de quele chose nous avons fait faire cestes noz lettres patentes. Don*e* souz nostre prive seal a Westm' le xxij jour de feverer, lan de nostre regne Dengleterre quarante quart' et de France trente primer.

b. Exchequer, K.R., Accounts Various (E. 101), 37/27/57

PRIVY-SEAL BILL of Richard II, ordering William Walworth and John Philipot, receivers for war, to pay certain wages and reward to John Haukyn, sergeant-at-arms, and others. There is no heading *Depar le roy*. Dated at Westminster, 3 May, regnal year 1 (1378).

Sealed with the privy seal in red wax applied on the face, below the dating-clause. [*Much reduced*]

Nous vous mandons que . . . Et ces presentes vous en serront garant. Don*e* souz nostre prive seal a Westm' le tierz jour de may, lan de nostre regne primer.

[*On the right of the seal*]: A noz bien amez William Walworth' et Jo-
han Philipot, receivours
de noz denier pur la
guerre.

c. Chancery Warrants (C. 81), 1339/5

SIGNET BILL of Richard II, ordering the issue of a protection with clause *volumus*. Dated at the manor of Kennington, 8 July, regnal year 1 (1377).

Formerly sealed with the signet in red wax applied on the face at the centre of a cross of red wax. Only traces of the seal remain. Here the signet was used as a substitute for the privy seal.

Full text above, p. 38. [*Much reduced*]

Fiat proteccio cum clausula volumus pro . . . usque ad festum natalis Domini proximo futurum duratura. Dat*um* sub signeto anuli ` nostri ´ in absencia privati sigilli nostri apud manerium nostrum de Kenyngton' viij die julii, anno regni nostri primo.

d. Warrants for the Privy Seal, Series I (P.S.O. 1), 2/87, dorse

SIGNET WRIT CLOSE of Henry IV to Nicholas Bubbewith, keeper of the privy seal, ordering him to issue a privy-seal writ to the treasurer and chamberlains of the exchequer. Dated at Woodstock, 28 April [1405].

The privy-seal writ issued in pursuance of this warrant has survived in Exchequer of Receipt, Writs and Warrants for Issues (E. 404), 20/209, dated at Westminster, 1 May, regnal year 6 (1405).

Formerly sealed with the signet in red wax applied at the centre of a cross of wax over a thong. Only traces of the seal and part of the thong remain. One horizontal and two vertical folds. Two sets of three horizontal slits, each set being placed along a horizontal line, for insertion of the thong. The address on the dorse reads: *A nostre tres[cher] clerc Nichol Bubbewith', gardein de nostre prive seel.* For the sealing method, see the drawings above on p. 38. [*Much reduced*]

SELECT INDEX